COLLECTED IMPRESSIONS

COLLECTED
IMPRESSIONS

by

ELIZABETH BOWEN

NEW YORK: ALFRED A KNOPF

1950

PRINTED IN GREAT BRITAIN BY
SPOTTISWOODE, BALLANTYNE AND CO LTD
LONDON AND COLCHESTER

FOREWORD

These pieces cover a term of time. Most of the book reviews date from the 1930's, though some were written during or since the war. With one exception, the prefaces represent later work. In Section V, the range of subjects and years is widest; the treatments are strikingly unalike. 'Anthony Trollope' was first broadcast only a few evenings before V-Day. 'Notes on Writing a Novel' and its companion were contributed to the second and third volumes of the memorable *Orion*: it is to that epoch that they belong.

As critic, the status of the novelist is uncertain. It might be argued that the habitual story-teller would do better not to enter the critical field at all. At the same time, pleasure and interest attach, for the writer himself, to the experiment—there is probably no one who is willing to rest until he has tried his pen upon everything. Few are the subjects upon which there can be nothing to say: the difficulty is in the manner of saying it. Criticism makes unexpected demands on what had hitherto been narrative style. Clearness, immediacy and honesty, in the expression, are what is wanted: that should be simple. But the writer whose type of mind is, by nature, practical is shy of (and possibly overrates) the necessity, in criticism, for theory. Mechanical difficulties with language are the outcome of internal difficulties with thought.

For a further reason, the change over from invention to analysis is not easily made. No creative writer lacks—can afford to lack— the critical faculty. He is, however, accustomed to keep the faculty bent, like a hooded lamp, on his own work—which must not be allowed to slip, for an instant, out of the orbit of that remorseless glare. To wrench the neck of the lamp in another, outward direction is not easy; and, even when that is done, the light may not focus with the required certainty. It is hard for the novelist to disengage himself from problems generic to his calling, and, more narrowly, peculiar to himself. He is aware, and may even exaggerate the magnitude, of problems confronting his fellow-craftsman; but in his attempt to define these, to be objective about them, he is handicapped. How, then, is he to estimate to what extent they have, or have not, been overcome? Recollection of his own exertions and anxieties haunts, for him, each page of the book by another hand. From which follows, that in attempting to judge the book he is likely to be morbidly over-clement.

I am conscious, in re-reading the book-review section of *Collected Impressions,* that I have written best, because most happily, about books whose claim was their subject rather than their style. Biographies, for instance, or histories of cities offer, without embarrassing consciousness of the literary medium, sorts of annexes to experience in actual life. Like any other experience, they are to be reacted to; and the reaction is agreeable to discuss. My criticism is impressionistic—its warrant being the present-day prevalence of the signed review. The anonymous critic must be impersonal, and formal, because inevitably his voice carries greater weight.

In my choice of a title for this book I have not so much intended to be disarming as hoped to be precise. These are impressions—of books, scenes or events—which, by force of continuing to be written and of having been kept in a folder, have collected themselves. Put together, they can but act upon one another: a book becomes something more than layers of print compressed between boards. *Collected Impressions* depends for any significance on its pattern: the order, to which I have given thought, is for me the equivalent of a style. The pieces have, by the fact of being placed in relation to one another, acquired something not present when, severally, they were first written. Each of them carries the colour of its year; each reflects, involuntarily, what was in that year a contemporary mood of thought or phase of feeling. They combine into something which is one of the many imponderable by-products of history.

The prefaces, and the 'Notes on Writing a Novel' put forward claims with which time has nothing to do. They were not journalism, and I stand by them as serious work, for which I would wish survival.

ELIZABETH BOWEN.

January, 1950.

CONTENTS

I
PREFACES

II
REVIEWS

WOMEN

VARIOUS

IRISH

III
TWO PIECES

IV
PLAYS, PICTURES, PLACES

V
A BROADCAST

VI
TWO PIECES FROM *ORION*

ACKNOWLEDGMENTS

Acknowledgments for permission to include Copyright material are due to the following:

The Editor of *The Bell* for THE BIG HOUSE; Messrs. Jonathan Cape Ltd., for an article from THE MULBERRY TREE edited by Graham Greene; The Cresset Press Ltd., for the Preface to *Uncle Silas* by S. Le Fanu; Messrs. Faber & Faber Ltd., for the Preface to *The Faber Book of Modern Short Stories*; Messrs. Alfred A. Knopf Inc., for the special Preface to the American Edition of IVY GRIPPED THE STEPS, Miss Bowen's volume of Short Stories, THE DEMON LOVER, Copyright 1946; Mr. John Murray for 'Post Victorian' from the *Cornhill Magazine*, and reviews as noted at foot of each; Messrs. Newforge Limited for *Folkestone* 1945 from *Contact*; *The New Statesman and Nation* for thirty articles and reviews, as noted at foot of each; *The New York Times Book Review* for a review of THE PORTABLE D. H. LAWRENCE which appeared on 9th February 1947 and for *The Achievement of Virginia Woolf* which appeared on 26th June 1949; *The Observer* for three reviews as dates noted at foot of each; The Editor of *Orion* in which the articles first appeared, for NOTES ON WRITING A NOVEL and OUT OF A BOOK; The Oxford University Press for ANTHONY TROLLOPE—A NEW JUDGMENT; Messrs. Martin Secker & Warburg Ltd., for the Preface to THE BLAZE OF NOON by Rayner Heppenstall; *The Spectator* for five articles and reviews, as noted at foot of each; *The Times* for a review of MYSELF WHEN YOUNG by H. H. Richardson from *The Times Literary Supplement*.

1
PREFACES

to

Uncle Silas by Joseph Sheridan Le Fanu

The Flaubert Omnibus

The Faber Book of Modern Short Stories

The Demon Lover by Elizabeth Bowen

The Blaze of Noon by Rayner Heppenstall

UNCLE SILAS

I

Uncle Silas is a romance of terror. Joseph Sheridan Le Fanu lets us know that he expanded it from a short story (length, about fifteen pages) which he wrote earlier in his literary life and published, anonymously, in a magazine—under the title of *A Passage in the Secret History of an Irish Countess*. As he does not give the name of the magazine I have not, so far, been able to trace the story. I should make further efforts to do so could I feel that its interest was very great: its initial interest, that is to say, *qua* story. It holds, it is true, the germ of the later novel—or, at least, of its plot. But about that plot itself there is little new. The exterior plot of *Uncle Silas* is traditional, well worn by the time Le Fanu took up his pen. What have we? The Wicked Uncle and the Endangered Heir. I need not point out the precedents even in English history. Also, this is the Babes in the Wood theme—but in *Uncle Silas* we have only one babe—feminine, in her late adolescence, and, therefore, the no less perpetual Beauty in Distress. Maud Ruthyn has her heroine-prototype in a large body of fiction which ran to excess in the gothic romances but is not finished yet —the distraught young lady clasping her hands and casting her eyes skyward to Heaven: she has no other friend. . . . No, it is hard to see that simply uncle and niece, her sufferings, his designs, compressed, as they were at first, into a number of pages so small as to limit 'treatment' (Le Fanu's *forte*) could have made up into anything much more than the conventional magazine story of the day.

What *is* interesting is that Le Fanu, having written the story, should have been unable, still, to discharge its theme from his mind. He must have continued, throughout the years, to be obsessed, if subconsciously, by the niece and uncle. More, these two and their relationship to each other became magnetic to everything strangest and most powerful in his own imagination and temperament. The resultant novel, our *Uncle Silas*, owes the pressure, volume and spiritual urgency which make it comparable to *Wuthering Heights* to just this phenomenon of accretion. Accretion is a major factor in art. Le Fanu could not be rid of the

3

niece and uncle till he had built around them a comprehensive book.

Something else draws my interest to the original story: its heroine, by the showing of the title, was Irish, by marriage if not birth. Joseph Sheridan Le Fanu (1814–73, grand-nephew of Sheridan the dramatist) was Irish; or rather Anglo-Irish. And *Uncle Silas* has alway struck me as being an Irish story transposed to an English setting. The hermetic solitude and the autocracy of the great country house, the demonic power of the family myth, fatalism, feudalism and the 'ascendency' outlook are accepted facts of life for the race of hybrids from which Le Fanu sprang. For the psychological background of *Uncle Silas* it was necessary for him to invent nothing. Rather, he was at once exploiting in art and exploring for its more terrible implications what would have been the norm of his own heredity. Having, for reasons which are inscrutable, pitched on England as the setting for *Uncle Silas*, he wisely chose the North, the wildness of Derbyshire. Up there, in the vast estates of the landed old stock, there appeared, in the years when Le Fanu wrote (and still more in the years of which he wrote: the early 1840's) a time lag—just such a time lag as, in a more marked form, separates Ireland from England more effectually than any sea.

Le Fanu was not, in his generation, alone in seeing the possibilities of the country house from the point of view of drama, tension and mystery. We may comment on 'atmosphere' : almost all the Victorians who were novelists used it without fuss. Wilkie Collins, for instance, wrings the last drop of effect from the woodgirt Hampshire mansion in *The Woman in White*, with its muffling, oppressive silence and eerie lake. The castles, granges and lonely halls back through romantic fiction are innumerable. One might, even, say that Le Fanu showed himself as traditional, or unoriginal, in his choice of setting as in his choice of plot. Only, while his contemporaries, the by then urbanized Victorian English, viewed the ancestral scene from the outside, the Irishman wrote out of what was in his bones.

Uncle Silas is, as a novel, Irish in two other ways: it is sexless, and it shows a sublimated infantilism. It may, for all I know, bristle with symbolism; but I speak of the story, not of its implications—in the story, no force from any one of the main characters runs into the channel of sexual feeling. The reactions of

Maud, the narrator-heroine, throughout are those of a highly intelligent, still more highly sensitive, child of twelve. This may, to a degree, be accounted for by seclusion and a repressive father —but not, I think entirely: I should doubt whether Le Fanu himself realized Maud's abnormality as a heroine. She is an uncertain keyboard, on which some notes sound clearly, deeply and truly, others not at all. There is no question, here, of Victorian censorship, with its suggestive gaps: Maud, on the subject of anything she does feel, is uninhibited, sometimes disconcerting. And equally, in the feeling of people round her we are to take it that, child-like, she misses nothing. The distribution of power throughout the writing is equal, even: the briefest scene is accorded brimming sensuous content. We must in fact note how Maud's sensuousness (which is un-English) disperses, expends itself through the story in so much small change. She shows, at every turn, the carelessness, or acquiescence, of the predestined person: Maud is, by nature, a bride of Death. She delays, she equivocates, she looks wildly sideways; she delights in fire and candlelight, bedroom tea-drinking, cosy feminine company, but her bias is marked. The wind blowing her way from the family mausoleum troubles our heroine like a mating cry. Her survival after those frightful hours in the locked bedroom at Bartram-Haugh is, one can but feel, somewhat ghostly: she has cheated her Bridegroom only for the time being. Her human lover is colourless; her marriage—unexceptionable as to level and in felicity—is little more than the shell of a happy ending. From the parenthesis in her 'Conclusion' (Maud writes down her story after some years of marriage) we learn that her first child dies.

Is, then, *Uncle Silas* 'morbid'? I cannot say so. For one thing, morbidity seems to me little else than sentimentality of a peculiar tint, and nothing of that survives in the drastic air of the book. For another, Maud is counterpoised by two other characters, her unalike cousins Monica Knollys and Milly Ruthyn, who not only desire life but are its apostles. And, life itself is painted in brilliant colours—colours sometimes tantalizing, as though life were an alternative out of grasp; sometimes insidious, disturbing, as though life were a temptation. I know, as a matter of fact, of few Victorian novels in which cosiness, gaiety and the delights of friendship are so sweetly rendered or play such a telling part.

Le Fanu's style, translucent, at once simple and subtle, is ideal for
such transitions. He has a genius for the unexpected—in mood as
well as event. One example—a knowing twist of his art—is that
Maud, whose arrival at Bartram-Haugh has been fraught with
sinister apprehension, should, for the first few months, delight
in her uncle's house. After Knowl—overcast, repressive, stiff with
proprieties—Bartram-Haugh seems to be Liberty Hall. She runs
wild in the woods with her cousin Milly; for the first time, she
has company of her own age. Really, it is the drama of Maud's
feelings, the heightening of conflict in her between hopes and
fears, rather than the melodrama of her approaching fate, which
ties one to *Uncle Silas*, page after page, breathless, unwilling to
miss a word.

II

Le Fanu either felt or claimed to feel uneasy as to the reception
of *Uncle Silas*. He mentions the genesis of the novel, not for its
interest as a creative fact, but in order to clear himself, in advance,
of the charge of plagiarism: his long-ago short story had been
anonymous. And, in the same 'Preliminary Word' he enters a
plea that the novel be not dismissed as 'sensation' fiction. *Uncle
Silas* was published in 1864: the plea would not be necessary
to-day. Sensationalism, for its own sake, does, it is true, remain
in poor repute; but sensation (of the kind which packs *Uncle
Silas*) is not only not disdained, it is placed in art. The most irre-
proachable pens, the most poetic imaginations pursue and refine
it. The status of the psychological thriller is, to-day, high. *Uncle
Silas* was in advance of, not behind, its time: it is not the last,
belated Gothic romance but the first (or among the first) of the
psychological thrillers. And it has, as terror-writing, a voluptuousness not approached since. (It was of the voluptuousness in his
own writing that Le Fanu may, really, have been afraid.) The
novel, like others of its now honoured type, relies upon suspense
and mystification: I should be doing wrong to it and the reader
were I to outline the story or more than hint at its end. To say
that a rich, lonely girl is placed, by her father's will, in charge
of an uncle who, already suspected of one murder, would be the
first to profit by her death is, I think, at once sufficient and fair.
But, the real suspense of the story emanates from the characters;

it is they who keep the tale charged with mystery. The people in *Uncle Silas* show an extraordinary power of doubling upon or of covering their tracks. Maud seldom knows where she stands with any of them; neither do we. They are all at one remove from us, seen through the eyes of Maud. The gain to a story of this nature of being told in the first person is obvious (but for the fact that the teller, for all her dangers, must, we take it, survive, in order to tell the tale). All the same, it is not to this device that Le Fanu owes the main part of his effects—you and I, as readers, constantly intercept glances or changes in tones of voice that Maud just notes but does not interpret aright. No, Maud has little advantage over you or me. Temperamentally, and because of her upbringing, she is someone who moves about in a world of strangers. She is alternately blind and unnecessarily suspicious. Her attitude towards every newcomer is one of fatalistic mistrust; and this attitude almost, but not quite (which is subtle) communicates itself to the reader. We do not, for instance, know, for an unreasonably but enjoyably long time, whether Milly, for all her rustic frankness, may not at heart be a Little Robber Girl, or Lady Knollys a schemer under her good nature.

You perceive [says Maud] that I had more spirit than courage. I think I had the mental attributes of courage; but then I was but an hysterical girl, and in so far neither more nor less than a coward.

No wonder I distrusted myself; no wonder my will stood out against my timidity. It was a struggle, then; a proud, wild struggle against constitutional cowardice.

Those who have ever had cast upon them more than their strength seems framed to bear—the weak, the aspiring, the adventurous in will, and the faltering in nerve—will understand the kind of agony which I sometimes endured.

And later, on receiving comforting news:

You will say then that my spirits and my serenity were quite restored. Not quite. How marvellously lie our anxieties, in filmy layers, one over the other! Take away that which has lain on the upper surface for so long—the care of cares—the only one, as it seemed to you, between your soul and the radiance of Heaven—and straight you find a new stratum there. As physical science tells us no fluid is without its skin, so does it seem with this fine medium of the soul, and those successive films of care that form upon its surface on mere contact with the upper air and light.

Who are the characters whom, in *Uncle Silas*, this at once nervous and spirited girl confronts? There is her father, Austin Ruthyn of Knowl, scion and reigning head of an ancient family, wealthy, recluse, widower, given up to Swedenborgian religion. There is Mr. Ruthyn's spiritual director Dr. Bryerly—'bilious, bewigged, black-eyed'—whose nocturnal comings and goings seem to bode no good. There is Mr. Ruthyn's first cousin Lady Knollys, woman of the world, who comes to stay at Knowl and interests herself in Maud. There is Maud's French governess Madame de la Rougierre, who, arriving early on in the story, gibbers in moonlight outside the drawing-room window.

Half-way through, story and heroine cross sixty miles of country. Austin Ruthyn is dead: his place in Maud's life is taken by his younger brother Silas, of Bartram-Haugh—reformed rake, widower and, again, religious recluse. Silas's marriage to a barmaid had dealt the first, though not yet the worst, blow to Ruthyn family pride. Children of the marriage are Milly ('a very rustic Miranda,' her father says) and Dudley, a sinister Tony Lumpkin. In the Bartram-Haugh woods dwell an ill-spoken miller and his passionate daughter. . . . In both great houses there is the usual cast of servants—at Knowl, correct, many and reassuring; at Bartram-Haugh few and queer. On from this point, characterization, in any full sense, stops: we are left with 'types,' existing, solely and flatly, for the requirements of the plot. A fortune-hunting officer, three clergymen, two lawyers and a thoughtful peer, Maud's future husband, come under this heading.

That last group, uninspired and barely tinted in, represents Le Fanu's one economy. In the main, it could be a charge against him that too many of the characters in *Uncle Silas* are over-charged, and that they break their bounds. There is abnormal pressure, from every side; the psychic air is often overheated. And all the time, we must remember, this is a story intended to be dominated by the figure of one man: Uncle Silas. All through, Uncle Silas meets competition. He is, I think, most nearly played off the stage by Madame de la Rougierre. Apart from that he is (as central character) at a disadvantage: *is* he, constantly, big enough for his own build-up? Is there or is there not, in scenes in which he actually appears, a just perceptible drop into anti-climax? Le Fanu, in dealing with Uncle Silas, was up against a difficulty inherent in his kind of oblique, suggestive art. He has overdrawn on his Silas in advance. In the flesh, Uncle Silas enters the story late: by this time, his build-up has reached towering heights. It is true that most of the time at Bartram-Haugh he remains off stage, and that those intervals allow of batteries being recharged. At Knowl, still only a name, he was ever-present—in the tormented silences of his brother, the hinting uneasy chatter of Lady Knollys, and Maud's dreams.

I don't [Lady Knollys admits, to Maud] understand metaphysics, my dear, nor witchcraft. I sometimes believe in the supernatural, and sometimes I don't. Silas Ruthyn is himself alone, and I can't define him because I don't understand him. Perhaps other souls than human are sometimes born into the world, and clothed in flesh. It is not only about that dreadful occurrence, but nearly always throughout his life; early and late he has puzzled me. . . . At one time of his life I am sure he was awfully wicked—eccentric indeed in his wickedness—gay, frivolous, secret and dangerous. At one time I think he could have made poor Austin do almost anything; but his influence vanished with his marriage, never to return again. No; I don't understand him. He has always bewildered me, like a shifting face, sometimes smiling, but always sinister, in an unpleasant dream.

Here is Maud, on arrival at Bartram-Haugh, fresh from her first meeting with her uncle:

When I lay down in my bed and reviewed the day, it seemed like a month of wonders. Uncle Silas was always before me; the voice so silvery for an old man—so preternaturally soft; the manner so sweet, so gentle; the aspect smiling, suffering, spectral. It was no longer a shadow; I had now seen him in the flesh. But, after all, was he more than a shadow to me? When I closed my eyes I saw him before me still, in necromantic black, ashy with a pallor on which I looked with fear and pain, a face so dazzlingly pale, and those hollow, fiery, awful eyes! It sometimes seemed to me as though the curtain had opened, and I had seen a ghost.

'What a sweet, gentle, insufferable voice he has!' exclaims, later, Lady Knollys, who, for Maud's sake, has tried to reopen relations with Bartram-Haugh. And, towards the end, we hear the beleaguered Maud: 'There were the sensualities of the gourmet for his body, and there ended his human nature, as it seemed to me. Through that semi-transparent structure I thought I could now and then discern the light or glare of his inner life. . . . Was, then, all his kindness but a phosphoric radiance covering something colder and more awful than the grave?'

Of the French governess, what is one to say? She is Uncle Silas's rival or counterpart. She is physical as opposed to metaphysical evil. No question of 'semi-transparent structure' here— the Frenchwoman is of the rankest bodily coarseness: one can smell her breath, as it were, at every turn. In the *Uncle Silas* atmosphere, bleached of sex, she is no more woman than he is man; yet, somehow, her marelike coquetry—that prinking with finery and those tales of lovers—is the final, grotesque element of offence. As a woman, she can intrude on the girl at all points. She is obscene; and not least so in the alternate pinchings and pawings to which she subjects Maud. While the uncle gains in monstrousness by distance, the governess gains in monstrousness by closeness.

Madame de la Rougierre is unhandicapped by a preliminary build-up: she enters the story without warning and makes growth, page by page, as she goes along. Le Fanu, through the mouths of his characters, is a crack marksman in the matter of epithets: nothing said of the governess goes wide. He had, it is true, with this Frenchwoman a great vein to work on: with Wilkie Collins and Dickens he could exploit the British concept of the foreigner as sinister. Her broken English (with its peculiar rhythm, like no other known broken English, specially coined for her) further twists, in speech, the thoughts of her hideous mind. Like Uncle Silas, Madame de la Rougierre is, morally, of an unrelieved black: considering how much we are in her company it is wonderful that she does not become monotonous—the variations Le Fanu *has* contrived to give her are to be admired. 'When things went well,' we are told, 'her soul lighted up into sulphureous good-humour.' The stress is most often upon this woman's mouth—a 'large-featured, smirking phantom' is Maud's first view of her, through the drawing-room window. We have her 'wide, wet grin.' She would 'smile with her great carious teeth.'

This creature's background is never fully given. Indeed, her engagement, as his daughter's companion, by Mr. Ruthyn of Knowl, is, with his obstinate tolerance of her presence, one of the first anomalies of the plot.

III

Uncle Silas, as a novel, derives its power from an inner momentum. In the exterior plot there are certain weaknesses, inconsistencies and loose ends. In this regard, the book has about it a sort
of brilliant—nay, even inspired—amateurishness; a sort of negligent virtuosity in which Le Fanu shows his race. This may be
the reason why *Uncle Silas* has never yet quite made the popular
grade. It has not so far, that is to say, moved forward from being
a favourite book of individual people into the rank of accepted
Victorian classics.

It cannot, I think, be said that most Victorian novels are guilt-
less of loose ends. But, in their elaborate plots with their sub-
structures, crowds of characters and varied, shifting scenes, there
is usually more to distract the eye: reader as well as author may
well overlook something. *Uncle Silas* is, in this matter, defence-
less in its simplicity: it has no sub-plots and contains comparatively few people. The writing is no less simple: this, its beauty
apart, is its great virtue. The effect of the simplicity is, that every
sentence of Le Fanu's—or, at least, its content—incises itself
deeply upon one's memory: one can forget not the slightest hint
or statement or question. And, the excitingness of the story keeps
one on the stretch, at once watchful and challenging, like a child
listener. Like the child, one finds oneself breaking in, from time
to time, with: 'But—? . . . But, I thought you *said*—?'

The omissions or inconsistencies of the plot are not psychological; they are practical or mechanical. They do not, to my
mind, detract from or injure the real story, because they are not
on its reallest plane. However, there they are. I do not feel it to
be the function of this Introduction to point them out to the reader
in advance—I intend, therefore, only to mention one, which
could hardly escape the most careless eye. *Who* was the concealed
witness who relayed to Maud the conversation between Madame
de la Rougierre and Dudley Ruthyn at Church Scarsdale? A
witness who must, by the way, have been no less observant and
subtle than Maud herself, for no inflection, gesture or glance is
lost. We are never told who it is. The most likely bid is Tom
Brice, the girl Beauty's lover and, at one time, Dudley's hanger-
on. Tom might have told Beauty, who might have told Maud.
But the account does not sound as though it had come through

the mouths of two peasants. . . . Elsewhere, the fact that the
degree and origin of the Frenchwoman's relationship with the
Bartram-Haugh Ruthyns is never stated may worry some
readers. We are left to infer that she was, already, their agent
from before the time she arrived at Knowl.

The plot is obfuscated (sometimes, one may say, helpfully) by
an extraordinary vagueness about time. This is a book in which
it is impossible to keep a check on the passage of weeks, months,
years. The novel is dominated by one single season in whose
mood it is pitched: autumn. Practically no other season is implied
or named. (Yes, we have a Christmas visit to Elvaston, and a
mention, elsewhere, of January rain. And after Madame de la
Rougierre's departure from Knowl Maud, in the joy of her release, is conscious of singing birds and blue skies—but those could
be in September.) The whole orchestral range of the novel's
weather is autumnal—tranced dripping melancholy, crystal
morning zest, the radiance of the magnified harvest moon, or
the howl and straining of gales through not yet quite leafless
woods. The daylight part of Maud's drive to her uncle's house
is through an amber landscape. The opening words of the
novel are, it is true, 'It was winter. . . .' But our heroine, con-
tradictory with her first breath, then adds: 'the second week in
November.' By this reckoning Maud, in telling Lady Knollys
that Madame de la Rougierre had arrived at Knowl 'in February'
is incorrect. The Frenchwoman, we had been clearly told,
arrived 'about a fortnight' after the opening scene. . . . No, there
is nothing for it: one must submit oneself to Le Fanu's hypno-
tizing, perpetual autumn. One autumn merges into another:
hopeless to ask how much has happened between! Yet always,
against this nebulous flow of time stand out the moments—each
unique, comprehensive, crystal, painfully sharp.

The inner, non-practical, psychological plot of *Uncle Silas* is,
I suggest, faultless: it has no inconsistencies. The story springs
from and is rooted in an obsession, and the obsession never looses
its hold. Austin Ruthyn of Knowl, by an inexorable posthumous
act, engages his daughter's safety in order to rescue his brother's
honour. Or rather, less Silas's honour than the family name's.
Silas Ruthyn is a man under a cloud: he has never yet been cleared
of a charge against him. Austin's having committed Maud to his
brother's keeping is to demonstrate, to the eyes of a hostile world,

his absolute faith in his brother's innocence. By surviving years under his lonely roof, Maud, whose next heir he is, is to vindicate Silas. Maud has, during her father's lifetime, agreed in principle to the trust. (She has still, be it said, to hear the terms of the will, and to learn the full story of Silas from Lady Knollys.)

I think [Austin says to his daughter] little Maud would like to contribute to the restitution of her family name. . . . The character and influence of an ancient family is a peculiar heritage—sacred but destructible; and woe to him who either destroys or suffers it to perish.

Call this *folie de grandeur*, or a fanaticism of the Almanach de Gotha. It is the extreme of a point of view less foreign to Le Fanu than to his readers. It was a point of view that they, creatures of an industrialized English nineteenth century, were bound to challenge, and could deride. It could only hope to be made acceptable, as mainspring and premise of his story, by being challenged, criticized—even, by implication, derided—in advance, and on behalf of the reader, by a person located somewhere inside the story. The necessary mouthpiece is Dr. Bryerly. Dr. Bryerly's little speech to Maud is a piece of, as it were, insurance, on Le Fanu's part. 'There are people,' remarks Dr. Bryerly, 'who think themselves just as great as the Ruthyns, or greater; and your poor father's idea of carrying it by a demonstration was simply the dream of a man who had forgotten the world, and learned to exaggerate himself by his long seclusion.' True—and how effective. The reader's misgivings, his fear of being implicated in something insanely disproportionate, have been set at rest. He is now prepared to lean back and accept, as Le Fanu wished, the idea on one—but that a great—merit purely: its validity for the purposes of the tale.

One more comment, before we leave the plot. In the disposition of characters (including what I have called functional types) about the field of the story, Le Fanu shows himself, as a novelist, admirably professional, in a sense that few of his contemporaries were. Not a single, even the slightest, character is superfluous; not one fails to play his or her part in the plot, or detains us for a second after that part is played. One or two (such as the house party guests at Elvaston) are merely called in to act on Maud's state of mind. But Maud's mind, we must remember, reflects, and colours according to its states, the action of the interior plot.

No person is in the story simply to fill up space, to give the Victorian reader his money's worth, or to revive flagging interest— Le Fanu, rightly, did not expect interest to flag.

IV

The background, or atmosphere, needs little discussion: in the first few pages one recognizes the master-touch. The story of *Uncle Silas* is, as I have indicated, as to scene divided between two houses: Knowl and Bartram-Haugh. The contrast between the two houses contributes drama. Knowl, black and white, timbered, set in well-tended gardens, is a rich man's home. It is comfortable; fires roar in the grates; pictures and panelling gleam; the servants do all they should. As against this, Knowl is overcast, rigid, haunted: Mr. Ruthyn is closeted with dark mysteries; there are two ghosts, and, nearby, the family mausoleum, in which Maud's young mother lies and to which her father is to be carried under the most charnel circumstances of death.

Maud, sitting with Lady Knollys after Austin's death, hears the wind come roaring her way through the woods from the mausoleum. The wind, Lady Knollys can but point out, comes, too, from the more really threatening direction of Bartram-Haugh. Uncle Silas's house, already the scene of one violent death, is, beforehand, invested with every terror. Bartram-Haugh, as first seen, demands a John Piper drawing:

I was almost breathless as I approached. The bright moon shining fully on the white front of the old house revealed not only its highly decorated style, its fluted pillars and doorway, rich and florid carving and balustraded summit, but also its stained and mossgrown front. Two giant trees, overthrown at last by the recent storm, lay with their upturned roots, and their yellow foliage still flickering on the sprays that were to bloom no more, where they had fallen, at the right side of the courtyard, which, like the avenue, was tufted with weeds and grass.

'The mind is,' as Maud elsewhere remarks, 'a different organ by night and by day.' Next morning's awakening is reassuring —a wakening to bright morning through bare windows, a cheerful breakfast, superb if neglected stretches of parkland, a blackberrying walk. Exploration, with Milly, of whole closed derelict floors and internal galleries brings only a fleeting memory of the ill-fated Charke. The psychological weather of those first Bartram-Haugh chapters is like the out-of-doors weather: gay and tingling. Till Milly is sent away, nothing goes wholly wrong. From *that* point, the closing in is continuous. The ruined rooms, the discovery of the ogress-governess in hiding, introduce the beginning of the end. . . . All through Le Fanu's writing, there is an ecstatic sensitivity to light, and an abnormal recoil from its inverse, darkness. *Uncle Silas* is full of outdoor weather—we enjoy the rides and glades, cross the brooks and stiles, meet the cottagers and feel the enclosing walls of two kingdom-like great estates. Though static in ever-autumn, those scenes change: there is more than the rolling across them of clouds or sunshine. Indeed we are looking at their reflection in the lightening or darkening mirror of Maud's mind.

V

Uncle Silas is a romance of terror, written more than eighty years ago. Between then and now, human susceptibilities have altered—some may have atrophied, others developed further. The terror-formula of yesterday might not work to-day. Will *Uncle Silas* act on the modern reader?

I think so, and for several reasons. Le Fanu's strength, here, is not so much in his story as in the mode of its telling. *Uncle Silas,* as it is written, plays on one constant factor—our childish fears. These leave their work at the base of our natures, and are never to be rationalized away. Two things are terrible in childhood: helplessness (being in other people's power) and apprehension— the apprehension that something is being concealed from us because it is too bad to be told. Maud Ruthyn, vehicle of the story, is helpless apprehension itself, in person: this is what gets under our skin. Maud, simplified (in the chemical sense, reduced) for her creator's purpose, is, we may tell ourselves, an extreme case. She has a predisposition towards fear: we are to watch her— and be her—along her way towards the consummation of perfect terror—just as, were this a love story, we should be sharing her journey towards a consummation of a different kind. Proust has pointed out that the predisposition to love creates its own objects: is this not true of fear? At the start Maud, in her unconscious search, experiments with Dr. Bryerly: she fears him. He acts as the forecast shadow of Uncle Silas—and, that he may play this rôle for the first act, he is given all the necessary trappings. Then, the Doctor discloses a character in point-blank reverse: he is levelheaded, a man of daylight, unfailing good counsellor, champion, friend. But by that time, what the Doctor is does not matter: using the love-fear analogy, he is an off-cast love. He has been superseded by Uncle Silas, past whom Maud has no further to look.

Maud had suspected in Dr. Bryerly a supernatural element of evil: his influence on her father appeared malign. This brings us to another terror-ingredient: moral dread. Should one call this timeless, or is it modern? Let us say, it is timeless, but that its refinement in literature has been modern. (By modern I mean, modern at the best.) Henry James inspired, and remains at the head of, a whole school of moral horror stories—I need not point out that it is the stench of evil, not the mere fact of the supernatural, which is the genuine horror of *The Turn of the Screw*. Our ancestors may have had an agreeable-dreadful reflex from the idea of the Devil or a skull-headed revenant popping in and out through a closed door: we need, to make us shiver, the effluence from a damned soul. In *Uncle Silas*, there is no supernatural element in the ordinary sense—the Knowl ghosts exist merely to key Maud up. The genuine horror is the non-natural. Lady Knollys, in her chatter, suggests that Silas may be a non-human soul clothed in a human body.

What Maud dreads, face to face with Silas, is not her own death.

Physically, Maud's nerve is extremely good. She stands up to Madame de la Rougierre, to whom her reactions are those of intense dislike, repugnance and disdain. She is frightened only of what she cannot measure, and she has got the governess taped. With the same blend of disdain and clear-sightedness, she stands up to Dudley. She shows, I think, remarkable nonchalance in re-exploring the top rooms alone, in the late dusk, after Milly's departure. As the plot thickens round her and door after door clangs to, she shows herself fanatically disposed, up to the very last minute, to give her uncle the benefit of the doubt. Were she, in fact, a goose or weakling, the story would lack the essential tension: *Uncle Silas* would fail. As it is, we have the impact of a crescendo of hints and happenings on taut, hyper-controlled and thus very modern nerves. *Is* there to be a breaking-point? If so, why, how, when? That, not the question of Maud's bodily fate, sets up the real excitement of *Uncle Silas*.

The let-up, the pause for recuperation, even the apparent solicitude: these are among the sciences of the torture chamber. The victim must regain his power to suffer fully. The let-ups in *Uncle Silas*—the fine days, the walks, the returned illusions of safety—are, for Maud and the reader, artfully timed. Nothing goes on for long enough either to dull you or to exhaust itself. And the light, the open air, the outdoor perspective enhance, by contrast, the last of the horror-constants—claustrophobia. On the keyboard of any normal reader *Uncle Silas* will not, I think, fail to strike one or another note: upon the claustrophobic it plays a fugue. The sense of the tightening circle, the shrinking and darkening room. . . .

Just as the outer plot of *Uncle Silas* is traditional, or unoriginal, Le Fanu does draw also, for fear or horror, out of the traditional bag of tricks—the lonely ruinous house, the closed rooms, the burning eyes, the midnight voices, the hired assassins, and so on. Maud herself, exploring Bartram-Haugh in the dusk, has in mind the romances of Mrs. Radcliffe. The induction of misery and despair preparatory to slaughter is Elizabethan. . . . In so far as *Uncle Silas* uses physical horror, the use is extremely sophisticated: Maud's quick and almost voluptuous reactions to sound, sight, touch and smell make her the perfect reagent. The actual sound of a murder, a messy butchery, has probably never, in any gangster story, been registered as it is here.

The function of an Introduction is, I think, to indicate the nature of a book and to suggest some angles for judgment. That judgment the reader himself must form. *Uncle Silas* will, in this new edition, reach, among others, a generation of readers who have grown up since the novel was last in print. They may read into it more than I have found. That it will have meaning for them I do not doubt.

1946.

C

THE FLAUBERT OMNIBUS*

I

(Madame Bovary. The Temptation of Saint Anthony.
Bouvard et Pécuchet)

Gustave Flaubert was born in Rouen in 1821, and died at Croisset, outside Rouen, in 1880. A life of inner dynamicism which covered, geographically, little space. His movements were deliberately circumscribed; it was not by chance that he died within a few miles of where he had been born; he had elected to live the greater part of his years inside one area of Normandy. He was as Norman in build as he was by breed—a striking fine big-shouldered blond young man upon whom the heaviness, baldness and veinous complexion of middle age were to settle unduly early. In temperament he was, like his native landscape, not untouched by the damps of Atlantic melancholy. His father was resident physician at the Rouen hospital: the little boy, playing in the hospital courtyard, used to climb up the creeper trellis to look in through the dissecting-room window. For Gustave it was decided, at the end of his Rouen education, that he should go to Paris and read law; but his studies were interrupted by the first attack of the nervous malady which was to disorganize his youth. Dr. Flaubert's second son, as a case, could and did command the attention of advanced medical circles of the time; but the seizures, followed by coma, eluded definition and cure. That they were *not* epileptic could be established: it would now be recognized that their root was psychic. Conflict, which he was to diagnose himself, made a shell of the young man's healthy frame.

Gustave himself was objective as to his symptoms: he owned to finding the tranquillities and exemptions of the invalid state not without charm. This could be hoped to mean, and did mean, no more of law in Paris. But the attacks, even their possibility, were not only a terror, they were an inconvenience. They had the effect of disabusing him—as an otherwise full-blown professing young Romantic of his day—as to there being anything advantageous, anything eclectic, anything inherently 'interesting' about

* This preface, having been written for a projected 'omnibus,' was intended to be an introduction to Flaubert for English readers who might not yet know his work, or his work's background. Therefore, the re-statement of what may seem, to other readers, obvious facts about Flaubert must be allowed for.—E. B.

18

hyperæsthesia. No, against that aspect of the Romantic cult he was indoctrinated. He was to say of poetry:

It has a calmer base. If having sensitive nerves were enough to make one a poet I should be greater than Shakespeare or Homer—the last I take to have been an un-nervous man. Such confusion is impious; as I should myself know—I who have heard through closed doots people whispering thirty feet away . . . who have felt in the space of a second a million thoughts, images, combinations of all kinds shoot through my brain like lit fuses of fireworks—which is all excellent matter for talk, and most moving. But this faculty for feeling beyond proportion is weakness. Let me explain—

If I had had a stronger brain the boredom of reading law would not have made me ill. I should have got something from it, not merely harm. Distress, instead of staying inside my skull, ran through my limbs and tightened them into convulsions. It *deviated*, in fact.

Surgical common-sense—disconcerting in love, making for that perpetual wariness, that in itself almost nerve-breaking application of the controls in art. He was to say: 'One should write more coldly.'

The pattern of human relationships in the life is simple—if not, like the movements, actually circumscribed. It must be true of most lives, and is true here, that nobody entering the scene late leaves a deep impression: the imaginative-emotional wax has set. The friends of the mature years, when Flaubert's full stature was reached, were valuable, stimulating, true—such friends are rewards, but they are not factors. The figures in the formative years were thus:—the father, the tired sceptical doctor; who, when Gustave (in the impassioned hope of proving his right to forsake law for the pen) read aloud from a manuscript, dozed off. Dr. Flaubert died when Gustave was in his middle twenties, leaving Mme Flaubert—sombre, controlled, rigid, vehemently centred upon her family, dreading breaks in the circle, a devotee and a sufferer. (Achille, the elder of the two sons, doctor also, was uncongenial to Gustave and hardly enters the picture.) There was Caroline, the beloved sister, playmate of the Rouen courtyard days, whose marriage inflicted the first blow and who was to die after giving birth to her first child. There was then the child, Caroline II, the niece who grew up at Croisset with her widowed grandmother and her uncle. There was one more full-blooded relative—dear 'licentious old uncle' Parain. There were the three close friends, dating from Rouen college days—Alfred le Poittevin, Maxime du Camp and Louis Bouilhet. And there was 'La Muse,' Louise Colet, mistress for eight years.

It was at Croisset that the novels were written. The old, low, pleasant-fronted house with garden running down to the Seine, had been bought by Dr. Flaubert before his death. For readers of Flaubert's letters, Croisset, in every detail, exists with an almost supernatural clearness. Actually, house and garden are gone now; the industrialism of Rouen has engulfed the site; only the little pavilion remains. Here at Croisset there came into being, to continue year after year, an existence of hypnotic routine, of hermetic quietness—a woman in black moving like a watchful shadow about the house, a little girl effacing herself, a man burning out his youth in a closed study. But not all the time: there were the tremendous visits—Alfred, Max, Louis coming to stay, from Rouen, later from Paris, in pairs or singly. Louis, in fact, only took his place in the inner circle after Alfred's death—a death which followed upon what was, for Flaubert, the second nightmare marriage of a beloved. With the friends' arrival, the quiet of Croisset splintered —nor was anyone gladder than Gustave to see it go. A wind of talk, fitful about the garden or at table, reached gale velocity in the five-windowed study at nights. Manuscript-reading, manuscript-gutting, analysis, rhetoric, argument, a gigantic sketching in of the plan, art, art, art. All the friends were writers. Also they spoke of love.

Gustave Flaubert's temperament bred his art out of dualities, with their attendant conflicts, more marked, more extreme, than has been often known. For us there remains the danger of seeing only one side of a picture that had two sides always. There was the monk of art; but there was, at the same time, the beau garçon. There was, at least in youth, a florid, rumbustious and noisy side to this lover of extravagance for its own sake, this playing-up Romantic, this pupil of Rabelais and congenial nephew of Uncle Parain. 'Overflow' remained a great word with Flaubert, and one can admire the overflow of the early years. He was by no means a delicate child of life. His relations with other men were characterized by zest and dash. His success with Mme Colet was instantaneous.

Louise Colet did not overlook her own value. The two met in Paris when Flaubert was twenty-four, just about the time of his family's move to Croisset. To Croisset, indeed, she was to prove, at least at the dizzying beginning of her reign, the ideal antidote or counterpoise. Seated on the sofa at the fashionable sculptor Pradier's studio party, enchantingly dressed and at the height of her voluptuous prettiness (it suited her to be thirty-five) she could have appeared, at the first glance, to be the very woman prescribed by Gustave's friends. Du Camp and Bouilhet, as on-lookers, had become alarmed by the tension of that solitary life—the relaxation to be found in a love affair, they had more than hinted, could but be beneficial, even to art. To which he had answered, he could not stand the tax of it. Time was to prove him right—but that afternoon at Pradier's the meeting could not have seemed to be more propitious. Mme Colet, in spite of rumours to the contrary, was heart-free: her relationship with the distinguished Victor Cousin, philosopher and former minister of France, had some time ago become, at his wish, platonic. He had, however, been delicate enough not to withdraw financial support; her child Henriette was his, and she continued to profit by her association with her ex-lover's name. Though also she was a celebrity in her own right: a poetess. Unhappily, she was, though up to now successful, as mediocre in gift as she was superb physically. And worse, this Venus was a campaigner, up to the neck in literary politics, a success fanatic. The blue eyes she turned on Flaubert that afternoon (in a Provençale, who had married an unpromising professor of music in order to be brought by him to Paris, her radiant degree of fairness was surprising) must have held a complex assessment: she saw at once the *beau garçon* and the young man introduced as having a literary future. Let it be to her credit that one does not doubt that it was to the former that she surrendered, and so soon.

For him, before Louise Colet there had been nothing between the ideal and the obtainable. The ideal had been 'the phantom of Trouville'—the young married woman, hardly more than sighted at the seaside when he was an adolescent, who had already inspired fragmentary novels and who was, years hence, to reappear in perfected form in the perfected *L'Éducation Sentimentale*. The obtainable had left him neither here nor there. Of the Flaubert and Louise Colet of the succeeding years it can be said that as lovers they were well matched, that there was one plane on which nothing could go wrong, but that there was a fatal dissonance between them as persons. Had he been less great and at all vulgar, her littlenesses and vulgarities would have exasperated him sooner: as it was he first overshot them, then wondered at them, then pitied them. A Flaubert at his most human and most humane appears in those letters to the poor *Muse*. He created the illusion of a sympathy that did not exist. He loved her, he loved his love for her, and he loved every evidence of her love. But from her point of view, there were too many letters and too few meetings: the raptures in Paris, the escapades at Mantes were interspaced by lengthening months of nothing. He could not, he said (*would* not, she bitterly felt) leave Croisset—leave, for to that it amounted, *Madame Bovary*. She would understand the sacrifice? She did not. Could she not, then, she asked, come to Croisset, meet his mother, enter that study? No; never; emphatically not; that would never do. She and Croisset not apart were unthinkable. When everything had deteriorated, when nothing could be worse, she crashed the barrier—arrived at Croisset without warning, forced her way into the house. He threw her out. That was the end.

She had no successor. If he, as it seems possible, hurt her more than she hurt him, she entered his life more deeply than he entered hers. He never forgot, as he never repeated, love. The letters he wrote to Louise during the writing of *Bovary* are like no others in the world: such letters could perhaps only be written, out of a burning brain, by a hand still carrying over the creative excitement, to a creature who did not exist. For us, it as though his skull were trepanned with glass: the process of *Bovary* is laid bare.

He assumed a passionate understanding of the passion, in which no other could interfere. He assumed too much. 'I tried,' he wrote to her in his last letter, 'to make a sublime hermaphrodite of you.' Her letters in answer have been destroyed.

The break came when Flaubert was thirty-two. *Madame Bovary* was not yet finished.

In number the works themselves are few, like the relationships —and perhaps for the same reason, that of enormous content. Almost every one of the novels has a complicated psychological history. Publication dates do not give a true idea of the order in which the novels were conceived. The official dates are as follows:—*Madame Bovary* serialized in the *Revue de Paris*, began to appear in the autumn of 1856. *Salammbô* was published in 1862;

L'Éducation Sentimentale in 1879; *La Tentation de Saint Antoine* third and final version, in 1874 (fragments of the second version having appeared in a review as early as 1857). *Trois Contes* was published in 1877, and *Bouvard et Pécuchet* in 1884, four years after Flaubert's death.

Madame Bovary, the first novel published, was not the first essayed. It was preceded in Flaubert's working life by two others; the embryonic *L'Éducation Sentimentale* (with which may be grouped the fragmentary *Novembre*) and the first version of *La Tentation de Saint Antoine.* Two obsessing themes, or subjects, had to be pushed aside in order that *Madame Bovary* should be written: Flaubert's powers only steadied themselves, only worked their way into the use of their full force, after what must have seemed an injurious sacrifice had been made. Later, he could afford to return to those two subjects: he was liberated from what had been strangling in their hold. In *Madame Bovary* there is nothing of the past (he wrote the greater part of that love novel in the atmosphere of his relations with Louise Colet) and nothing of the East.

For years the East dominated the greater sensuous part of Flaubert's imagination. Exoticism, colour, violence, languor, voluptuousness with which was associated a mystique—it was a dream which enervated, intoxicated and, as dreams do, drained him. It was a dream with the power of attracting images to itself, a dream fed by inexhaustible reading, identified with the love for Alfred le Poittevin, who had shared it, and emotionally forever fixed by his death. Did this dream also serve as an outlet for the hyperæsthesia Gustave had reason to dread? As a fantasy, it was the evident antithesis to Normandy—such a compensatory continuous picture is not rare; it is a commonplace of the imaginative nature. What was rare in this particular nature was its intensifications, in any of the few directions it took. 'Real' life was left to be a residuum— not in, and not worth bringing into, focus.

It would be too simple to say that Flaubert got the East out of his system by going there. For two years (1849–51) he travelled the Near and Middle East with Maxime du Camp: nothing was disappointing—in fact, there was fulfillment beyond hope. But what did happen during those two years was that he began for the first time to 'see' Normandy. Partly, there was a natural setting in of nostalgia. It was more than a case, here, of distance lending enchantment to the view: with Flaubert, distance was necessary for vision. (As, indeed, it was for love: Alfred was always to be desired, being dead; Louise was loved with most exaltation when she was not there.) It was while he was in the East that the nebulous psychic mass which was to be Bovary-Normandy formed itself. All to be now awaited was, still, the story.

This supplied itself almost immediately, on his return home. Mme Flaubert numbered among her few and sombre acquaintances a certain Mme Delamere, a widow prostrated by the loss of her only son—young Delamere, a country doctor, had committed suicide after learning of the infidelities of his wife. How many references to the Delameres Flaubert may have heard before the story 'took' with him, one cannot say: it was the story which, for the next five years, was to become his life: *Madame Bovary*. A story whose lowness he was to lament, under the 'uninterestingness' of whose people he was to groan, in the depiction of whose monotonous trivialities he was to weep and sweat. A story of adultery in the provinces. He was to take as heroine a woman beautiful only by inadvertence, trailing her way towards disaster not worth a tear, full of tawdry wishes, without a thought. He was to surround his Emma with a decent oaf of a husband and, as lovers, a sentimental clerk and a flashy squireen. He was, it is true, as against this, to have fun—a fun due for full expansion in *Bouvard et Pécuchet*—with the creation of Homais, the pharmacist. . . . Everything stood or fell by how this was *seen*—a relentless test of the vision, this 'realistic' story.

Madame Bovary, in its unforeseen and imperative demand to be written, displaced an already projected book. Flaubert, off and on, had discussed with Maxime and Louis the idea of a novel that should have a Flemish setting and be about a young girl who was a mystic and died a virgin. And there had been more: the idea had begun to collect matter. From this to the story of an adulteress may seem a far cry—yet, does one not see in *Bovary*, never quite submerged, the young girl's face? That the soul of Emma should be without virtue does not make it less a palpable soul—of whose pitiful fluttering candescence, at the most carnal moments, one is aware. She is a guilty innocent, for whom rightly or wrongly one must weep. It is terrible for her, coming home to the null little roadside house at Tostes the day after the ball. It is terrible when she receives the basket of apricots; and when, at table with her husband that same evening, she sees the lights of Rodolphe's carriage driving away across Yonville square. Running through the early morning sunshine to Rodolphe's house, singing on the Seine with Leon, in the ray of moonlight coming between the iron shutters of the boat, to the metronome-sound of the oars, she is happy. Is Emma a 'character'? Not, I think, in the English novelist's sense. She consists in sentiments and sensations, in moments for their own sake.

Flaubert and the proprietors of the *Revue de Paris*, in which *Madame Bovary* appeared, were prosecuted for immorality. They were acquitted; but the fact that the charge was brought procured for the novel, when in 1857 it appeared in book form, a notoriety as disgusting to Flaubert as it was unforeseen. '*Bovary*,' he had once remarked, '*c'est moi*.' At any rate, it had not occurred to him to denounce her. Must one, then, be 'for' or 'against' a character? Apparently. His dislike for the French middle-classes (with which we must deal further) did not decrease.

The report of the 'Bovary trial,' with the defence speech, appended to most of the French editions, is worth reading.

It had been in September 1849, that du Camp and Bouilhet received an awaited summons to Croisset. The occasion was to be solemn; a culmination of their so far tripartite life in art. Flaubert had completed *La Tentation de Saint Antoine*—that this version was to be the first of three was not then (how should it be?) foreseeable —and was to read out *Saint Anthony* to the two others. The study doors were closed; they seated themselves at the round table; there was a silence, then the reading began. It occupied eight sessions of four hours. At the end there was once more a silence, ice-cold—du Camp remained with his eyes down; it was left, as so often happens, to the more pleasant nature, to Bouilhet, to say the unpleasant thing. 'We think you should throw it into the fire and never speak of it again.'

Everything, it came out under their analysis, was wrong with that *Temptation of Saint Anthony*—beginning and ending with the fact that they found it impossible to make out what Flaubert was driving at. Whatever the hermit had or had not done, Gustave, it seemed, had yielded to all temptations—obscurity, 'diffuseness of pathos,' over-decoration, exaggeration, bombast, verbosity. To cap everything, was this not an imitation of Faust? . . . Mme Flaubert, sleepless, haunted the outside of the study door:

inside the study, her son continued to bare his breast to knives.

Into the fire *Saint Anthony* did not go. Flaubert, who abandoned nothing, would of all books never abandon this. It was 'Alfred's book'; it was his own magnetic East; it was the reply to the picture once seen in Genoa. That obstination as to *Saint Anthony* has so many layers; one cannot drill down past a point. To simplify, one might call this his symbol book: the book that it was inevitable that one should want to write early and that one would not be capable of writing properly till late. Half-way between the time wished and the time due, in fact in 1857, during the serialized appearance of *Bovary*, he once more brought out the manuscript and began to revise it—then came the Bovary trial: in revulsion he even turned from *Saint Anthony*. 1874 gives us the final version (*Salammbô* and *L'Éducation Sentimentale* had intervened). Flaubert's books seem bound either to project across or retreat from what may be taken as the average, medium line of popular favour—*Saint Anthony*, I should judge, is the extreme case of recession: it is the book for few. The antithesis on which it is built is simple, but the erudition, the panorama of mythology is frightening: one must know too much in order to understand. The ascetic, the abandoner of the world for one thing, on trial, his own judge—there was an adolescent melodramaticism in Flaubert's first seizing on the Anthony image. The anchorite in the desert, the hut in the amphitheatre of rocks. . . . *Here*, we have the third version, burned quite pure: no, he did not throw the *Saint Anthony* of the Croisset reading into the fire, but he did fire it. What the process was, the student of writing can and should learn by comparison of this last *Saint Anthony* with the preceding two.

Hatred of the bourgeois must either sour one or become mirth. With the Romantics of Rouen, young, the shared fury had been from the first enjoyable. Life, collisions and the enormities of experience were to harshen it, but could one forget?—Flaubert did not—that this had begun in games, with hyperboles, conspiracies, the collection of 'cases,' the exquisite compilation of a *cliché* dictionary (for additions to which one strained one's ears at gatherings) and, best of all, with the erection and breathing of life into a Magog of middle-classness, the 'Garçon'. This 'Garçon' stalks through the Flaubert books—nor can one believe that his entrance was ever unaccompanied by that smile which Proust (as a writer on writing not unlike Flaubert) in the writer denounces: one should not amuse oneself. This 'Garçon' is Homais in *Bovary*; he is to be seen in play among the 1848 prisoner-prodders of *L'Éducation Sentimentale*. Flaubert was spared living to watch him salute in ranks in a coloured shirt—but, equally, he was not allowed to finish his 'Garçon' masterpiece, *Bouvard et Pécuchet*, that overdue expansion of all his, perhaps all, intellectual fun. This book, begun in age (age was premature with him) should be read in youth. Or, no: perhaps one requires two-thirds of life behind one, already, to relish it to the full?

Bouvard et Pécuchet is a Little Man story, written with a sympathetic, all-embracing destructiveness which would not have done well in Britain during our recent war. Impossible, all the same, not to like these fellows, these two clerks, dropping down beside one another on a boulevard bench, discovering their first sympathy in the fact that they have both written their names inside their hats. The fortuity is to deepen into a bond; the result of the conversational sniffings proves reassuring—both are good fellows, dealers in the received idea. Bouvard inherits a fortune; he buys a property between Caen and Falaise—is it inappropriate that Bouvard's domain should have provided a battle-ground for a war arising from the perversion of just such ductile chaps? Both move to the country, to try out received ideas, and others to be receivable, on Nature. . . . We can but suffer with them as we suffer with Emma Bovary—Nature taxes their ingenuity to the last. Early comes the fiasco of the party to show off the 'architected' garden. (The dilution in whimsey of the received idea is not to be overlooked.) . . . Flaubert documented himself for *Bouvard et Pécuchet* with a thoroughness even the preparations for *Saint Anthony* could not equal; he is said, for instance, to have read more than a hundred books on arboriculture to supply what reduced to hardly more than a paragraph. Intellect tracked, checked and justified, all the way, the writing of this last obsessional book.

II

Salammbô. L'Éducation Sentimentale. Trois Contes

'I think,' observed Flaubert, writing to Sainte-Beuve, 'that I have been less hard on humanity in *Salammbô* than in *Madame Bovary*.

The curiosity, the love which impelled me towards vanished religions and vanished peoples have about them something moral and sympathetic, it seems to me.'

To us, this could seem possible. *Salammbô*, published in 1862, could be felt by the reader of the late 1940's to be the most, from his point of view, contemporary of the Flaubert novels. But this story of Carthage, with its operatic resplendence, its unremitting heat and, most of all, its brutalities, clanged on the nerves and distressed the senses of the senior critics of Second Empire France. Its characters, each intolerably dominated by a fixed idea, over-charged, never moving otherwise than in a fury or in a trance, were found unintelligible—particularly, as the author foresaw, by ladies. The book, he had estimated, would annoy the bourgeois—'which is to say, everyone.' And indeed, in so far as *Salammbô* did have in Flaubert any convulsive source, there was that 'suffocating' hatred of his own epoch and its stupidities of which he spoke to Bouilhet. A young generation, sharing this point of view, countered the attacks with enthusiasm.

It is not to be assumed that Flaubert would have found us less detestable. But it does seem likely that we, present-day readers of *Salammbô*, have nerves and senses differently keyed. If we are not, as it is to be hoped, more callous, we are more resistant. Consciously suffering our own epoch, we have a Carthage in our present-day sense of life. The psychic note of *Salammbô* is in our compass; the story presents analogies we cannot ignore, and the characters, if still forbidding, are not inscrutable.

At the time when *Salammbô* was written, the world had reason to consider itself still within bounds; the European ideal engaged confidence. It was not merely the bourgeois who recoiled from this Carthaginian blast from the Croisset writing-table: the book shocked the finer liberal mind, the responsible sensibility of its day. In us, that recoil can still, and should, be felt. But a recognition is forced upon us: *Salammbô* was not only historic but prophetic.

In a letter written while he was at this work, Flaubert anatomizes the difficulties of the historical novel. In general, and with exceptions to be found, the historical novel is, from the point of view of art, a hybrid, ever-doubtfully satisfactory; and as a form of psychological exploration it is not less dubious in its results. One can but think of the centuries as one must of races, as infinitely estranging to and estranged from one another. To perceive the people of any distant past as they were needs, virtually, clairvoyance—or, at least, the acceptance of Croce's view that the historic sense is an intuition. Granted the clairvoyance or intuition—upon which, by his own showing, Flaubert in part relied—how, still to render the past in terms comprehensible (if not acceptable) to one's own time? For Flaubert, looking further into the novel than most writers, this doubled a for him ever-existing problem—how to deliver, most immediately and with the least loss, the novel's idea. 'The difficulty,' he said, 'is in finding the *right* note. This is to be obtained by an excessive concentration on the idea, whether naturally or by force of will; but it is not easy to imagine a constant truth. . . . Moreover, in order to be understood it is necessary to make a sort of permanent translation, and what a gulf that opens between the absolute and the rest of the work! And then, the good French reader, who "wants to be respected" has a ready-made idea as to antiquity: he will have it in on me for giving him what does not resemble that. . . .'

How does *Salammbô* open? With Carthage, still a resounding name but a Carthage at bay, her nominal exceeding her actual power. Now, at the end of the war in Sicily, she finds it impossible to pay off the Mercenaries, the hired Barbarian army, who have got her the victory by their brute force. These thousands, increasingly disaffected, have streamed back into Carthage, where they await their due. Their animal alien presence is to be felt among the terraces, the temples, the shops, the wine-cellars, arsenals and bakeries, and the immune garden-cooled houses of the rich. Hamilcar, who commanded the Mercenaries, is away: to-night, however, by his orders, they are being feasted, as a propitiation, in his gardens. Wine flows, a pent-up frenzy breaks out. Ligurians, Lusitanians, Balearics, Greeks, fugitives from Rome work each other up, burn and surge and wreck. In the gardens' treetops the monkeys dedicated to the moon are roasted by the climbing fires; trunks are hacked off elephants; slaves are let out to run free; there is a holocaust of the jewelled sacred fish from the lake in front of the palace. Out from the palace comes Hamilcar's dedicated daughter Salammbô. Virgin, hierarchical, ignorant of everything but her own cult, Salammbô comes down the terraces step by step, singing to her lyre, heading a procession of eunuch priests. Walking among the revellers, she continues to sing Carthage's mystic story and vanished puissance. Pausing beside the table of the captains, she reproaches them for the murder of the fish. Her look, by falling upon, seems to single out Mâtho, the young Libyan chief, who from now on is to be haunted by love and terror. It is Mâtho who, counselled by Spendius, the released slave, the wily Greek, is to become a leader of the Barbarians when, after their sortie from Carthage, they make an enraged return. It is Mâtho who, led by Spendius, makes away with the sacrosanct veil of Thanit. It is to Mâtho's tent in the Barbarian encampment that Salammbô journeys alone to retrieve the veil. We are to have the return of Hamilcar, his scourging anger against Carthage, his campaign against the Barbarians in the tributary countries. . . .

One might say, a scenario. But not for Hollywood; these battlepieces and tortures, sacrifices to Moloch, crucified lions, vultures' wings brushing the faces of dying crucified men are outside the vocabulary of the New World. One might say, the outline of a poetic drama, for Marlowe if not Shakespeare. But under Flaubert's treatment poetry displaces itself from the declaimed word to the scene and movement: there is no soaring speech; the personages are muted and taciturn. The unrolling and flashing are for the eye, in the cast of Carthage in sun or moonlight, in the ridges of open landscape and the sinister narrowness of passes, in fateful massing of men or their resigned defiling across country. Here is visual rhetoric: this is an overpowering visual book.

'Do not,' Flaubert said to Taine, 'compare the interior vision of the artist with that of the truly hallucinated man. I know both states perfectly: there is an abyss between them. In hallucination, within the meaning of the act, there is always terror; you feel your personality escaping you; you think you are going to die. In the poetic vision, on the contrary, there is a joy; it is something which enters into you. It is none the less true that one no longer knows where one is.'

When it is said that *Salammbô* was the result of a sustained, gigantic act of imagination on Flaubert's part, it must, at the same time, be understood that the function of the imagination, by his rule of art, had to be no less limited than it was intensive. Which meant, that imagination should illuminate but should not supply—in the sense of faking or improvizing—facts. Anything ascertainable must be ascertained: there must not be the slightest haziness, chanciness, incorrectness in any picture he gave of the outside world, whether past or present. He documented himself for *Salammbô*, as for *St. Anthony*, by hard, wide, insatiable reading which would appear to have left no source untouched. He had reason, he could say with equanimity, to believe his Carthage to be as near to Carthage as it was possible to come. To an interrogatory he stood up with zest. Ultimately, the Carthage that works on us is the psychic concept. But he could not have given the concept that full force had he remained uncertain, and thus uneasy, as to any historic or concrete detail able to be verified after two thousand years. Unlike Proust, he could make no æsthetic use of the blurs and distortions of half-memory. He broke off in the early chapters of *Salammbô* to revisit Tunis, first seen during his travels with du Camp.

To research, as thorough but of a different kind, for *Bouvard et Pécuchet* we have referred already. For *L'Éducation Sentimentale* (published, after seven years of work, in 1869) it was to be a question of a not distant past which had, none the less, had time to become historic. Frédéric, hero of this novel, views the Paris scenes of the 1848 Revolution with only sporadic interest, sometimes with apathy. Frédéric, so far as one can compute, would have been by only a year or two Flaubert's junior; and Frédéric's creator was, twenty or so years hence, to regret his youthful vagueness as to the Revolution. His scheme for *L'Éducation Sentimentale* confronted Flaubert, in middle age, with reconstructing what he ought *then* to have watched—the political, revolutionary, social, intellectual, commercial and more prosperous *demi-monde* Paris of 1848. He succeeded in doing this, and in adding more. The barricade fighting, the mob in the Tuileries, the shot-spattered façades, the convocations of enthusiasts, the encampment and action of the National Guard have an unnerving verisimilitude. These scenes are more than cinema; they play off as though recorded, at the time of their happening, on nervous wax. But not for these only went the research: Frédéric's movements in and out of Paris were checked as for a dossier—there were consulted dusty old coach and train time-tables for the relevant year. And, was it essential, one might ask, that Frédéric and Mme Arnoux should have one, one only, of their many interviews in a china factory? Those few pages were to involve Flaubert in the technicalities of an entire process.

It must have been essential. To examine the structure and motivation of *L'Éducation Sentimentale* is like opening the back of a clock. Here is an interrelation of coils and tensions, springs and weights, cogs and hammers. In the plot, nothing does not act upon something else. This is the longest, the most complex and, in its action, deliberately the slowest of Flaubert's novels. (One cannot, it is to be noted, call it the most ambitious; each was the most ambitious in its turn; each offered unique difficulties upon which he was to impale himself; each opened up vistas of possibility before which he quailed.) *L'Éducation Sentimentale* inherited the title of an early work, and represents the recasting, in his maturity, of a youthful idea. This putting of emotion into perspective could not be done other than unemotionally. This novel, drawing more than any other upon Flaubert's personal experiences as a man, could not but be the supreme test of his impersonality as an artist.

It has been said by some that *L'Éducation Sentimentale* fails because of a dullness or insipidity or lack of emotional range in its central figure. Actually, what may be disconcerting is the detachment of Flaubert's own attitude—a detachment which, even, subdues irony. The reader's demand to be engaged emotionally is not met—nor, even, with Frédéric does one become, as one did with Emma Bovary, a reluctant confederate. To admire, as it deserves, and to enjoy to the degree due to oneself *L'Éducation Sentimentale*, one has to release oneself from the idea that character is the real subject of any novel—the subject of this one is not the nature of Frédéric, but the nature of feeling. Frédéric Moreau, in his interknit four relationships with four women— Mme Arnoux, Louise Roque, Mme Dambreuse and the gallant Rosanette—seems dull in being will-less, passive. But so is a mirror passive; and Frédéric is in the mirror sense anything but dull—he reflects, records. He records an amazing, if not the whole, range of the sensations of love. He has been given by Flaubert, out of Flaubert and for Flaubert's purpose, susceptibility—accordingly, every scene, face or object which passes Frédéric's eyes—from the start, when the changing banks of the Seine are drawn past the river-steamer on whose deck he stands— stands out in a purity of distinctness, almost stereoscopic. And more, each scene is charged with its own moment—the foggy winter evening streets through which Frédéric walks beside Mme Arnoux seal up in themselves the ambience of an unspeaking love; Fontainebleau, château and forest with Rosanette, holds the charm of a sensuous acquiescence.

As draughtsman and painter the Flaubert of *L'Éducation Sentimentale* is at his most superb. Few novels hold such interiors or such landscape. Here he captures, still more than in *Madame Bovary*, everything that is lyrical in provincial France—gardens, islands, riversides, flowing water, fluttering leaves, summer-houses. (It seems fitting that the garden pavilion of Croisset should survive him.) He renders in words, as did his contemporaries the Impressionists in light-filled colour, the joy, more than half unconscious, of the beholding eye. He shows, even, an adorable touch with dress—Mme Arnoux's gowns, Rosanette's bonnet-ribbons, the mock-emerald pin in little Louise's hair. As for the Paris of this book, one can say that a young man's Paris had, for the Flaubert into his 'forties, acquired distance. By which gained, not lost. The necessariness, for Flaubert, of distance for vision, of vision for art, is stated.

He laid aside *Bouvard et Pécuchet* for two years in order to write the *Trois Contes* (published in 1877). These three short stories have something more endearing than their perfection of form—though, as to that, the perfection is to be marvelled at: one may wonder why Flaubert had not turned to this genre before. Their simplicity and their humanness—for there is humanity even in the harsh *Hérodias*, remote little cousin, as it were, of *Salammbô*—make the *Trois Contes* suggest themselves as an ideal first approach, for any would-be reader, to Flaubert: it seems a pity that they are so often sought out so late, if at all. *Un Cœur Simple*, the life-story of a servant, is moving—a word to be used advisedly but used here. Something religious and tender in Flaubert's attitude to the simple person appears, in this short story, as never before. And this lovingness remains near the surface in *La Légende de Saint Julien l'Hospitalier*, mediæval, inspired, he says, by a stained glass window in a church 'in my own country.' The story of the hunts-man-saint rustles with life, like the forests in it, full of savagery and holiness, pride and sorrow, animals and a soul. It is beautiful. *Hérodias*, it is said, came from a carving as did *Saint Julien* from a

D

window; and is, indeed, stone-sharp rather than translucent. The anxious Tetrarch, his haggard scheming wife, the cold greedy visiting Romans, the indomitable John the Baptist roaring up from the bottom of his dungeon, and Salome (stripped of the tawdriness which has been allowed to surround her since), a very young girl dancing at a banquet, walking round a balustrade on her hands. . . . The *Trois Contes*, were they a holiday of the imagination, a dwelling on what was cool and sweet, a stay with lyricism, before the resumption of work on the old anger? He went back, as we know, to *Bouvard et Pécuchet*, to the remorseless comedy, to the contemplation of fatuity and futility, to the furious elaboration of the joke which never wore itself out of him, but which wore him out.

'I have, myself,' he had written to Louise Colet when he was thirty-one, 'a certain concept of style: a style that should be beautiful, that someone will make someday, ten years or ten centuries hence. A style to be rhythmic as verse, precise as the language of science. . . . Prose was born yesterday, that's what one should remind oneself. All combinations in prosody have been already arrived at; those of prose are still to be found.' And, in another letter,'. . . there are neither beautiful nor bad subjects. One could almost establish as axiomatic that there is no such thing as a subject at all, style being in itself an absolute manner of seeing.' And elsewhere: 'I am convinced that everything is a question of style, or, better, of presentation.'

These *dicta*, taken from the background of his mind while he was at grips with the writing of his first effective novel, may offend by sounding priggish or calculating. There are persons, indeed, to whom Flaubert's whole theory of writing is antipathetic. To the Anglo-Saxon, particularly, there is something unseemly in the idea of a man sobbing and sweating over a manuscript. (One cannot, either, excuse or write off Flaubert as 'an excitable Frenchman': he was hardly Latin—he had, as a Norman, much in common with the English in the matter of physique, temperament and even, if one goes back far enough, heredity.) The idea of an artist as someone joyous, easy and disengaged, blown through by the rushing mighty wind of his inspiration, is more appealing. But there is this to be said: Flaubert, in the course of those very struggles, drew off into *himself* every fever that struggle breeds.

No trace of what he suffered in making art was allowed to pass through to the art itself—which may be found, if anything, too God-like, too glassily impassive, too calm and clear. The difficulties he, as a writer, faced were partly those generic to all writers, partly his own—of his own seeking. The analysis he made of the difficulties (always, it should be remembered, in letters to his most intimate friends) eased and cleared his mind. He was not pretentious, he was impassioned; he had neither time nor desire to be didactic. I do not find it possible to classify Flaubert as an 'æsthete'; there was no aspect of life, however prosaic or vulgar, upon which he willingly turned his back; and he was involved deeply, at every turn, with his exacting morality. The letters quoted in this Introduction were written, mostly, when he was a young man, but no ideas or ideals voiced in them were abandoned later: on the contrary, he held to those more closely with every year that he continued to live and write. Live and write?—the two were synonymous. A sin against art, for him, was a moral sin. He was not, it may be argued, moral in his judgments of life. But how could he be?—a point (not necessarily *the* point) of his art is that on life it passes no judgments of any kind, good or bad.

Virtue in art, for him, was impersonality. To be personal, he said, was to be weak. He spoke to Louise Colet of that puissant exaltation possible for the writer once he was clear of *himself*. One must not—it amounted to simply this—allow one's self, one's feelings, one's desires, one's point of view, to enter one's book at all. The idea, which since his day has gained so much ground, that writing is 'self-expression' was shocking to him. He praised Shakespeare's 'superhuman impersonality.' 'Does one know if Shakespeare were sad or cheerful? The artist should so arrange as to make posterity think he has never lived.'

Flaubert, however, man of big frame and nature, could not hope, on his way through life, to cover his tracks. His emergences from the Croisset study became events for a widening circle of friends. In his later life, nothing succeeded the early intimacies— Alfred, the beloved romantic who died young, was never forgotten; Flaubert grew nearer to Bouilhet, of the solid and just intelligence, and further away from slick and worldy du Camp— typical man of letters about-town. Bad relations, in fact, with du Camp had set in early: it had been exasperating, at thirty-one, to be lectured, in a string of letters from Paris, on the evils of running to seed in the provinces, to be adjured to come to Paris and 'meet everyone.' '*To be known*,' replied Gustave promptly, 'is not my first business; that only satisfies the most mediocre vanities. I am out for something better; to please myself. . . . Shadow for shadow, give me the greater.' The implication could not be lost on Maxime. Whereupon: '*Mon cher*,' came the bland voice from Croisset, 'I am sorry to find you so sensitive.'

To Paris, when he did choose to come, Flaubert brought an avowed, undiluted sturdy provinciality: they could take him or leave him. His sociability (as so often happens) became greater as, with the advance in years, his faculty for intimacy became less. His relations with Sainte-Beuve, Taine, Gautier, Turgeniev, the Goncourts, Zola, Renan, Daudet were congenial, expansive, reciprocally warm. The now elderly George Sand (the '*Chère Maître*' of the letters), counted for much: she came, as woman friend, to the Croisset which to the poor '*Muse*,' the mistress, had been forbidden; and another great correspondence fills in the gaps between. The young Guy de Maupassant had, as Alfred's nephew and as a pupil-writer, a double claim: that relationship demands a book to itself.

But a picture of any one mellow period would be false. Of trouble—loss, change, grief—there was more rather than less in the later years. Bouilhet, having established considerable fame as a dramatist, broke down in health, then, in 1869, died: that death drew from Flaubert a moving letter, after the silence of many years, to du Camp, 'Now there is only you. Do you remember how we' [we *three* by implication] 'used to write to each other, *Solus ad Solum?*' . . . There was the 1870–71 Franco-Prussian war: Flaubert the Frenchman was spared none of the bitterness of the defeat, Flaubert the Norman, here in the Rouen area, none of the chagrins and strains of the occupation. The Croisset house was occupied by Prussian officers: Mme Flaubert, finished by shock and hardship, died in 1872. The niece Caroline's marriage, some years before, not only left Flaubert now quite alone at Croisset; it was to involve her uncle in years of worry—Flaubert sacrificed the greater part of his capital in an attempt to stave off the collapse of Caroline's husband's business. A novelist so uncompromising could not, and never did, expect to live by his pen: sheer existence,

for the remaining years, was not easy. Moreover, health failed
again; there were recurrences of the original malady. He worked,
if anything, harder; ate, as the strain and his physical size demanded, heavily, and ceased altogether to take exercise—it is hard
to keep up the heart for solitary walks. Apoplexy appears to have
been the cause of his death at Croisset in 1880.

We should be remembered by what we in the end remember:
our good days. 'Sometimes,' he had said long ago, 'on my good
days of sunshine, I have sighted . . . a state of soul to which fame
would be nothing and even happiness useless.'

1947.

THE FABER BOOK OF MODERN
SHORT STORIES

The short story is a young art: as we now know it, it is the child of this century. Poetic tautness and clarity are so essential to it that it may be said to stand at the edge of prose; in its use of action it is nearer to drama than to the novel. The cinema, itself busy with a technique, is of the same generation: in the last thirty years the two arts have been accelerating together. They have affinities—neither is sponsored by a tradition; both are, accordingly, free; both, still, are self-conscious, show a self-imposed discipline and regard for form; both have, to work on, immense matter—the disorientated romanticism of the age. The new literature, whether written or visual, is an affair of reflexes, of immediate susceptibility, of associations not examined by reason: it does not attempt a synthesis. Narrative of any length involves continuity, sometimes a forced continuity: it is here that the novel too often becomes invalid. But action, which must in the novel be complex and motivated, in the short story regains heroic simplicity.

An art having behind it little tradition is at once impetuous and halting, and is very affectable. Its practitioners are still tentative, watching each other: some positive and original mind is wanted to renew impetus, or to direct it. The short story as an art has come into being through a disposition to see life in a certain way. But the writer himself may stay unaware of this new disposition if he have not already seen it made evident elsewhere in art: only the rare writer does not look for a precedent. In England, the limitations of narrative prose with its *longueurs*, its conventions dangerous to truth, had appeared for a long time to be impassable: oblique narration, cutting (as in the cinema), the unlikely placing of emphasis, or symbolism (the telling use of the object both for its own sake and as an image) were unknown. The short story was once the condensed novel; it needed a complex subject and depended for merit on the skill with which condensation had been effected. The short stories of James and Hardy show, in their excellence, a sober virtuosity: they are *tours de force* by practised executants, side-issues from the crowded imagination. They show, *qua* the short story, no urgent æsthetic necessity; their matter does not dictate their form. Their shortness is not positive; it is non-extension. They are great architects' fancies, little buildings on an august plan. They have no emotion that is abrupt and special; they do not give mood or incident a significance outside the novelist's power to explore. Their very excellence made them a dead end: they did not invite imitation or advance in any way a development in the short story proper. That impetus that it needed, the English short story had to get from abroad. Rumour, the translation and easier circulation of foreign books, also a widening curiosity, brought Tchehov and Maupassant into the English view.

The influences of two foreign masters on an affectable new form have necessarily run counter to one another. Tchehov stands (or stands with us) for an emancipation of faculties, for a romantic distension of the form of the story to let in what might appear inchoate or nebulous. Maupassant stands for astringency, iron relevance. Tchehov opened up for the writer tracts of emotional landscape; he made subjectivity edit and rule experience and pull art, obliquely, its way. His work was a system of irritations beautified; he secreted over the grit inside his shell. His hero was the sub-man; he crystallized frustration, inertia, malaise, vacancy, futile aspiration, shy or sly pretentiousness. He dragged that involuntary sub-life of the spirit up into the impassive light of art. The suffering, too-intelligent and submissive bourgeois is typified in him; he came of that class which fosters its own annihilation, and which revolution cannot obliterate. He was, in art's sense, a political force in art, revolting against the aristocratic rejection of matter for manner's sake. He made his own manner, commanding it so completely as to suggest less discipline than it had—and this has, on the whole, made him a dangerous influence. He has been made to sponsor self-concern, licence, fortuity.

Maupassant was the born popular writer, battered by Flaubert into austerity. His themes were simple: lust, cruelty, money and that sort of rose-pink fancy that has such a charnel underneath. He transcribed passions in the only terms possible—dispassionate understatement. There was an uninterrupted communication between his thought and his senses; his sort of erotic nearness to what he wrote of give him a cautious language that never exceeds art. He saw life in a glare; life composed itself for him into pictures in primary colours, outlines in black chalk. His writing was energetic, ruthless, nervous and plain. Tchehov sustained with his subject a sensitive, sometimes painful, flirtation: Maupassant touched nothing of which he was not the prey. His hardness and capability made him that rare thing—the first-rate *unliterary* writer.

Till lately, Maupassant has repelled the bulk of the English, or has been read for reasons not connected with art. His work shows unhuman fire, like an animal's eye; his uncomplexity is not sympathetic. His finish appeared to have a touch of the shop about it, a faded smartness not yet fully 'period.' He had not been taught impersonality for nothing: the artist without tricks very seldom starts a school. Tchehov's cloudy detachment, charged with pity, has been more acceptable here; his deceptive looseness got him imitators. Tchehov started in England a new, a prose romanticism, romanticism of suburbs and provinces. He influenced at second-hand, through the work of Katherine Mansfield, a group of writers who did not know him directly, or only turned to him later. This group is now in turn exerting an influence, so that Tchehov may be indirectly copied by writers who do not read, or intend to read, him at all. It is arguable that, had Tchehov not been translated and first given his vogue by a few eclectics, a large body of English stories might have remained unwritten. He was a great incentive, but should not be a model. He has been devoutly and unconsciously parodied; we have suffered outpourings of minor dismay, of mediocre sentiment. From the dregs of his influence our most vital short story writers now seem to revolt.

This cult of Tchehov has had, however, its natural boundaries. The Irish Sea makes a bigger break in sentiment than the Atlantic, and Irish and American writers of the short story have—for all their differences in temper—strong common qualities. Extraverted coldness in art, objectivity, may be the fruit of a life that is, or has been lately, physically exciting or uncertain, life that is quick, rough or lived at high nervous tension, in which either sexual or political passion makes society unsafe. Precipitate feeling makes for hard form in art. The younger Irish writers have almost all carried arms; American civilization keeps the Americans, nervously, armed men: fact there overtops fantasy. There is a state of living in which events assault the imagination, stunning it:

such a state of living enforces its own, a now no longer unique, literature. Amazement—involuntary and to a degree fathomed—is part of poetry. In the short story, semi-poetic, amazement is not only not fathomed but not stated; but has to be made evident. The writer must so strip fact of neutralizing elements as to return to it, and prolong for it, its first power: what was in life a half-second of apprehension must be perpetuated. The extraverted short story—bare of analysis, sparse in emotional statement—is the formula for, never the transcript of, that amazement with which poetry deals. The particular must be given general significance. Narration is bound to be exact and impassive. This method, which was Maupassant's, is now in the hands of the Irish, the Americans, some of the younger English. Liam O'Flaherty, Hemingway have perfected it. It has dangers, which are now becoming apparent—style may be too much deflated, feeling is threatened with an over-simplification that makes it savage and dull.

Properly, this collection—which invites the reader to study the development of the short story in English since, roughly, 1910, to notice its variations and watch its trend—ought to include the work of Americans. The superiority, in general, of the American short story to the British has been too eagerly claimed on the far side of the Atlantic, but this is not enough to make the claim invalid. The American level of workmanship is higher; also, to-day, from the American pen our used language starts with new vitality. The American story writer has as his matter a hybrid psychology, city life at once slick and macabre and a wide continent not yet at all fully explored by art—and he has the habit of travel. The inclusion, here, of American short stories would heighten the standard of the collection and make for a wider view. But it would mean the exclusion, to make space, of a number of English stories equally vital and serious, if not so finished in their carrying-out. Moreover, the best American writing is as positively American as French writing is French: its imposing foreignness must raise all sorts of issues not relevant to the study of English work. The English short story—however much it may have owed, initially, to abroad—must advance always inside the national limitations. Irish short stories are included because the tie between the two countries, however irksome, has made some kind of affinity, however artificial. On the Irish side, indignation has been fruitful;

the long, hopeless, romantic quarrel has bred literature. And in Ireland the English language is not yet stale.

Protection in art is only justified by a fairly strong claim for the home product. Such a claim the stories here will have to substantiate. To select them was not easy. In this country, within the past fifteen years, the non-commercial or free short story—that is to say, the story unsuitable, not meant to be suitable, for the popular, well-paying magazines, and free, therefore, not to conform with so-called popular taste—has found a wider opening: it has come to have an eclectic vogue. Production in this department has consequently increased. But, unhappily, the free story is being fostered with less discrimination than good faith. It is too generally taken that a story by *being* non-commercial may immediately pretend to art. Emancipation from commercial conventions was excellent—but now a fresh set of conventions threatens to spring up and to prove as tyrannous, dangerous to living work. Too many free stories show, both in technique and subject, a desolating and nerveless similarity. The public gets slated by the free short story's promoters for not giving such stories a more grateful reception, or supporting the magazines in which they appear. But why should anyone tolerate lax, unconvincing or arty work—work whose idiom too often shows a touch of high-hat complacency? The commercial short story writer had his own, hard-learnt, competence: the new, non-commercial story, if it is to be important, should be able to make its way, any distance, on its intrinsic merits—it still has to be, in one sense or another, subsidized. Subsidy dishonours what ought to be, in the great sense, a popular art. At present, a very large number of free stories lack verisimilitude, are pompous, dissatisfying—they are not up to the mark. But what is the mark?

The mark is, the completeness, or spherical perfection, latent in any story that is projected rightly; a completeness to which any story having the germ of real life should be capable of expanding, but which too few reach—at an indefinable moment the writer's purpose slackens, or some adventitious emotion starts to deform the story. The first necessity for the short story, at the set out, is *necessariness*. The story, that is to say, must spring from an impression or perception pressing enough, acute enough, to have made the writer write. Execution must be voluntary and careful, but conception should have been involuntary, a vital fortuity. The sought-about-for subject gives the story a dead kernel, however skilfully words may have been applied: the language, being *voulu*, remains inorganic. Contrived, unspontaneous feeling makes for unquickened prose. The story should have the valid central emotion and inner spontaneity of the lyric; it should magnetize the imagination and give pleasure—of however disturbing, painful or complex a kind. The story should be as composed, in the plastic sense, and as visual as a picture. It must have tautness and clearness; it must contain no passage not æsthetically relevant to the whole. The *necessary* subject dictates its own relevance. However plain or lively or unpretentious be the manner of the story, the central emotion—emotion however remotely involved or hinted at—should be austere, major. The subject must have implicit dignity. If in the writer half-conscious awe of his own subject be lacking, the story becomes flooded with falseness, mawkishness, whimsicality or some ulterior spite. The plot, whether or not it be ingenious or remarkable, for however short a way it is to be pursued, ought to raise some issue, so that it may continue in the mind. The art of the short story permits a break at what in the novel would be the crux of the plot: the short story, free from the *longueurs* of the novel is also exempt from the novel's conclusiveness—too often forced and false: it may thus more nearly than the novel approach æsthetic and moral truth. It can, while remaining rightly prosaic and circumstantial, give scene, action, event, character a poetic new actuality. It must have had, to the writer, moments of unfamiliarity, where it imposed itself.

The writer's imagination must operate in the world, whether factual or fantastic, that is most natural to it. The one nineteenth-century writer, in English, of the short story proper, Edgar Allan Poe, dealt almost wholly in fantasy: in England, in the same century, the much humbler F. Anstey, with a few little-known stories, followed. Since Poe's day, it has been the English rather than the Americans who have occupied the fantastic domain. Pure, objectified or projected fantasy (as opposed to private, escapist fantasy, or to *Bovaryisme*) stays, on the whole, with our older writers, or writers early in time, such as Richard Middleton, who died young by his own act. Rudyard Kipling and H. G. Wells, with some of their greatest stories, Walter de la Mare, E. M. Forster, Algernon Blackwood and M. R. James have each added to a terribly likely world, whose oddness has a super-rationality, which is waiting just at the edge of normal experience. Younger writers have, now and then, each projected his own ray into it. The fantasy story has often a literary beauty that is disarming; the one test one can apply is: does the *imagination* find this credible? Any crazy house against moonlight might, like the House of Usher, split right down to show the moon: there is assent at once, but no way to check up. Fancy has an authority reason cannot challenge. The pure fantasy writer works in a free zone: he has not to reconcile inner and outer images.

There is only one pure (or externalized) fantasy story in this book: the separate nature and problems of the fantasy story set it apart; also, the general trend of the short story has been, lately, towards inward, or, as it were, applied and functional fantasy, which does not depart from life but tempers it. Pure (as opposed to applied) fantasy has, it is true, reappeared in the apocalyptic writing of Dylan Thomas: the delirium or the dream. This may be another beginning. Up to now, however, and during most of the period this collection covers, writers have, rather, tended to explore and annotate different kinds of escape or of compensation. The retreat from fact that private fantasy offers has been as grateful in life as its variations are fascinating to art. Man has to live how he can: overlooked and dwarfed he makes himself his own theatre. Is the drama inside heroic or pathological? Outward acts have often an inside magnitude. The short story, within its shorter span than the novel's, with its freedom from forced complexity, its possible lucidness, is able, like the poetic drama, to measure man by his aspirations and dreads and place him alone on that stage which, inwardly, every man is conscious of occupying alone.

Omissions from this collections should be accounted for. I have omitted stories by two of our major writers, Rudyard Kipling and H. G. Wells: stories already classic, too well known and well liked to want further prominence or a given place. Both a Wells and a Kipling story are, however, intended to be taken as present, in the sense of other work being seen in relation to them. Somerset Maugham, whose preface to a collection of his own stories had so much matter, is represented not in proportion to his importance, by a very short tale. He, with the Kipling of *Plain*

Tales from the Hills the later *Phantom Rickshaw* and other stories, has most stably continued in the de Maupassant tradition. A Katherine Mansfield story was not available. H. E. Bates has, as a short storyist, already a substantial body of work to his name: its quality is so much recognized, its character so distinctive that he has become a term of comparison. He is less disabused than Tchehov. His work, which exercises, or has transmitted, an influence, should be kept in mind in the reading of stories here. Short stories by almost every English novelist of merit exist, and few are no more than by-products. But I have given preference to stories by writers who, whatever else they may or may not have written, show in this form a special, unique release of their faculties, or who by their use have given the short story new direction and force. Lack of space has made for other exclusions I do not propose to defend but must regret: several stories I wanted have had to be dropped out. In so far as this collection is to offer for a survey the short story since 1910, I cannot but feel that the period is not evenly covered. There is a preponderance of later work. This disproportion (given the scheme of the book) was to an extent inevitable, is to an extent deliberate—there has been increased production, a stronger impetus, inside the last ten years. Also, most recent stories have a close interest in so far as they show, up to date, the short story's trend. The short past of this art can, at the most, hold a no more than equal balance against its future.

The future lies, as in all arts, not with the artist only: the reader and critic have a share in it. If the short story is to keep a living dignity, and is not to be side-tracked into preciousness, popular impatience on the one hand and minority fervour on the other will have to be kept in check. The present state of the short story is, on the whole, healthy: its prospects are good. It shows on the plane of fact a better documentation, on the plane of feeling less showy uneasiness. Manner, once threatened with over-elaboration, has been simplified, subordinated to subject. The attack on convention is being better directed. There is a revulsion against 'rare' or inflated feeling—this revulsion, however, is sometimes dangerously strong. For it must be kept in mind that the short story, while rightly eschewing the false-poetic, cannot from its very nature be completely prosaic. Political bias, more and more appearing, has been to the good: it makes for a new heroicism.

This century's emotion, dislocated and stabbing, has at least this value: it makes a half-conscious artist of every feeling man. Peaks of common experience soar past an altitude-line into poetry. There is also a level immediately below this, on which life is being more and more constantly lived, at which emotion crystallizes without going icy, from which a fairly wide view is at command. This level the short story is likely to make its own.

1936.

THE DEMON LOVER

[Preface to the American Edition]

The stories in this collection, *The Demon Lover*, were written in wartime London—between the spring of 1941 and the late autumn of 1944. They were written for the magazines or papers in which they originally appeared. During these last years, I did not always write a story when I was asked for one; but I did not write any story that I was not asked for. For, at the same time, I have been writing a novel; and sometimes I did not want to imperil its continuity.

Does this suggest that these stories have been in any way forced or unwilling work? If so, that is not the case. Actually, the stimulus of being asked for a story, and the compulsion created by having promised to write one were both good—I mean, they acted as releases. Each time I sat down to write a story I opened a door; and the pressure against the other side of that door must, I found, have been very great, for things—ideas, images, emotions—came through with force and rapidity, sometimes violence. I do not say that these stories wrote themselves—æsthetically or intellectually speaking, I found the writing of some of them very difficult—but I was never in a moment's doubt as to *what* I was to write. The stories had their own momentum, which I had to control. The acts in them had an authority which I could not question. Odd enough in their way—and now some seem very odd—they were flying particles of something enormous and inchoate that had been going on. They were sparks from experience—an experience not necessarily my own.

During the war I lived, both as a civilian and as a writer, with every pore open; I lived so many lives, and, still more, lived among the packed repercussions of so many thousands of other lives, all under stress, that I see now it would have been impossible to have been writing only one book. I want my novel, which deals with this same time, to be comprehensive. But a novel must have form; and, for the form's sake, one is always having to make relentless exclusions. Had it not been for my from-time-to-time promises to write stories, much that had been pressing against the door might have remained pressing against the door in vain.

I do not feel I 'invented' anything written here. It seems to me that during the war in England the overcharged sub-consciousnesses of everybody overflowed and merged. It is because the general subconsciousness saturates these stories that they have an authority nothing to do with me.

These are all wartime, none of them *war*, stories. There are no accounts of war action even as I knew it—for instance, air raids. Only one character (in 'Mysterious Kôr') is a soldier; and he only appears as a homeless wanderer round a city. These are, more, studies of climate, war-climate, and of the strange growths it raised. I see war (or should I say feel war?) more as a territory than as a page of history: of its impersonal active historic side I have, I find, not written. Arguably, writers are always slightly abnormal people: certainly, in so-called 'normal' times my sense of the abnormal has been very acute. In war, this feeling of slight differentiation was suspended: I felt one with, and just like, everyone else. Sometimes I hardly knew where I stopped and everyone else began. The violent destruction of solid things, the explosion of the illusion that prestige, power and permanence attach to bulk and weight, left all of us, equally, heady and disembodied. Walls went down; and we felt, if not knew, each other. We all lived in a state of lucid abnormality.

Till the proofs of *The Demon Lover* came, I had not re-read these stories since they were, singly, written. Reading the stories straight through as a collection, I am most struck by what they have in common. This integrates them and gives them a cumulative and collective meaning that no one of them, taken singly, has by itself. *The Demon Lover* is an organic whole: not merely a collection but somehow—for better or worse—a book. Also, the order in which the stories stand—an order come at, I may say, casually—seems itself to have a meaning, or to add a meaning, I did not foresee. We begin with a hostess who has not learned how with grace to open her own front door; we end with a pair of lovers with no place in which to sleep in each other's arms. In the first story, a well-to-do house in a polite square gives the impression of having been organically dislocated by shock; in the last, a pure abstract empty timeless city rises out of a little girl's troubled mind. Through the stories—in the order in which they are here placed—I find a rising tide of hallucination.

The stories are not placed in the time-order in which they were first written—though, by chance, 'In the Square,' placed first here, *is* the first in the book I wrote, in a hot, raid-less patch of 1941 summer, just after Germany had invaded Russia.

The hallucinations in the stories are not a peril; nor are the stories studies of mental peril. The hallucinations are an unconscious, instinctive, saving resort on the part of the characters: life, mechanized by the controls of wartime, and emotionally torn and impoverished by changes, had to complete itself in some other way. It is a fact that in Britain, and especially in London, in wartime many people had strange deep intense dreams. 'Whatever else I forget about the war,' a friend said to me, 'I hope I may never forget my own dreams, or some of the other dreams I have been told. We have never dreamed like this before; and I suppose we shall never dream like this again.'

Dreams by night, and the fantasies—these often childishly innocent—with which formerly matter-of-fact people consoled themselves by day were compensations. Apart from them, I do not think that the desiccation, by war, of our day-to-day lives can be enough stressed. The outside world war news was stupefying: headlines and broadcasts came down and down on us in hammer-like chops, with great impact but oddly little reverberation. The simple way to put it was: 'One cannot take things in.' What was happening was out of all proportion to our faculties for knowing, thinking and checking up. The circumstances under which ordinary British people lived were preposterous—so preposterous that, in a dull way, they simplified themselves. And all the time we knew that compared to those on the Continent we in Britain could not be said to suffer. Foreign faces about the London streets had personal pain and impersonal history sealed up behind the eyes. All this pressure drove egotism underground, or made it whiten like grass under a stone. And self-expression in small ways stopped—the small ways had been so very small that we had not realized how much they amounted to. Planning pleasures, choosing and buying things, wondering and wandering, dressing yourself up, and so on. All that stopped. You used to know what you were like from the things you liked, and chose. Now there was not what you liked, and you did not choose. Any remaining

E

choices and pleasures shot into new proportion and new value: people paid big money for little bunches of flowers.

Literature of the Resistance is now steadily coming in from France. I wonder whether in a sense all wartime writing is not resistance writing? In no way dare we who were in Britain compare ourselves with the French. But personal life here put up its own resistance to the annihilation that was threatening it—war. Everyone here, as is known, read more: and what was sought in books—old books, new books—was the communicative touch of personal life. To survive, not only physically but spiritually, was essential. People whose homes had been blown up went to infinite lengths to assemble bits of themselves—broken ornaments, odd shoes, torn scraps of the curtains that had hung in a room—from the wreckage. In the same way, they assembled and checked themselves from stories and poems, from their memories, from one another's talk. Outwardly, we accepted that at this time individual destiny had to count for nothing; inwardly, individual destiny became an obsession in every heart. You cannot depersonalize persons. Every writer during this time was aware of the passionate attachment of men and women to every object or image or place or love or fragment of memory with which his or her destiny seemed to be identified, and by which the destiny seemed to be assured.

The search for indestructible landmarks in a destructible world led many down strange paths. The attachment to these when they had been found produced small worlds-within-worlds of hallucination—in most cases, saving hallucination. Writers followed the paths they saw or felt people treading, and depicted those little dear saving illusory worlds. I have done both in the *The Demon Lover* stories.

You may say that these resistance-fantasies are in themselves frightening. I can only say that one counteracts fear by fear, stress by stress. In 'The Happy Autumn Fields,' a woman is projected from flying-bombed London, with its day-and-night eeriness, into the key emotional crisis of a Victorian girlhood. In 'Ivy Gripped the Steps,' a man in his early forties peers through the rusted fortifications and down the dusty empty perspectives of a seaside town at the Edwardian episode that long ago crippled his faculty for love. In 'The Inherited Clock,' a girl is led to find the key to her own neurosis inside a timepiece. The past, in all these cases, discharges its load of feeling into the anæsthetized and bewildered present. It is the 'I' that is sought—and retrieved, at the cost of no little pain. And, the ghosts—definite in 'Green Holly,' questionable (for are they subjective purely?) in 'Pink May,' 'The Cheery Soul' and 'The Demon Lover': what part do they play? They are the certainties. The bodiless foolish wanton, the puritan 'other' presence, the tipsy cook with her religion of English fare, the ruthless young soldier lover unheard of since 1916: hostile or not, they rally, they fill the vacuum for the uncertain 'I.'

I am sorry that the stories in *The Demon Lover*, now going to readers on the other side of the Atlantic, do not contain more 'straight' pictures of the British wartime scene. Such pictures could have been interesting: they *are* interesting in much of the brilliant reportage that exists. I know, in these stories the backgrounds, and sometimes the circumstances, are only present by inference. Allow for the intensely subjective mood into which most of the characters have been cast! Remember that these impulsive movements of fantasy are by-products of the non-impulsive major routine of war. These are between-time stories—mostly reactions from, or intermissions between, major events. They show a levelled-down time, when a bomb on your house was as inexpedient, but not more abnormal, than a cold in your head. There was an element of chanciness and savageness about everything—even, the arrival at a country house for Christmas. The claustrophobia of not being able to move about freely and without having to give account of yourself—not, for instance, being able to visit a popular seaside resort, within seventy miles of London, between 1940 and 1944—appears in many: notably, in 'Ivy Gripped the Steps.' The ghostly social pattern of London life—or, say, the conventional pattern one does not easily break, and is loth to break because it is 'I' saving—appears in the vacant politeness of 'In the Square' and in the inebriate night-club conversation, and in 'Careless Talk.' These are ways in which some of us did go on—after all, we had to go on *some* way. And the worthless little speaker in 'Pink May' found the war made moratorium for her married conscience. Yes, only a few were heroic purely: and see how I have not drawn the heroic ones! But everyone was pathetic—more than they knew. Owing, though, to the thunder of those inordinate years, we were shaken out of the grip of our own pathos.

In wartime, even in Britain, much has been germinating. *What*, I do not know—who does, yet, know?—but I felt the germination; and feel it, here and there, in these stories now that I read them through. These are received impressions of happening things; impressions that stored themselves up and acquired force without being analysed or considered. These, as wartime stories, are at least contemporary—twenty, forty, sixty years hence they may be found interesting as documents, even if they are found negligible as art. This discontinuous writing, nominally 'inventive,' is the only diary I have kept. Transformed into images in the stories, there *may* be important psychological facts: if so, I did not realize their importance. Walking in the darkness of the nights of six years (darkness which transformed a capital city into a network of inscrutable canyons) one developed new bare alert senses, with their own savage warnings and notations. And by day one was always making one's own new maps of a landscape always convulsed by some new change. Through it all, one probably picked up more than can be answered for. I cannot answer for much that is in these stories, except to say that I know they are all true—true to the general life that was in me at the time. Taken singly, they are disjected snapshots—snapshots taken from close up, too close up, in the middle of the *mêlée* of a battle. You cannot *render*, you can only embrace—if it means embracing to suffocation point— something vast that is happening right on top of you. Painters have painted, and photographers who were artists have photographed, the tottering lacelike architecture of ruins, dark mass-movements of people, and the untimely brilliance of flaming skies. I cannot paint or photograph like this—I have isolated; I have made for the particular, spot-lighting faces or cutting out gestures that are not even the faces or gestures of great sufferers. This is how I am, how I feel, whether in war or peace time; and only as I am and feel can I write. As I said at the start, though I criticize these stories now, afterwards, intellectually, I cannot criticize their content. They are the particular. But through the particular, in wartime, I felt the high-voltage current of the general pass.

1945.

THE BLAZE OF NOON

The Blaze of Noon is a story told in the first person by a man in whom one sense is suppressed: the 'I' is a blind man. His profession—he is a *masseur*—brings him to Mrs. Nance's house in Cornwall; he is to give treatment to Mrs. Nance. He brings with him into the group he finds at Rose Gwavas his private normality, the normality of a person with whom adjustment has become a lifelong act, for whom the four active senses are working overtime. His arrival at Rose Gwavas, his sojourn, his departure, and its aftermath, make the time-plan, though not the scope, of the book.

Such a novel could be an aggressive *tour de force*. I do not consider *The Blaze of Noon* to be a *tour de force*; it is, rather, the extraordinary extension (extraordinary because this has never been done before) of experience of which the sheer *matter* is ordinary—a visit, the impact of new surroundings, penetration into a new group of people, one realized and one unrealized love affair. With Louis Dunkel the hyper-activity of the four functioning senses is stressed in the first passage only; after that this is taken for granted —emphasized only when in the five-sense person there *would* be heightening: in the apprehension of something new, in the love approach. Curiousness, incalculability, variation exist in the 'normal' characters, not in Dunkel himself. If he shows arrogance it is the arrogance of the over-sound, not of the sufferer. Dunkel has, in fact, 'dominated' his blindness, as Montherlant's Pierre Costals proposed to dominate his leprosy.

What comes of this domination? First of all the suppression of the ordinary wish to dominate in any other field. Towards other beings he has no power-wish; in fact, the wish seems to be to withhold power. There is an absence of that *anxiety* directed upon the self, that sense of inexplicable inner disablement, of inefficacy for life that the 'normal'—or five-sense—person feels, and for which he cannot account, and which ravages him *because* he cannot account for it. Here, the patent outer disability, blindness, shifts the centre of being, and stabilizes it. In Louis Dunkel is evident, as in the stoical cripple, the physical self-possession and impersonality of the person dependent in small things—the blind man, alighting at the Cornish station, must wait on the platform like a package till the Rose Gwavas party claim him—but independent in large. Dunkel's blindness cancels out some factors in his intercourse with people, and heightens others. The handshake, for instance, at the first meeting, is with him the step over the frontier into what may prove an enormous territory. He is, from the first, made conscious of Sophie Madron by the fact that, unlike the rest of the party who come to meet him, she does not shake hands. She has taken her place beside him in the back of the car while he can still create no definite image of her. 'And that was dangerous.'

I must have seemed a creature utterly distant, alien and withdrawn from the world of three young people who had come to meet me. And the woman who does not immediately seek to bridge distances like that between herself and a man, either by touch or by a torrent of solicitous words, is unusual.

Unusually plain, perhaps, and therefore diffident in the sense that a conviction of her own inferiority stifles her spontaneous impulses. But I did not think Sophie Madron was plain. There had been a trace of diffidence in her voice, but it was superficial and of a kind that goes rather with too much rather than too little emotional readiness.

No, it was something quite different from this. Either she was a woman in love and obsessed, and therefore devoid of any outgoing impulse towards other men (but I felt something a little too vague and tremulous about her for this to be altogether true). Or she might be a woman so fastidious, superficially, and at bottom so erotically self-conscious, that she had considered beforehand how important and therefore how compromising to herself is the touch of a man whose eyes are in his fingers and had been shy and aloof for that reason.

This detective work of the senses continues, not only in relation to Sophie, before love, but in relation to the environment—the new atmosphere charged with the scents and sounds of glaring April, with unexpected surfaces to be touched—and to the other characters. Then with the coming of Amity Nance, the young blind deaf-mute, to Rose Gwavas, there is a change of gear. In the extraordinary communication between Louis and Amity, the extraordinary approach, all senses and faculties except touch are suppressed. The Amity-Louis passage is the final touchstone of *The Blaze of Noon*.

This is not primarily a book about blindness: Louis's blindness is an accessory, to create the conditions in which a man can speak

of direct love. Here, the experience is perfectly generalized. The
blind narrator imposes blindness: the unseenness of Sophie is
therefore absolute. Every sentiment, every phantasy, every
romantic particularization that, in love, goes with the act of seeing
is, accordingly, stripped away. Since Lawrence there has been
little writing in English on the subject of Love, as apart from the
surround of the love affair. And this is writing very unlike Lawrence's—much less emotional, much more ascetically sensual, or
sensually ascetic, more disabused. The disabusedness, and the absence of conflict, make this un-English writing: Dunkel posits, in
love, a whole set of laws and conditions which may be very repugnant to the English mind. Most of all, he may offend, or frighten,
by the very suppression of the romantic-particular, the *personal*
motive, the hunt for *unique* experience that is supposed, with the
English, to excuse, or to elevate love to 'a higher plane.'

In a country where the romantic-particular rules, the personal
coldness and calmness of these lovers may be found more shocking than their erotic simplicity.

As a novel *The Blaze of Noon* is remarkably integrated. The
articulate, fluctuating Sophie, and Amity, unhearing in her shell of
unseeing silence, balance each other. The unseen scene is felt.
The dialogue, not able (since it comes to us through Louis) to be
illustrated by expression or gesture, has the spare, even sharpness
of something purely heard. This novel, by knocking away devices, by moving beyond the known terms of reference, looks like
—and I think is—the beginning of something new. Unlike most
English novels, it is unprovincial: coming now, it may come a
little in advance of its time—it is more like a novel one might
imagine being written ten, or even twenty, years hence. We may
all be more European by then. If personal experience is to survive
and have any value, and continue to be communicated by art, it
must be cleared of the twilight of vague romanticized feeling and
of the received idea. I do not believe there will be any revolution
—at least, any effective revolution—in English writing: the change
in manner and purpose will come on us gradually. I believe *The
Blaze of Noon* to be an early sign of the change.

1939.

II
REVIEWS

Women

Various

The Irish

THE GIRLS*

George III's three eldest daughters, Matilda, Augusta, Elizabeth, were born within four years; they were unreservedly welcome, for when they began to arrive there were already three princes to assure the succession. Three more princes followed Elizabeth, making a space of six years between her and Mary, the next and fourth princess. A year after Mary came Sophia; then two more short-lived princes created another space before Amelia, the last of the family. The princesses thus fell into two age-groups of three, and this grouping of interests held good throughout their lives. In turn, each grew from a dignified, dressy baby into a blonde, pretty child, then up into a fine girl. Their figures filled out, their features coarsened a little, and still the girlhoods had to protract themselves. In those days of early blooming and early marriage, the protraction was cruelly out of order; the Princess Royal took it as special mortification, the five others seemed to take it as fate. The princesses were admired; they had showy complexions, they were all big-limbed except Sophia, 'the elf,' who was *petite*. None of them inherited Queen Charlotte's dark colouring, her aplomb or her *méchanceté*. As young girls they inspired delicious portraits: the two Gainsboroughs, of Princesses Augusta and Mary, depict gazelle-like creatures, pouting, mysterious. And in the Copley group an impossibly happy light falls on the younger trio, Mary and Sophia, as little girls in fichus, Amelia the plumed baby, with a tambourine and puppies, gambolling under a vine.

In real life their gambols were muted. Adulation and constant delicious food (they were all hearty, happy eaters, up to their old ages) does not supply everything, even for little girls. From their mother they got that untender and rigid love some very fecund women keep for their growing young. George III's recurrent, then chronic, illness of mind kept the Queen in a fierce, tense mood, and she saw to it that the girls were tensed up too. Their family life at Kew, at Windsor, at Weymouth, was constantly shadowed and always sequestrated. Enthusiastic and sympathetic

* 'The Daughters of George III.' By DOROTHY MARGARET STUART. (*Macmillan*.)

ladies surrounded the Queen and the girls; the princesses had no
Court pleasures; their only public appearance was the detested
formal promenade, on the terrace at Windsor, along the Weymouth front. The brothers, as they grew up, became *affairés*,
important, and with their tutors left for a wider world. The
princesses remained, and their sensibilities burgeoned, in that
steam-heated, hyper-feminine atmosphere. Their father's condition became a charge on their pity—through this, and their royal
training, the King-father myth continued to dominate them. With
the Queen their relationship, as they all grew up, was emotional,
subtle, profoundly uneasy beneath the smother of 'love.' Pious,
ardent and plain, the Queen knew how to employ, with her girls
at least, the arts of a spoiled beauty. She took a defeat finally—
but then died, and the old neurosis sprang up again: in chapel,
they had to go past her empty chair. The Princess Royal stayed
locked up in herself, in the blushing awkwardness, in her longing
to marry—and she was happily married and out of it when the
final clash with the Queen came. With the other five girls, foun-
tains of sensibility, brother-worship developed—and what an outlet it was. They wrote letters to all their brothers, but wrote most
of all to G. P., the Prince Regent. G. P. reciprocated their tender
kindness—as an elder brother he was quite admirable.

The princesses' buoyancy, gusto and dignity are surprising,
given the circumstances. They write to G. P. of illnesses (mostly
of nervous origin), frustrated loves and incurable money-troubles
—they had allowances which they all of them overspent. They
were not dangerously neurotic, and only Sophia appears a little
smugly silly—even she had palpable 'go' and charm. On the
whole, they had sound natures. Did education do much? The
Queen herself instructed them in religion, but the rest of their
education was supervised by the clear-headed and amiable Lady
Charlotte Finch, and her two indomitable lieutenants, and buffers,
Miss Goldsworthy and Miss Gomm. From appropriate masters
they learned languages, and each princess except Sophia wrote a
clear, stylish hand—they learned means, in fact, to express if not
to order their thoughts. They were taught the accomplishments
—drawing, music, the ingenious use of the needle. No teacher
seems to have claimed for any one princess spectacular talent in
any one of the arts. But how foolish to decry the accomplishments—the sheltered woman's sole tactile hold on life. The bore,

the yearner, the introspective woman, the woman tiresome to herself and others has increased since accomplishments were discredited. The futility of the achievement counts less than the virtue achieving gives. Accomplishments—and they were very mediocre—shored the princesses up in a cloudy, insane world. The Princess Royal, once married, settled down to paint china at Würtemberg. Princess Augusta, at her piano, pleased herself and pleased those who liked her better than music with her 'compositions,' mild reminiscent airs. A brother stood charmed by the piano, in the autumn dusk at Frogmore, and Tom Moore listened with great ease. Vehement Princess Elizabeth, for years 'wishing to settle,' solaced herself with arts and crafts, 'japanning' entire rooms at Frogmore, publishing series of drawings on noble themes. Princess Mary wept at her wedding to Silly Billy, then took to gardening at Bagshot. Princess Sophia thanked heaven she was never at a loss for something to do. In her old age, when she was blind, she endlessly tore up paper into fine scraps, to fill pillows for invalids. Ill health and love for Fitzroy occupied Princess Amelia during her short life, but she loved to read novels. All the sisters had their charities, impetuous spending, kindly solicitudes.

Nurses, foster-mothers, stayed in the princesses' backgrounds, comforted sickbeds, wept at belated weddings. All the girls found a confidant in Lady Harcourt—visits to Nuneham make some delicious scenes. Lady Harcourt, indefatigable optimist, indefatigable would-be matchmaker, raised their spirits with talk of possible marriages. For the girls, at once so eager and natural, the years, those years of disenchanted seclusion, went by at once too slowly and too fast. To love was fatally easy; it was not easy to 'settle.' Their religion restricted the royal marriage market. Eligibles were chiefly in Germany, mostly widowers, mostly pretty uncouth. Elizabeth made a bid for Louis Philippe; the marriage she did in the end make was the cue for one of Napoleon's spiteful remarks. In simple terms, the girls, sequestered even from brothers, met very few young men. Gentlemen holding office near the family circle were not young, were the acme of steadiness, and were properly conscious of their position as commoners. But on three of such gentlemen, three princesses fixed their hearts. Princess Augusta's love for General Sir Brent Spencer was returned fully, and was (we are given reason to hope) consummated

in a secret marriage. It was love of the *Persuasion* quality, patient
and dignified. Sophia's rape of respectable General Garth (of
which the incredibility led to a scandal later) and Amelia's infatuation for the blockish Fitzroy were less happy, in fact were regrettable. Sophia carried off her rôle of unmarried mother with remarkable cheek and style, and sustained the Cumberland scandal
with elderly stoicism; poor Amelia, succumbing, left an unfortunate will. To what extent the sisters were in each other's confidence it is not possible to be quite clear: the Prince Regent took
the full blast of the love troubles—at all events, it must all be kept
from the Queen.

The characters of the six princesses emerge in Miss Stuart's six
chapters. Miss Stuart could not have used her material better—
with less portentousness, with more dispassionate reasoning, with
fewer flights. The princesses' characters, as is the case with most
women, are more interesting than their destinies. The crux, for
the Princess Royal, was marriage—which, though late, unroman-
tic, childless, was fulfilment: she did well as a queen.

But the crux for the five others was not marriage, not even love
(except for Princess Amelia), it was the intense drama of their
break with the Queen. This great revolt of the girls, this group of
girls in their thirties, could have been epoch-making had it been
widely known. Princess Augusta penned the joint ultimatum
letter, and it was she who came in from her ride that morning to
take the brunt of the storm. G. P. had backed the girls up, but
G. P. was somewhere else. Successions of nerve storms swept the
younger princesses, but Augusta, the most truly sensitive of them,
could not permit herself sensibility. . . . Princess Elizabeth was
always too fat—she was 'artistic,' positive, loved yellow ostrich
feathers and once wore eleven standing up in her hair. Her personality is a shade repellent. She married, at a mature age, the
Hereditary Prince, later Landgrave, of Hesse-Homburg. Princess
Mary the beauty, the 'perfect Miny,' tactful, patient, serene, married her cousin the Duke of Gloucester, alias 'Silly Billy,' 'the
Cheese,' 'the Slice,' and tided over little troubles he made. Sophia's
elfishness got her into a double scrape, and Amelia, the King's
darling, was sickly, loved vainly, died.

The Daughters of George III could have filled six volumes; Miss
Stuart's one volume is a *tour de force* of compression, which ex-
pands in the memory. Her method is straight and lucid, and she

has overlooked nothing that could be significant. Her choice of quotations from letters shows a strict intelligence, and her analysis could not be better done.

The New Statesman and Nation.

HORRIBILE DICTU*

1939

Other people's vicissitudes are fascinating—fascinating to read about, to be told of, to witness, to do anything but share. Nothing is more agreeable than the story of things going wrong at the So-and-Sos'. To hear of an occasion going off perfectly smoothly leaves one a little flat. The untoward is popular: children like stories to be as dreadful as possible; later, we all like to have some unfortunate friends. Love, money, health, social ambition or home life will never cease to make topics, because in these spheres things are constantly going wrong. It is nicer to hear of *contretemps* than to assist at them—to be present always may mean to be involved. And ideally, small disagreeablenesses should happen to friends' friends, not to friends of one's own. The small awful things that do happen should seem likely, never too probable. In fact, the occurrence should stay set back at a distance: it is then not too painful, and more easy to see.

> It almost makes me cry to tell
> What foolish Harriet befell. . . .

Struwwelpeter has model openings, and *Struwwelpeter* should be the narrator's model, in the long run.

Mrs. Mary Wylde's book about her vicissitudes has got this kind of threatening note on the cover, and is absorbing most of the way through. It is (I suppose) a book written to inculcate pity for women and kindness to the middle class. It should also explain why women, well-to-do women, look so obsessed or aggrieved,

---

* 'A Housewife in Kensington.' By MARY WYLDE. (*Longmans.*)

and why they are never having a nicer time. The middle class looks to its women to keep the flag flying: they do. Exactly what flag, and why? This Mrs. Wylde, wisely, does not begin to explain, and why should she? As a character, she is vigorous rather than sympathetic. She shows what a woman with two boys away at public schools, a husband, two maidservants, a four-storied house in Kensington, a fur coat, a Dutch garden, an old Morris has to stand up against. Constantly let down, done down, played up and put upon—you only begin to know what Kensington women suffer when you are into the pages of Mrs. Wylde. And the conclusion you reach, if you do reach a conclusion, is that this part of London should have a Mothers' Day. Any house in any one of those streets and squares may be being the scene of a *supplice* like Mrs. Wylde's. At the same time, Kensington is a matriarchy, and over the door of every home might be graven: 'Remember, this all comes very hard on *me*.'

She opens:

Behold a late-Georgian house with cream stucco walls, blue front door, shining brass knocker, Dutch garden all abloom, and a window-box gay with pink ivy-leaf geranium.'. . . . You are interested in houses? Then come into mine and see what happens beyond the blue-painted door with the gleaming knocker. Like the man in the fairy-tale, put on the cloak of invisibility, keep close to my elbow, and you may follow my adventures in housekeeping and share such thoughts as I wish to disclose.

As an invitation, this is sufficiently sinister; in fact it is rather more like a challenge.

Kensington looks inscrutable because it looks dull, and one is willing to let the dull stay inscrutable. There is so much of it, all façades and trees. It is a neighbourhood, or a quarter, about which many people have already been fairly funny and rather spitefully rude. It represents so much money, pretty soundly invested and dully spent. It is a mentality in architecture: you wonder what it might look like as an extensive ruin, and like to leave it at that. But when Mrs. Wylde—obligingly, and with a sort of gloomy mixture of resignation and pride—rolls back on a hinge the entire front of her house, the world inside (is it inside all these houses?) immediately springs into existence, and is very frightening indeed. Here is a world governed by class neurosis, in which employed

and employers are hyper-conscious of each other's hostile exist-
ences the whole time. Mrs. Wylde is a plucky woman; she displays
reserves of culture, humour, idealism. Her maids lack culture,
humour, idealism: in fact, they seem to be simply sluttish and
warped. Maids come and go, but they all turn out just like this.
Mrs. Wylde loves order but, no doubt rightly, does not attempt
style. At most, she 'indulges in a little mild entertaining,' but
though she lunches alone she always has pudding for lunch. The
trouble is that order bores almost all maids, but they will do anything for a bit of style. Can it be possible, also, that maids do
not care for culture, humour, idealism?

Inevitably, Mrs. Wylde has her pessimistic moments. She asks
herself if, in a generation or two, there will be many of 'our kind'
left. At intervals during the year this journal covers she shuts herself up in an upper floor of the house in what seems to be an acute
state of nervous siege. Once or twice she is shot right out of the
house by some sheer malevolent pressure. At times, she shows
persecution mania—and really, who can wonder? The plumber
bungles her boiler, the furrier bungles her fur coat, the maids of
course bungle everything, woodlice get at the Dutch garden,
poison gets at the cat, the flap comes off the gateleg table before a
small tea-party, the acid content of a battery gets upset on the
drawing-room carpet and all the way up the stairs. All this
means expense.

None of these troubles can be peculiar to Kensington—perhaps, though, the so very acute reaction to them is? To suffer in
this way, one must be a woman of character, a woman intended
for better things and at the same time distinctly not getting them.
Mrs. Wylde is a writer, as well as a great reader—when she feels
played out she goes to bed with a book. 'In my last year at school
I had to choose whether I would specialize in botany or literature,
and I never ceased to be glad that I chose the latter. It is a peren-
nial interest.' It is not only this, but it breeds a view of oneself.
Seeking peace in the old nursery from the banging and hammering
that are endemic in her house—for these Kensington homes
always seem to be cracking up, flaking off, smoking, warping or
leaking—she pegs away at her writing. Though: 'I am no Mrs.
Jellyby, I am afraid, to neglect the family and let extraneous
interests take first place.'

Mrs. Wylde goes out now and then, and how I wish she would

F

tell us more about parties she goes to. She does tell us about the musical society, whose practices took place in a converted public house, and about her dustman who whistled Vaughan Williams and appeared at the society's festival in a dinner jacket, 'looking as fresh and smart as any public school man. Dustmen, I know, are well paid nowadays, but a dustman in a dinner jacket is an unexpected sight.' Mrs. Wylde, being a writer, is interested in human nature; she has a conversation with a fishmonger about his mad wife, with a plumber who turns out to *be* a public school man, with a hair-dresser girl about marriage and home-making, while she is getting her hair waved. The vividness of these conversations makes me wish more and more that Mrs. Wylde would tell us about her own set. Here is one picture only:

I enjoy a good laugh as much as anything. I don't know many women who are devoid of humour, and often their appreciation of the incongruous is sharper than that of men, as the following anecdote will perhaps illustrate.

A friend was being presented with the head of a tiger by the man who had shot it in India. Dramatically he described how his bearer saw the beast and tried to shoot, but the safety catch of the gun was down. Quickly he seized the gun from the native—aimed, and brought down the animal. Whereupon another man who was listening to the story, immediately countered, in all solemnity, 'Talking of safety catches on guns, I was out shooting rabbits the other day . . .' He did not finish the sentence, for it was drowned by the laughter of his wife.

Once one has read Mrs. Wylde, she becomes a companion. *A Housewife in Kensington* contains all sorts of passages you are certain to want to mark. It is not, in the strict sense, a very useful book, not a book to turn to for household hints—in fact, there are hints that one could give Mrs. Wylde. *Should* she have been so flummoxed when she had to do the cooking, and, in that case, why insist on a treacle sponge? Why is it wicked to go to a restaurant when you have not, for the time being, got any cook and make such heavy weather about cooking yourself? Why all this cellar trouble; what about Mr. Therm? . . . No, this is a chatty more than a helpful book. It is an addition to vicissitude literature; I take it to be a fair picture of Kensington, and it is a most striking self-portrait of a lady, by Mrs. Mary Wylde.

The New Statesman and Nation.

MANNERS*

1937

Behaviour—social behaviour—is partly an art, partly instinct. In what is called our freer modern life, manners have come to count for a good deal less, which makes sheer manner count for a good deal more. Now that it is less vital to be correct, it becomes far more important to be acceptable. In fact, the decline of manners in the grand and fixed sense has made behaviour infinitely more difficult. A perpetual, forced recourse to instinct (the art element being discredited) gives our friends a harassed, unstable air. There is no longer the safety of a prescribed world, of which the thousand-and-one rules could be learnt, in which one could steer one's way instructed and safe. The world, even the great world, can have, in an age of manners, held no more terrors than does the Hyde Park Corner traffic, with its apparent complexity, for the unassuming driver who has passed his test. For each of the occasions of society, one of the thousand-and-one rules you had learnt fitted. You knew what to do, and did it. Society went like clockwork.

This held true not only of the great world, but to any world in which people had time to meet—in which leisure, money, interest went to make a society. Societies were distinct and delimited— 'Society' proper, business, professional, artistic, provincial, county, military, and so on. If marriage, a freak of taste or some sudden access of fortune caused you to move from one society to another, to take what you considered a step up in the world, you went for instruction, more or less admittedly, to some authorized person in the new society. Inappropriate behaviour was, of course, fatal, and provided, as it still does, agreeable matter for comedies and *Punch* jokes. Politeness was to an extent an affair of symbols, and an unexplored ethic lay behind. This ethic, with a recognition of the values prevailing in his particular world, was inbred in the young person—who was less likely than we are to leave the particular world into which he had been born. He stayed where he was, and knew what he must comply with. That is just

* 'Can I Help You?' By VIOLA TREE. (*Hogarth Press.*)

the crux of the matter: we move about. The lives of most people now, say, in their thirties have changed inconceivably since childhood. Tradition is broken. Temperament, occupation, success or failure, marriage, or active nervous hostility to an original *milieu* have made nomads of us. The rules we learnt in childhood are as useless, as impossible to take with us, as the immutable furniture of the family home. And often, that first single world with its accepted currency has been left for not one new world (or set) but for half a dozen. These may overlap, but at points are widely apart: each is a little nucleus of feeling, each is quick to find the inept person or the person indelibly stamped with the stamp of another world either 'queer,' up-stage, a worm, a fake or a crook. The one-world man or woman, rare and often enviable, may be recognized by his or her assurance, surprised but not nonplussed silence in an unknown *milieu*, and palpable contempt for the unknown. They are less subject to feelings of persecution, and therefore make a solid minority.

Straightforward people—who tend to be one-world people: the outdoor, the extroverted or those whose standards are set by money, of which they have a safe supply—are certain they are not crooks, and therefore cannot be unnerved. They feel a simple contempt for unusual manners. But complex people are never certain that they are not crooks, never certain their passports are quite in order, and are, therefore, unnerved by the slightest thing. They are touchy judges of manners in other people, because anyone doing the wrong thing precipitates an embarrassment it is hard to forgive. They do, fundamentally, wish to please, and are therefore affectable to a fault. Their own bad manners when positive are often savage evidence of a sense of failure, when negative (such as the not answering of letters) are generally rooted in some inhibition: they have either a claustrophobic dread of committing themselves, or dread to say or write what may not be found agreeable. They are unobjective with regard to society; their standards are entirely personal.

But this personal attitude is becoming more general, and largely rules society—or societies—outside the shrinking, traditional grand world. For that world, with its classic and unpersonal simplicities, more and more of us may be coming to feel a nostalgia to which we have no right. Or one might feel the same nostalgia for provincial societies, in which behaviour is equally exact—set. It

is a case, there, of 'whose service is perfect freedom.' Outside
the set observances, which become instinctive, which cost little,
which have the value of art, one might be free to *be*, but not bound
to exhibit, oneself. There were far more 'personalities' in the ages
of manners. But so-called free, or intelligent, society imposes a
constant tax on all the powers. There is no guide here. To please,
even to conform to what is expected, one must constantly draw on
a private natural genius, meant for one's own pleasure or for the
intimacies of love. Exhaustion, a sense of spentness and deflation,
follows in many people the unconventional supper, the *longueurs*
of the free-and-easy week-end. You can go wrong at any point,
and by going wrong drag up a host of agonies: here too much is
involved. Manners were a protection; they also stabilized one.
How much more gladly would one observe ritual than be put
through a series of daunting hoops.

It would be less difficult if there were not still vestigial remnants
of manners. Good general-purpose manners nowadays may be
said to consist in knowing how much you can get away with. Be a
shade too punctilious and you are sticky; make a little too free and
you are a pariah. Fresh adjustments have to be made in every
room you enter. Such good manners as we have left are, clearly,
functional—they have a direct application to the routine of life.
For instance, it is still a fault to be late, because you waste someone's time or risk spoiling a dinner—provided they wait for you.
It is still grievous to interrupt or to talk down, because your
neighbour also wishes to do his piece, and you should do as you
would be done by. It is rude not to answer letters because that
makes inconvenience. Questions from which the tabu has been
partly lifted, and which are the questions you chiefly wish to ask—
such as: How old are you? How much money have you got?
What sort of people do you fall in love with?—are still doubtful,
and must be faultlessly timed. There is still a fine line between
intimacy and impertinence. It is rude to stay too long, because
then you begin to intrude. Love of privacy—perhaps because of
the increasing exactions of society—has become in many people
almost pathological. The polite person, nowadays, treats his
friends as one once only treated the great: he inquires (by telephone) whether his visit at such-and-such an hour will be acceptable. The practice of 'calling'—fantastic invasion—lapsed with
the poker-faced servant and the leisured hour. Where these

persist one may still keep cards and call. But the person who has only one living-room, or who often answers his own door, depends for his privacy on the right feeling of friends. He is likely to live keyed up to a dizzy point of busyness, or to be leading an intensive emotional life. It is unpardonable to walk in on a *tête-à-tête*.

In short, there are still manners, but obvious manners are suspect. This is a transitional period, and for a transitional period Miss Tree's book, *Can I Help You?* is written. Miss Tree has a flair for living, for enjoying herself, for getting the best out of people. She infects her book with all this: it is inspiring rather than strictly helpful in a *terre-à-terre* way. She must be a woman who sails through life. Her own method of living merges the traditional and the spontaneous. There are few worlds she does not know, and few she has quite discarded. She is detached, vital, accomplished, poised. For years she has been replying to etiquette queries out of the outer darkness for the *Sunday Dispatch*. I am sure her replies to the *Sunday Dispatch* queries must be at once more pertinent and more concrete than the delicious and rambling disquisitions in chapter after chapter of her book.

Otherwise, my reply to Miss Tree's *Can I Help You?* would be, quite firmly: No. No, I would reply, you are an exceptional person with a heritage of intelligence, dash and grace, and you know just how far the exceptional person can afford to deviate from the ways of the world. But you cannot tell me how I am to behave. I live (say) in Brixton: my friends are not so far *éblouis* by my presence that I can get away with anything I like. I live in Brixton, and am asking you how I should arrange the forks when my husband brings his boss home to dinner. You obviously *do* know how this should be done, but you insist on telling me of a prettier way. It is all very well for you to say: My mother used to arrange them in a sort of fan, and I remember she often put a camellia between each. . . . Or, I live in Chelsea: my friends, though they affect to be Bohemian are pretty bourgeois really, and I cannot get away with the parties you describe. . . . Or, the note I copied from your model, inviting a distinguished person to dinner, got me into trouble with my husband, who said it was too perky: that is not at all *your* type, he said. . . . Or, I live in Wimbledon and, following your instructions, cleared the drawing-room and asked sixteen friends to a studio high tea, giving them the sausages to grill on forks, like you said. I thought it would be a romp, but they all went home early and none of them have invited us out since.

Everyone will enjoy reading Miss Tree's book, but it is, most decidedly, a book for people who have already taken a line of their own—these will be amused by comparing their line with hers. This entirely free book is full of tact and wisdom. But those, alas! cannot be taught. This is a manual for the new society, a society loosened up by the telephone. If Miss Tree does help, in this maze of new behaviour, it is by example rather than by advice. She does, now and then, it is true, emit a conventional fact or two: I am in no sort of position to check up on these, but they seem to me valid. She is encouraging in so far as she shows what pleasant times may be had. Her moral is: Be yourself.

But how this can take it out of you!

The New Statesman and Nation.

VIRGINIA WOOLF*

1941   I

The scene of *Between the Acts* is Pointz Hall, a country house built a little too low in a hollow under a hill, but whose terrace, all the same, commands a wide view. The action takes place within 24 hours—the eve and the day of the village pageant, work of the solitary, masculine Miss La Trobe. The time is June, 1939. Pointz Hall is inhabited by old Mr. Oliver, of the Indian Civil Service, retired, his sister Mrs. Swithin, his daughter-in-law Isa, and her two young children. Isa's husband, Giles Oliver, who is in business in London, comes to join the family at week-ends: he is there for lunch on the pageant day. As they move in to lunch the Olivers are invaded, and pervaded, by *soignée*, impulsive Mrs. Manresa, 'the wild child,' who arrives in a car with her own champagne and her supercilious companion, William Dodge. Next, the county neighbours arrive, and from rows of chairs watch the villagers act the pageant against the view. The pageant, with its tea-interval, is played out: it occupies the middle part of the book. In the course

* 'Between the Acts.' By VIRGINIA WOOLF. (*Hogarth Press.*)
* 'The Death of the Moth.' By VIRGINIA WOOLF. (*Hogarth Press.*)
* 'Virginia Woolf.' By E. M. FORSTER. (*Cambridge University Press.*)

of the afternoon Giles, out of temper, responds to Mrs. Manresa just enough to trouble his wife, whose own distant rhyming thoughts are in their turn disturbed by desire for Mr. Haines, the gentleman farmer, who has been at Pointz Hall the night before and is on the terrace this afternoon. The pageant over, everyone goes away; Miss La Trobe, still without speaking, disappears into a public-house. After dinner the old people withdraw; Giles and Isa, alone for the first time, big with the quarrel that must precede love, are left confronting each other in the summer darkness in which *Between the Acts* began. The cycle of hours has completed itself.

This is the plot of the book—important because this time, in *Between the Acts*, Virginia Woolf has integrated plot and vision. The characters are involved in the central action, compromised (one might say) and motivated by it: there are few, and no final, single movements away. The plot is, thus, organic; very much more so than in any other novel of hers. Awkward but vital discord, friction, collision between the outer and inner are not only not stressed, but hardly present at all. To this reconciliation—a reconciliation so new in Virginia Woolf's writing that one is aware of it here from the first page—certain elements in the writing might be said to be sacrificed; there is less anguish, less desire and less surprise. The thickets of mystery between person and person have been thinned, though in no place levelled down. There is less speculation—but, in its place, a perceiving certainty. One might say that the characters behold each other and the scene round them more calmly, and are beheld by Virginia Woolf more calmly, than in the other books. Actually, in this very calmness, anguish, desire, surprise have reached rim-level: the miracle is that they are contained.

The pageant at once fixes into the centre, epitomizes and limits the idea of time that has been circumambient in all the other books. Artificial consciousness of the past is induced, by the mechanics of Miss La Trobe, upon the immense, dramatic unconsciousness of the present—upon the rows of people on their chairs on the terrace facing the sun-changed landscape and the approaching war that is too imminent to be realized. And the pageant is not only time by art—and, as art, is a sort of war in itself; the confrontation of two armies, the actors and the acted upon. That art, here, should be at the Miss La Trobe level is immaterial; the question or challenge is put to art itself, from both sides, by the audience upon the terrace and by Miss La Trobe, at her distance, watching her idea shrink as it unrolls. The degree of the imperfection is not examined—Miss La Trobe's script is given without satire—the point is, that the fate of imperfection *is* present, in the attempt to render, in the attempt to eternalize even for one moment, in the attempt to speak. The limitation, the downward pull on the power is agonizing to the poor village highbrow—to the others it was a foregone conclusion, known. Clouds and cows, however, the village idiot, light on a distant spire and unpredictable fancies among the onlookers perfect moments that perish for Miss La Trobe. Her designed silence falls flat, but the cows save it. Her crux, 'the Present,' the trick with the running mirrors throwing back at the audience their own faces, succeeds, but shatters the planned whole. After this break with illusion the vicar rises to speak, but does not know what to say.

Here is Miss La Trobe at the end of the afternoon:

At last Miss La Trobe could raise herself from her stooping position. It had been prolonged to avoid attention. The bells had stopped; the audience had gone; also the actors. She could straighten her back. She could open her arms. She could say to the world, You have taken my gift! Glory possessed her—for one moment. But what had she given? A cloud that melted into the other clouds on the horizon. It was in the giving that the triumph was. And the triumph faded. Her gift meant nothing. If they had understood her meaning; if they had known their parts; if the pearls had been real and the funds illimitable—it would have been a better gift. Now it had gone to join the others.

'A failure,' she groaned, and stooped to put away the records.

Then suddenly the starlings attacked the tree behind which she had hidden. In one flock they pelted it like so many winged stones. The whole tree hummed with the whizz they made, as if each bird plucked a wire. A whizz, a buzz arose from the bird-buzzing, bird-vibrant, bird-blackened tree. The tree became a rhapsody, a quivering cacophony, a whizz and vibrant rapture, branches, leaves, birds syllabling discordantly life, life, life, without measure, without stop devouring the tree. Then up! Then off!

. . . Miss La Trobe nicked the lock and hoisted the heavy case of gramophone records on to her shoulder. She crossed the terrace and stopped by the tree where the starlings had gathered. It was here that she had suffered triumph, humiliation. ecstasy, despair—for nothing. Her heels had ground a hole in the grass.

Round the dead centre that is the pageant the high moments are in individual lives. The young people tack garlands of paper roses round the barn, in which, if it rains, the pageant may have to be. The fish for lunch arrives, and is received by the cook. Isa, who thought about Mr. Haines while brushing her hair, continues to feel for her husband angry desire. Mrs. Swithin, reading an Outline of History, sees mammoths in Piccadilly, damp-rooted rhododendrons growing along the Strand. While Mrs. Swithin is showing William Dodge over the house they lean from a window to watch the pageant people arriving: a breeze suddenly blows and the muslin blinds flutter out down the whole façade. These individual people, dwellers at Pointz Hall, visitors, deliberately not made complex, are keys to the mystery of the afternoon. Over them, like fate, their fate itself, hangs the weather that is Virginia Woolf's mind.

Because *Between the Acts* is Virginia Woolf's last book, the reader may search it for some touch of finality. Of this I find, as I expected to find, none. The form and the combination of elements are, as always, new; she never used any combination or form twice. When the book ends it is, as at the end of the other books, as though a lamp had been switched off at its base, but the current is still waiting along the flex. *Between the Acts* in no sense completes her work, which is incapable of being completed. One envisages or desires completion only upon a level upon which she neither wrote nor lived.

The distinction made, at the start, between plot (or action) and vision may be a dangerous one. It may be one that she would not have allowed. But to allow it makes possible one sort of discussion of her work. One can only think of the vision in terms of height, light and aerial pressure. In *The Waves*, vision consumes everything else. So great is its power that there are no concessions; the book is what Flaubert might have called a *débordement*. Through *Jacob's Room*, *Mrs. Dalloway*, *To the Lighthouse*, we have marked the sweep and quickening of the ascent to the perhaps too high point of *The Waves*. In *The Years*—*The Waves'* successor, complement, inverse—there is, in the sense of vision, a steep drop. Plot, which had been a great natural part of the two earliest novels, *The Voyage Out* and *Night and Day*, re-emerges, but seems strained, as though, throughout, some other important entrance were being denied: one feels, in *The Years*, the effort to confine vision to each character's possible register. Upon the plots of *The Voyage Out* and *Night and Day* inundations by vision had been unchecked; impetus rather than resolution carried forward the narrative. Now, in *Between the Acts* Virginia Woolf has balanced her plot and vision, and each a little partakes of the other's kind.

Through all the books runs the theme of time. Or, rather, all time encircles the moment, from page to page. Death is there, as something not to be borne, not to be borne; there in the evocation of dead people by a shell, a chair, a window or the eternity of a remembered scene. The characters, under their veil of gentleness, violently oppose themselves to fate, and to each other even in love. The threat of pain to come is in every caress of hand or mind, and yet behind this waits the solution, the reconciliation to be reached, or, if not reached to be, as in *To the Lighthouse*, seen.

To the Lighthouse is the most humanly perfect of the novels. But *The Waves* remains the key to them all, and, both before and after the book in its time order, is present throughout the others. In *The Waves* what is gradual truth in the other books is ejaculated in a succession of cries. It is not only Rhoda who cries out, but it is Rhoda who is remembered:

What dissolution of the soul you demanded in order to get through one day!... How you chained me to one spot, one hour, one chair, and sat yourselves down opposite! How you snatched from me the white spaces that lie between hour and hour.... Yet those were my life.

But I yielded.... I did not go out into the street and break a bottle in the gutter as a sign of rage. Trembling with ardour, I pretended that I was not surprised. What you did, I did. If Susan and Jinny pulled up their stockings like that, I pulled up mine like that also. So terrible was life that I held up shade after shade. Look at life through this, look at life through that; let there be rose leaves, let there be vine leaves—I covered the whole street, Oxford Street, Piccadilly Circus, with the blaze and ripple of my mind, with vine leaves and rose leaves.... With fleeces, with vestments I have tried to cover the blue-black blade. I implored day to break into night. I have longed to see the cupboard dwindle, to feel the bed soften, to float suspended, to perceive lengthened trees, lengthened faces, a green bank on a moor and two figures in distress saying goodbye. I flung my words in fans like those the sower throws over the ploughed fields when the earth is bare. I desired always to stretch the night and fill it fuller and fuller with dreams.... Walking on the embankment, I prayed that I might thunder for ever on the verge of the world where there is no vegetation, but here and there a marble pillar. I threw my bunch on to the spreading wave.

The New Statesman and Nation.

1942   II

'She liked writing,' E. M. Forster says of Virginia Woolf, 'with an
intensity which few writers have attained, or even desired.' He
recurs to the statement, and he develops it. It was, he says, a life-
line, when, having made her the subject of the Rede Lecture to be
delivered in the Senate House, Cambridge, he found himself in the
May of last year confronted by the necessity of summing up her
achievements in an hour. By chance the appearance of the lecture
in print has synchronized with the appearance of *The Death of the
Moth*, a collection of Virginia Woolf essays.

E. M. Forster and Virginia Woolf are two novelists likely to
understand one another. This could have held good had they
never met—in fact, I am still not clear, and I suppose it never will
be decided, whether a personal friendship between two writers
helps the mutual judgment or distorts it. 'Let us love each other
in art,' Flaubert suggested, 'as the Christians loved one another in
Christ.' (Unhappily, he made the suggestion to a woman incapable either of love or art.) E. M. Forster, in his lecture on Virginia
Woolf as an artist, seems to me to have taken her nature—a nature
to be discovered only through friendship—into an at once fair and
loving account; whereas, she opens her essay on his novels on a
note of almost masculine hesitation. She is, here, unusually impersonal; it is the contemporary she writes about, not the friend.
Either because, as she says and he says, she found difficulty in
judgment of her contemporaries, or because friendship set up
some inhibition, that essay, though grave and reasoned, is not her
best.

I say 'grave' because her critical essays fall into two groups—
the grave (which are completely impersonal) and those written
with a smile. On the whole, she smiled most when she could look
at her subject down a fairly lengthy perspective of time. The
actual moment exerted too much pressure; she could live it only
when it became the past. From the past her art could retrieve the
moment, make it again the present, but a present to be lived without any pain. Her novels, like her essays, are full of moments
which exactly this process has purified, crystallized, placed in
time's light but completely outside time. Such moments (beginning in *Jacob's Room*, at their height in *Mrs. Dalloway*, *To the Lighthouse* and *The Waves*) were at once the novels' subject and their

poetic essence—but, at the same time, warred with the novel form.

Popular taste has, therefore, agreed her novels, *qua* novels, to be works of an inspired imperfection. Taste of that order finds little fault with what might be called her visionary criticism. Myself, I love the novels' impulse to synthetize better than the flawless unities of the essays. I am glad that *Between the Acts* was the book she wrote last, and that *The Death of the Moth* is her 'last' book only by the fact of its publication date.

Most of the essays in *The Death of the Moth* had already been published in periodicals. There are included, however, some which remained in abeyance in her drawer. All, Leonard Woolf lets us understand, would, had she lived, have been subjected to revision before their appearance as this book. Those not yet published were due to be most worked on: she let nothing into print that did not satisfy her—she could bring this to the point of re-writing nine or ten times.

Her liking for writing—civilized understatement of her passion —made this demand. By this creative revision, what did she add, or what did she eliminate? Pieces of work which had still not satisfied her are here in *The Death of the Moth* to suggest answers. I believe that in her work on them she had meant to use the apparently humble quality of discretion. There appears, in these pieces, seldom a surface roughness but often a sort of inner intemperance—lovable, possibly, in a nature but derogatory, as she would see it, in art. She did not by nature write coldly—and, poetically speaking, it was neither possible nor desirable that she should. Each draft—was this so?—was a stage in the cooling off from the original white heat of the first. In so far as this white heat had made for pureness of vision, nothing could have stood out to be sacrificed. In so far as it made for an impure judgment there was much to which censorship could apply.

In content *The Death of the Moth* offers much the same fare as did its predecessors, the two volumes of *The Common Reader*. There are essays on Gibbon, Walpole, Coleridge, Sara Coleridge, Madame de Sévigné, Shelley, the Rev. William Cole—these all in the smiling division—and more serious essays on George Moore, E. M. Forster, and Henry James. There are village pieces (including an air raid), a talk on professions for women, a London monologue, 'Street Haunting,' and a reprint of the 'Letter to a Young

Poet.' 'The Art of Biography' discusses the achievement of Lytton Strachey, and a letter not sent to *The New Statesman* defines her enemy, 'The Middlebrow.'

The Observer.

THE ACHIEVEMENT OF VIRGINIA WOOLF*

1949

Bernard Blackstone offers his *Virginia Woolf* as 'a commentary.' 'I have aimed,' he says, 'at presenting Virginia Woolf as an explorer of different worlds of experience—different, but intricately related, as they all are the creations of a human mind working upon the phenomena which veil reality. This kind of exploration was, it seems to me, her main preoccupation; and the result was her supreme contribution to the English novel.'

Accordingly, he has considered her work under three divisions —Love and Freedom, Marriage and Truth, the World and Reality. The grouping imposed itself upon him as he read through the novels in their time-order; and the free development of the study, as it proceeds, shows the frame to be less arbitary than it might appear.

I would claim three main merits for Dr. Blackstone's book. He disposes of the charge that Virginia Woolf's art was the product of an aerial remoteness from the human norm; he reverses the judgment (current at least in England) that she was ideally critic rather than novelist, and he places her as, essentially, a creature of her environment and her time.

This third achievement may be the most important. A certain magic, which in continuous circuit travelled out from her personality into and through her art, to be reabsorbed by her and sent out again, has perhaps escaped him; if so, he is aware of this— there are dancing motes or elements in genius which are impossible to pin down. One can only note their action, marvel at what they leave behind. The analogy to the painter has been well

---

* 'Virginia Woolf.' By BERNARD BLACKSTONE. (*New York: Harcourt, Brace.*)

brought out; the analogy to the poet one can no more than state—
quotation, however, makes that self-evident.

Virginia Woolf affected, one might say recreated, the consciousness of the age in which she wrote. She extended and
deepened, to a degree perhaps not measured yet, human susceptibility to sensation; ironically, she was to do this at a time
when, because of the pressure put on it by events, sensation could
be an insupportable tax. She was the extreme and final product
of the English liberal mind: a mind whose values and structure
Dr. Blackstone shows in his exposition—phase by phase, novel
by novel—of her beliefs, her insistences and her refusals (such as
that of religion).

She was of a seriousness possible to anatomize: George Eliot's
lends itself to the same process, Jane Austen's does not. Dr.
Blackstone does well in forcing into our notice the thought and
morality in the novels: overlooked, never strongly reacted to, *that*
side of her could have been forgotten soon. Freedom, Truth,
Reality—he says, and can indicate—preoccupied her. But, in her
art at its purest, these were consumed: all went up in the smokeless
visionary flame. In effect, then, was she purely æsthetic?

No. Dr. Blackstone is fascinated by the paradox. His analysis
of the novels, in their order, follows the changes in her technique
as she moved forward—not so much from subject to subject as
from one to another manner of seeing. She was to begin with,
then to abandon, plot; to develop, then eliminate, character; to
perfect scene (almost completely in *To the Lighthouse*), then to
dissolve it in *The Waves*. Her forward course, it is suggested,
zigzagged: she experimented, but never pursued the same line
of experiment for long—with the completion of each book the
experiment it stood for had been concluded.

It could be argued that each new novel derived its impetus from
a reaction against the one before. Thus, while an abstract concept of 'Virginia Woolf writing' can be formed, there is no one
'typical' Virginia Woolf novel. Having begun traditionally, with
The Voyage Out and *Night and Day*, she was to approach or sheer
away from the comprehension of what might be called the average
reader according to a rhythm of her own.

Dr. Blackstone's verdict that *Night and Day* (1919) was retro-
gression from *The Voyage Out* (1915) will not, I imagine, be dis-
agreed with. Virginia Woolf, he remarks, had not yet found her

technique. *Monday or Tuesday* (short stories, 1921) marks a turning-point; or, one might better say, the first of her striking emergences.

She is trying [Dr. Blackstone writes] to find a form and a style adequate to convey her individual vision of life: and not only of life on the objective plane, but also of that 'taste of eternity' which keeps breaking through at odd moments and seems to give her vision all its value.   To convey that taste certain barriers of prose fiction have to be broken down; that is now obvious to her. The current form of the novel, in which she has been working up to now, will not do. She was hampered by the convention of an intricate continuous plot; by set descriptions of people and scenes from without; by the necessity to provide link passages. But when she examined the technique of poetry, she found that these mechanical devices were not essential. . . . By rapid transitions, by allusions and imagery, poetry could give precisely that complexity of impressions, that sense of the eternal glowing through the momentary, which was the essence of her experience.

The short story was not for her the ideal form; yet *Monday or Tuesday* brought about her release: this was her embarkation upon the 'stream of consciousness.' And upon this followed the novel with its own kind of perfection, *Jacob's Room* (1922)—the last book, according to Dr. Blackstone's grouping, of the first, or the 'Love and Freedom' phase. The discovery of technique had been, for her, most of all the discovery of technique's fluidity.

The three novels of the second, or 'Marriage and Truth,' group are high points of a dazzling virtuosity: at the same time, they are incomparably works of the heart. With *Mrs. Dalloway* (1925) and *To the Lighthouse* (1927) Virginia Woolf was to demonstrate what the novel could do. Tangible and transparent at the same time, these two satisfied absolutely. *Orlando*, a whimsical deviation, followed in 1928.

In the third—'The World and Reality' group—*The Waves* and *The Years* (1931, 1937) presented the reader with two kinds of ordeal, inherent in two extremes. Of *Between the Acts* (1941) one might ask, how consciously was this a last novel? It offers, more simply than any had so far done, a synthesis. A group of Virginia Woolf characters, watching a village pageant from a terrace, overhang history: this is a June afternoon in a world on the brink of war. This was the novel published after her death.

She was a woman writer: Dr. Blackstone notes her extreme

consciousness both of the predicaments and of the inherent genius of her sex. Genius for life; disability, it might appear, in art.

'The point about women,' he says, 'which Virgina Woolf's novels emphasize is not that they despise truth but that they see something beyond truth, which we may call reality; and they see other roads of approach to this reality than the path of verbal logic. If verbal logic (which is what men generally mean by "truth") gets in the way of kindness, or vision, it has to be given up; the human values are worth more than the purely intellectual.'

She was the child of a particular world—intellectual, liberal, civilized—in which feminine disparity, one would have imagined, would least appear: the eclectic world of her brothers' Cambridge friends, which was to perpetuate itself in Bloomsbury, London. Masculine brutishness, strength-philosophy, the fascism of which she was to be conscious before it had a name, can, one would have imagined, have seldom touched her life. Her novels, with the exception of *Mrs. Dalloway,* were as much (and, æsthetically, as rightly) circumscribed by the milieu of her own life as were Jane Austen's.

From whence, then, came this obsession of hers that women were being martyrized humanly, inhibited creatively, by the stupidities of a man-made world? What must inevitably be called Virgina Woolf's feminism appears most strongly in her doctrinal, non-fiction books; most notably in *A Room of One's Own* and *Three Guineas*—it was a bleak quality, an aggressive streak, which can but irritate, disconcert, the adorer of Virginia Woolf the artist. One cannot, and I do not, blame Dr. Blackstone for letting irritation appear.

This woman, enchantingly beautiful no less in person than in mind, lived (as all of us who knew her will remember) in a sort of ambience of ideality—an ideality never to be thickened over by sentiment because of the purity of its crystal air. Out of this orbit she—partly because of actual delicacy, partly from distaste— seldom moved. Or seldom moved, at any rate, socially: she was a tireless solitary walker about London, looking in at windows, listening to scraps of talk. Frustrated intellectual women took up, in person, little of her time: in person, I should not hesitate to say, they would have afflicted, bored her. Yet, she burned for their sorrows without rest.

One may suppose that Virginia Woolf saw the 'outside' world

with the more horror from the very fact of seeing it at one remove. She did not exaggerate its griefs; possibly she remained unaware of its immunities and its compensations. It is possible—nay, more, I know it to be a fact—that she reproached herself for being privileged, sheltered. The second World War, beginning with the Spanish war, was to her the material culmination of something she had always seen latent, dreaded. It was her doom as a person —she was too great an artist for it to have been her doom as that —to live at a time when the intolerable must be faced.

That, had she lived, had the dreaded return of illness not driven her to the decision of death, she could have faced the intolerable, I do not doubt. Had she not, after all, preconceived everything? That 'taste of the eternal' that she transmitted remains with us. Her art, though it registered dismay and en-visaged defeat, triumphed: it is the strongest incentive to suc-ceeding artists to take in all, to transmute all, to continue to ride the waves.

                                   The New York Times Book Review.

IVY COMPTON-BURNETT*

1941   I

'It is the intangibility of the distinction that gives it its point,' says Luce, on an early page of *Parents and Children*, discussing whether her father should join her grandfather, or wait for her grandfather to join him. The residing of Fulbert, his wife Eleanor and their nine children, with Luce at the head, in the house of Fulbert's parents, Sir Jesse and Lady Sullivan, in itself creates a situation in which distinctions are bound to appear. The family fabric of pride and feeling, in which the thirteen Sullivans and their dependants all play their part, has no ordinary ground-work: it starts to rise from the level that Miss Compton-Burnett's novels, in their depiction of living, always assume. There are, that is to say, none of the obvious squalors and enmities. For instance, Lady Sullivan (Regan), of whose three children Fulbert only sur-

---

* 'Parents and Children.' By I. COMPTON-BURNETT. (*Gollancz.*)
* 'Elders and Betters.' By I. COMPTON-BURNETT. (*Gollancz.*)

vives, is a furnace of motherhood, whose interior roar can be heard when some incident opens the door of her nature. But her attitude to Fulbert's wife is not hostile.

She looked at Eleanor with a guarded, neutral expression. She could not see her with affection, as they were not bound by blood; and the motives of her son's choice of her were as obscure to her as such motives to other mothers; but she respected her for her hold on him, and was grateful to her for the children. And she had a strong appreciation of her living beneath her roof. . . . The two women lived in a formal accord, which had never come to dependence; and while each saw the other as a fellow and an equal, neither would have grieved at the other's death.

Eleanor's maternity is less positive. In fact, her lack of gift for this rôle is commented on by her children, constantly in her presence and unfailingly when she has left a room. Eleanor Sullivan has, at forty-eight, 'a serious, honest, somewhat equine face, and a nervous, uneasy, controlled expression.' She passes from floor to floor of the house, moves to and fro between the schoolroom and nursery, plucking upon the harp-strings of her young's sensibility with an inexpert but always hopeful hand. Throughout the early part of the book she is attempting to rally the children's feeling— attempting, in fact, to drill the nine Sullivans for climax of a sort of ballet of sorrow—for their father's forthcoming departure for South America. But Eleanor, if she does not captivate, exercises a pull of her own. She enjoys, without intermittence, Fulbert's ironic affection. And, immediately upon Fulbert's reported death, she is wooed by a neighbour, the inscrutable Ridley Cranmer.

The nine children fall into three groups—Luce, Daniel and Graham, young adults; Isabel, Venice and James, the schoolroom party, under the passive control of Miss Mitford, the governess, and Honor, Gavin and Nevill, the nursery children, under the dispensation of the nurse Hatton, her underling Mullet (of the fox-like features and the dramatized youth) and in a state of skirmish with Miss Pilbeam, the nursery governess, whose ingredients are honestness and faith. Actually, Hatton's dispensation extends a good way beyond the nursery bounds: a woman of fewer words than most of the characters, she has the Sullivan make-up perfectly taped. To say that the Sullivans have a Nannie-complex would be to speak on a lower level than the novel deserves. The relationship of the family with the two governesses is—as is

usual with Miss Compton-Burnett—perfectly done: it does not
cease to be analysed, from both sides, with an imperturbable lack
of feeling and zest for truth. 'I like all cold; I like even ice,' says
one of the children—though in another context. And an icy
sharpness prevails in their dialogue. In fact, to read in these days
a page of Compton-Burnett dialogue is to think of the sound of
glass being swept up, one of these London mornings after a blitz.
There are detonations in the Sullivan home—Fulbert's departure,
his letter to Isabel, the news of his death, his widow's engagement,
the show-down with Ridley, the discovery of Sir Jesse's illicit
paternity—each creates a momentary shock of dullness, each is
measured by this mortality of fine glass.

With each novel, Miss Compton-Burnett adds to her gallery.
Figures she has already, in another novel, created, she is content—
and content with deliberation—to rename and to put, in *Parents
and Children*, to a this time purely formalized use. For the Cranmer
family (with the exception of Faith, who is new), for the three
mysterious Marlowes and for the three eldest of the nine Sullivans,
Miss Compton-Burnett seems to me to rely, and rightly, on our
progressive acquaintanceship with one kind of person—what one
might call the illustrative rather than the functional character. In
Parents and Children, these play subsidiary parts. In *Parents and
Children* the high light falls on, and genius is evident in, the
younger Sullivan children and their immediate world. Especially
James and Nevill. I know no children like James and Nevill;
there may be no children like James and Nevill—in fact, the point
of this author's genius is that it puts out creatures to which it
might defy life to approximate. James and Nevill, of a beauty
divorced from sentiment, *are*, in *Parents and Children*—one cannot
question them; they are more living than life. There are also
Honor, Gavin, the tearful, complex, articulate Isabel, and Venice
—this last more lightly, though as surely, touched in. To say that
this book depicts the repercussion of grown-up crisis on children
would be incorrect. The children's intensive, moment-to-moment
living is for each a solitary crisis, that each maintains: grown-up
sense of crisis, grown-up drama do no more than splinter upon
these diamond rocks. It is the strength of Lady Sullivan, the
strength of Miss Mitford, the strength of Hatton that they recognize the children's inviolability.

In this novel, as in the others, relationships remain static. The dialogue, in less than half of a phrase, in the click of a camera-shutter, shifts from place to place. The careless reader, for instance, must look back twice to discover at which point the departing Fulbert's carriage drives off. Scenes, on the other hand, are played out without mercy, to an attentuation felt by each of the characters. Most notably, the scene of Fulbert's departure. 'Well, it cannot go on much longer, boys,' Fulbert says to his elder sons, as they all stand in the hall. 'If there were any reason why it should stop,' says Graham, 'surely it would have operated by now.' Luce says: 'The train will become due.' The train is the only artificial interference, by Time.

Is this a book for now? Decidedly, yes. And for the 'now' not only of already avowed readers of Miss Compton-Burnett. *Parents and Children*, coming at this juncture, is a book with which new readers might well begin. Miss Compton-Burnett, as ever, makes a few concessions; she has not, like some of our writers, been scared or moralized into attempts to converge on the 'real' in life. But possibly, life has converged on her. Elizabethan implacability, tonic plainness of speaking, are not so strange to us as they were. This is a time for *hard* writers—and here is one.

The New Statesman and Nation.

1944   II

The great Victorian novelists did not complete their task, their survey of the English psychological scene. One by one they died; their century ended, a decade or two before its nominal close. Then—as after one of those pauses in conversation when either exhaustion or danger is felt to be in the air—the subject was changed.

There came, with the early 1900's, a perceptible lightening, if a decrease in innocence: the Edwardian novelists were more frivolous, more pathetic. Their dread of dowdiness and longwindedness was marked; content to pursue nothing to its logical finish, they reassured their readers while amusing them, and restored at least the fiction of a *beau monde*. They were on the side of fashion: to shine, for their characters, was the thing. Competent, nervous, and in their time daring, they redecorated the English literary haunted house. Their art was an effort to hush things up. Curiously enough, in view of that, almost all the novels I was forbidden to read as a child were contemporary, which was to say, Edwardian. They were said to be 'too grown up.' (To the infinitely more frightening Victorians, no ban attached whatsoever: a possible exception was *Jane Eyre*.) When, therefore, I did, as I could hardly fail to, read those Edwardian novels, I chiefly got the impression of being left out of something enjoyable. Here was life no longer in terms of power, as I as a child had seen it, but in terms of illusion for its own sake, of successful performance, of display. Yes, and here the illusion bent on the grown-up state, on its stylishness, its esoteric quality. The fashions of the day, that I saw round me—artful silhouettes, intricate mounted hair-dressing, the roses, violets or cherries heaped high on hats—the constant laughter I heard in other rooms and the quick recourses, in my presence, to French, all contributed something to this. The Edwardians, perhaps to mark the belated accession of their King, did, however speciously, build up the grown-up idea. The distant existence of that *élite*, that group of performers that I approached so slowly and who might be no longer there by the time I reached them (a premonition which was to be justified) tormented me, in common with other children. I should like to know how the Edwardian novel affected its grown-up readers. In them too, I suppose, it played on the social nerve, the sensation of missing something.

That the Edwardians were, in fact, on the retreat, that they were fugitives from the preposterous English truths of Victorianism, putting up the best show they could, probably did not appear in their own day. Their shallowness was a policy, however unconscious. We owe it to them to see not only the speciousness but the ingeniousness of their contrived illusion. This was only not stronger because they were poor in artists: it reaches a worthy level in the best of the novels of E. F. Benson; it attains to a sublimation, nothing to do with fear, in the later novels of Henry James.

What, then, was this task the Victorians failed to finish, and that the Edwardians declined to regard as theirs? A survey of emotion as an aggressive force, an account of the battle for power that goes on in every unit of English middle-class life. The Victorians' realism and thoroughness, with regard to what interested them, has perhaps been underrated: where these do not operate,

where they are superseded by jocose patter or apparent prudery, I
think we may assume the Victorians' interest flagged—for instance, I think it arguable that they were not, imaginatively,
interested in sex, and that they were hardly aware of society. Their
blind spots matter less than their concentration, from which some
few blind spots could not fail to result: they concentrated on
power and its symbols—property, God, the family. Of these,
their analysis was unconscious: the order was one to which they
fully subscribed; they had no idea that they were analysing it, or
that, carried far enough, this must be destructive. In that sense,
their innocence was complete.

For what they required to work on, for what magnetized them,
the Victorians had no need to look far beyond the family. The
family was the circuit: the compulsory closeness of its members to
one another, like the voluntary closeness of people making a ring
of contact to turn a table, generated something. Society was, for
the Victorian novelists' purpose, comparatively negligible: as a
concept they could and did ignore it; it might just exist as a looser
outside ring, a supplementary system of awards and penalties, or
an enlarged vague reproduction of the family pattern. Love was
recognized as either promising an addition to the family structure
by a right marriage, or threatening damage to it by a wrong one;
apart from this, desire was sheer expense, and the lover from
the outside, as a late-comer, must be either a nincompoop or a
pirate. . . . This would seem to hold good of Dickens and
Trollope (whose personal sociability committed them to nothing
stronger in writing than a good word for a good time had with
good fellows, and left them derisive about any *beau monde*) and of
the Brontë sisters, for all their stress on the isolated passion of
individuals. As to George Eliot it seems doubtful: her analysis
was more conscious, which makes her less Victorian. The most
obvious instance is Charlotte M. Yonge, and the major exception
Thackeray, whose sense of society was acute, and whose families
are in a felt relation to it.

Thackeray was in another sense an exception: in his novels
there do exist grown-up people. For elsewhere, with the Victorians, we are in a world of dreadful empowered children. The
rule of the seniors only is not questioned because, so visibly, they
can enforce it; meanwhile, their juniors queue up, more or less
impatiently awaiting their turn for power. The family gradations,

though iron, are artificial: inwardly, everyone is the same age. The Victorians could not depict maturity because they did not believe in it. The father of the family was the extension of his youngest son's impotent buried wish, the mother, with her mysterious productivity, that of her daughter's daydream. How far the Victorian family was falsified by the mirror of Victorian art, or how far its characteristics were merely exaggerated, cannot be settled here: it is the art not the family that we study. For that matter, were the Victorian artists influenced by the passionate conjugality, and later equally passionate widowed seclusion, of their Queen? In its subjectivity, in its obsession with emotional power, the age was feminine: the assertions by the male of his masculinity, the propaganda for 'manliness' go to show it. The apronstring, so loudly denounced, was sought, and family life, through being ostensibly patriarchal, was able to cover much. Trollope, in whose own youthful experience family life had stood for debts and deathbeds, and Dickens, in whose it had stood for debts and disgrace, were active in forwarding the ideal.

Or, so it seemed to their readers and to themselves. It can be seen now that Victorian novel-writing, had it continued upon its course, would have endangered, not by frankness but by its innocent observations, the proprieties by which we must hope to live. It can be seen why the Edwardians took fright, and sought refuge in the society fairy-tale. It was certainly not the Edwardians who were the *enfants terribles*. As it happened, the Victorians were interrupted; death hustled them, one by one, from the room. We may only now realize that these exits, and, still more, the nervous change of subject that followed them, were a set-back for the genuine English novel. Its continuity seems to be broken up. Since then, we have a few brilliant phenomena, but, on the whole, a succession of false starts.

Have we, to-day, any serious novelist who has taken up, or even attempted to take up, at the point where the Victorians left off?

A possible answer might be, Miss Compton-Burnett, whose latest novel, *Elders and Betters*, calls for some fresh discussion of her position. She, like the Victorians, deals with English middle-class family life—her concentration on it is even more frankly narrow. In form, it is true, her novels are ultra-Edwardian; their pages present an attractive lightness, through all the weight being thrown on elliptical dialogue; but, beyond that, their unlikeness to the Edwardian is infinite—to begin and end with, they allow no place for illusion. They are, at the first glance, unlike the Victorian in being static (time is never a factor in them), in being unsensuous and unvisual, in refusing to differentiate between comedy and tragedy, in being without remorse. They resemble the Victorian in their sedateness, and in their atmosphere of physical and social security. Her avoidance of faked, or outward, Victorianism, however, is marked: we find ourselves with this, and more, guarantees that Miss Compton-Burnett is not merely copying but actually continuing the Victorian novel.

She continues it, that is to say, from the inside. Her being in the succession shows in her approach to her subject, rather than in her choice of it—for the family as a subject has never been out of fashion; there is no question of its being reinstated. What Miss Compton-Burnett revives is a way of seeing; she sees, with hyperacute vision, what the Victorians saw, and what they had still to see. She has been too clever, or too instinctively wise, to set her novels inside any stated time: the idiom of talk is modern, the way of living dates from thirty to forty years back. Costume and accessories play so little part that her characters sometimes give the effect of being physically, as well as psychologically, in the nude, and of not only standing and moving about in but actually sitting on thin air. For some reason, this heightens their reality. In space, they move about very little: they go for short walks, which generally have an object, or advance on each other's houses in groups, like bomber formations. They speak of what they will do, and what they have done, but are seldom to be watched actually doing it—in *Elders and Betters*, we do see Anna burning the will: on examination, we find this to be necessary, for this act she will not admit, and so can never describe. . . . This bareness, which starves the reader's imagination and puts the whole test of the plot to his intellect is, surely, un-Victorian? Miss Compton-Burnett has stripped the Victorian novel of everything but it's essentials—which must have been fewer than we thought. Her interest is in its logic, which she applies anew.

As a title, *Elders and Betters* is ironical: everyone in this novel is the same age, and nobody is admirable. In a Victorian novel, the characters fail to impose upon the reader; here, they fail to impose upon each other. The revolution, foreseeable, long overdue, has arrived—without disturbing a single impalpable cup on the impalpable drawing-room mantelpiece. It has been succeeded by this timeless anarchy, in which meals are served and eaten, visits paid, engagements to marry contracted and broken off. Everything that was due to happen in the world the Victorians posited, and condoned, has happened—but, apparently, there is still more to come: such worlds are not easily finished with, and Miss Compton-Burnett may not see the finish herself. For one thing, that disrespect for all other people underlying Victorian manners (as Victorians showed them) has not yet come to the end of its free say, and fear has not yet revenged itself to the full. The passive characters, almost all young men, marvel at the others, but not much or for long; they return to marvelling at themselves. Only the callous or those who recuperate quickly can survive, but in *Elders and Betters* everyone does survive—except Aunt Jessica, who commits suicide after the scene with Anna. In this we are true to the masters; in the Victorian novel people successfully die of their own death-wishes (as Aunt Sukey dies in *Elders and Betters*), but nobody ever dies of an indignity.

Miss Compton-Burnett shows, in *Elders and Betters*, that she can carry weight without losing height. She has been becoming, with each novel, less abstract, more nearly possible to enclose in the human fold. *Elders and Betters* is, compared, for instance, with *Brothers and Sisters, terre à terre*; but with that I greet a solid gain in effect. The more she masters what I have called her logic, the more material she can use. Her technique for melodrama has been by degrees perfected, and is now quite superb: I know nothing to equal Chapter X of this book—the duel in Aunt Sukey's death-chamber, after Aunt Sukey's death. Only second to this is the lunch-party, at which two families voice their disgust at old Mr. Calderon's engagement to Florence, the governess's young niece. There is an advance, too (again, a logical one), in the articulateness of employed persons: nothing protects the Donnes against Cook and Ethel, with whom even Anna is placatory. The importance of money has not budged, but dependence is now felt by the monied side—also, there is, with regard to employed persons, either a weakening or a belated dawn of grace. In one of the earlier novels, it seemed consistent that a child of the house should laugh every time the governess eats; in *Elders and Betters*, a child suffers because he has left a governess out in the dusk and rain. And religion, the worship in the rock garden, for the first time enters the scene.

The post-Victorian novel, in Miss Compton-Burnett's hands, keeps its course parallel with our modern experience, on which it offers from time to time, a not irrelevant comment in its own language. To the authority of the old, relentless tradition, it has added an authority of its own.

Cornhill Magazine.

SUCCESS STORY*

1942

Authoress of a best seller that made history, Mrs. Beecher Stowe would appear to owe much to the unhappiness of her youth. It is from the ranks of ill-adjusted people that crusaders most often emerge. If *Uncle Tom's Cabin* is not a work of art, it is the explosion of a remarkable temperament. Her humane indignation was real enough. But, with that sublime unscrupulousness to be found in even the minor artist, she cashed in on a real abuse to express her own passions—passions which a blameless, indigent marriage, motherhood, and one or two female friendships had not, so far, released.

It may be too much to say that the American Civil War would not have occurred if Harriet, sixth child of the New England Calvinist minister, Lynham Beecher, had had a better break as a young girl. Born at Litchfield, Connecticut, in 1811, she had the environment which has forced up so many natures at once brilliant and warped. Fanaticism salted the family bread. Her father's zeal showed in the variations of his nervous dyspepsia. In Harriet, the self-searchings of adolescence were elevated to a religious duty; she racked herself unremittingly—was she saved, or not saved? At twenty-two she wrote:—

I have been reading the life of Madame de Staël and *Corinne.* I have felt an intense sympathy with many parts of that book, with many parts of her character. But in America feelings vehement and absorbing like hers become still more deep, morbid, and impassioned by the constant habits of self-government which the rigid forms of our society demand.

* 'Crusader in Crinoline.' The Life of Harriet Beecher Stowe. By FORREST WILSON. (*Hutchinson.*)

They are repressed, and they burn inward till they burn the very soul, leaving only dust and ashes.

At Hartford she taught school, and hated it. Even her own sex denied her romantic friendship, and, in those days of early marriage or none, no suitor for some years came her way. As a child she had been pretty; success was to bring her into bloom as a woman. But when the Beechers moved West, to Cincinnati, on a (financially guaranteed) crusade, life still showed no promise for Harriet. Her physical being was, consequently, forbidding and tense.

Her good days began with her marriage to Calvin Stowe, one of her father's staff at Lane Seminary. He was the still mourning widower of one of her few glamorous friends. Her career as a writer, which had just opened, was to be halted by a career of maternity. In raw Cincinnati, threatened by recurrent waves of cholera, hard-worked young Mrs. Stowe stored up her powers of vision. She was close enough here to slavery, with its hideous facts: her imagination had only too much to bite on. She was already near the centre of a journalistic group that was pressing for Abolition. But not till her return, with her husband, to New England—Brunswick, Maine—did Uncle Tom spring, full-armed, from a vision she had in church.

Harriet, sending her novel off to the publisher, had expressed the hope it might earn her a silk dress. It did, in fact, earn her a world ovation—hysteria is not confined to our age. Her two tours in England were the occasion for orgies of denunciation of American vice. The abuses of our own industrial system, at that time, were kept tactfully out of view; rows of children, hymning under her windows, thanked the God who had made each A Happy English Child. This became the theme-song of her first trip. Only Thackeray sounded a sour note. Mrs. Beecher Stowe, radiant and dressing well, ignored all breaches of international tact. Fundamental innocence made her the born lion. She was disillusioned when, after the outbreak of the Civil War, England, enraged by the Yankee closing of cotton ports, veered without warning to the delinquent South. Not the least of Mrs. Stowe's gratifications in England had been the confidences of Lady Byron. And not the least of her blunders back in America was to be her dragging up of the old Byron scandal, intended to clear Lady

Byron of La Guiccioli's charge of coldness of heart. In two continents, Mrs. Beecher Stowe's shares went rapidly down. . . . As a biography, *Crusader in Crinoline* is packed with matter. It could have more style but could not be more clear.

The Observer.

ANNE DOUGLAS SEDGWICK*

1936

Anne Douglas Sedgwick, born in 1873, was the child of American parents living in London. The Sedgwicks came from New England, her mother's family from Ohio: she visited America as a child, twice in the five years preceding her marriage to Basil de Selincourt in 1908, then once more with her husband in 1930. Like many people whose lives are divided by water, who feel indigenous nowhere, she had to play consciously, strongly on her impressions and memories to give life a continuity that should be accidental, to give her conception of life, which preoccupied her, form. Appreciation became her most active faculty. In these letters her emotion attaches itself almost desperately to scenes, objects and people inside its scope, like a land bird to the railings and funnels of a liner it has followed too far and dare not leave now. Her dread for chaos, her desire not only for form but for a sense of any purpose behind it was immense; she wished to settle, and to settle without being deceived. Calm with a sort of tremor, tender, impetuous, arbitrary, yet with something behind them oddly *voulu* and cool, these letters to her friends have something dwelling about them, a delicate and penetrating greed that makes them like love-letters. She writes in an early letter to Mrs. James Pitman:

By *feeling*, by *instinct*, I am intensely pessimistic and altogether sceptical; my natural outlook on things is a despairing one; life seems to me a succession of moods dependent on external impressions, and death to end all.

* 'Anne Douglas Sedgwick.' A Portrait in Letters Chosen and Edited by BASIL DE SELINCOURT. (*Constable*.)

And in the following letter:

We have bought a mirror—*I* have rather, for mine it is. . . . I saw it in an old shop; my whole nature had been *hungering* for just such a mirror over our little white mantelpiece. . . .

And in 1914:

Just a year ago to-day . . . you in your purple dress, the softly glowing house, the glass bowl of nasturtiums in the hall, the roses and carnations and violets—how it all comes back! and the silvery lawn next morning from my window.

She was a New Englander in her formality and her charm. Not a hint of her perplexity can have shown. Her will, her moral æsthetic, her need to communicate humanly through small beauties, ordered her life as a woman exquisitely, as it directed her pen. Her possession took on something from the delight of her eye. To visit Far End was to enter one of her novels—but a novel of hers with any drama suspended—the tea-table with yellow roses on it, the sitting-room door at the head of the steep stairs had a precise silver-point line round them, and mattered more than a table or door in real life. She was gracious and natural in her relations with younger people. With everyone she must have been inexorably gentle: it is impossible to determine from these letters which lay deeper in her, irony or sentiment. But the letters have, I feel, inevitably been edited with a bias, and give an incomplete view of her character. Development may be a myth: there is at any rate no effect of development inside the thirty-seven years this collection covers. She does not defeat or exorcise her uneasiness, but learns to minister to it. The end of a century formed her, but she was a born Edwardian, tuned to her age, its charm, its privileges and its unconscious ruthlessness as only a woman could be— it is interesting that she should have found Jane Austen 'distinctly *dashing*, bold, even coarse.' Bunk had silted up slowly in the century between them, and Anne Douglas Sedgwick, for all her seriousness and courage, never stood wholly clear of it: loyalties made that impossible. She, like her generation, faced the indictment of 1914 without a tremor: she never ceases to see the War in heroic terms. Her good faith must have been absolute in 1941, when she wrote: 'So many of the finest types in Britain one feels are *meant* for a crisis like this. . . . One hopes that, after such a *lifting* and such a trying in the crucible, people can never again sink to quite such levels of squabbling and misunderstanding,' Nobility made her one of those luxuries for which we others are still paying the bills.

As a young woman she was an intellectual of her day: anxious but not militant, pious in the exact sense, given to study, to self-cultivation, to the desire to arrive at the truth. At the end of her twenties, when the letters begin, she is reading Huxley, Newman, William James and *Personal Idealism*—'a collection of essays on Philosophy by eight Oxford men. The value and meaning of personality, its power and right of interpreting life, is the basis of their thought.' Her poets were George Herbert and Emerson. As she grows older, her own thought becomes at once more personal and more objective, and shows less need of direction or companionship: metaphysics preoccupy her less. In the early letters she declares herself a regretful agnostic; just before her death, to another Mrs. de Selincourt, she defines her religious position in a letter that, because of its highly personal idiom, it would be unfair or at least misleading to quote. She faced death as she faced the War, with impassably well-bred courage, and a height of her frightening humour that nothing could defeat. Here was something more than the liner, a rock, more noble and static, for the lost bird to settle on.

Her integrity appears most in her own comments on her novels. Anne Douglas Sedgwick perfected, without pretension or fever, an art within her own scope. Her novels were the Edwardian novel at its best: one cannot too much honour her skill, their integrity—for integrity they must have, or their charm would make one uneasy. She delighted in personality, and in drawing round it an unfaltering moral line—she was too smiling, worldly and adept to be a prig; she was sadly incapable of fanaticism. 'I can express *nothing*,' she wrote, 'except in character, as it were. . . . I still feel so unable to say what I myself think of "Valeria" or "art" in general. I've no theories, you know; never think at all as to what "school" I belong to; my books, I know, when they are at all good, are a phase of myself, and perhaps a deeper phase than I am able to express in my personal capacity . . . the only instrument I'm aware of is a *smile*.' The smile, with its qualifications, its friendliness, its isolated and faintly barren delight in life, persists now, in her books, as a physical memory of her—persists growing yearly more foreign and distant, now when all smiles are changing their quality. Would she have desired her letters to be published? She had a strong sense of privacy, and must surely have wished to be remembered, as she is worthy to be remembered, as a novelist above all. She stands on the slope of New England writers, with Mrs. Wharton above her half-way to Henry James— the novelist of intelligent, smiling drawing-rooms, of security, of one's precocious childhood. She inspires nostalgia already: her novels are monuments, minor monuments, but they are cut cleanly and the stone is good.

The New Statesman and Nation.

FANNY BURNEY*

1938

Mr. Tourtellot has written the story of a decline: its moral appears to be: 'Beware of having too many nice friends.' Fanny Burney should have been her own heroine; her life exceeded her fancy; the illusions, triumphs and predicaments that beset her were more striking than any she could have devised. To an extent, no doubt, she was her own heroine; she can never have failed to see what was happening to her, and she always had the resource of quiet enjoyment. She should have written more novels—as it was, she became more deeply embroiled with life than could have been the most interesting of those young females who failed to follow *Evelina* and *Cecilia*. She assisted at scenes of an excruciating delicacy; she was chased round Kew Gardens by a dotty king; she put in those final weeks at Brighton with Johnson and the renegade Mrs. Thrale—weeks whose tension and squalor must have been without parallel. Her prepossessing qualities as a young person, her ability to play up to success were, apparently, the ruin of her career. Winning, unostentatious, she enjoyed—as which of us would not—exercising discreet power in illustrious sets. She remained the young person *par excellence* up to the end of her thirties. She then fell in love with d'Arblay, during an inter-

* 'Be Loved No More.' The Life and Environment of Fanny Burney By A. B. TOURTELLOT. (*Allen and Unwin.*)

mission, when a promising new attachment, to Mme de Staël, had been, by Dr. Burney, untimely nipped in the bud. Her marriage isolated her: for the first time, she had to live her own life, instead of other people's. As a social person, she came to an end.

From the title on, Mr. Tourtellot's book has an emotional quality. This is clearly a period, a society in which his fancy loves to dwell. Nostalgia has inspired very careful research; also, he seems to have bathed in the doubtful charm of these beings with every pore open. He does not, for some reason, render this charm well—for that something more is needed than nostalgia and diligence. His style is far from happy; it is too heartfelt—but on the other hand, how honest not to affect irony. Of laborious irony, and of 'atmospheric' writing *Be Loved No More* is quite innocent: this is, indeed, its greatest, if negative, merit. Also, he has assembled his matter well; as the book proceeds he vibrates less and the narrative gains much in compactness and speed.

As for the absence of atmosphere, does this arise from a proper strictness, or does Mr. Tourtellot lack some susceptibilities? He shows little sense of time-colour. He seems quite unaffected by the nature of places in which events occurred—or has he perhaps not visited some of them? In an outlying part of Chesington, now Chessington, garden, away from the small, gay zoo, a miniature train, chuffing through an arch in a beech hedge, dashes past the mulberry tree under which, so the label says, Fanny Burney sat to write *Evelina*. The train, the band from the circus and the zoo-cries fail to ruffle the well-like calm of this retreat at the end of the walled garden. It is at Chessington that Fanny can be remembered most happily; it was here that she wasted least of her time—till she had lost what she owed to the vigilance of Samuel Crisp. Had there been less of Streatham she would have done better. Her martyrdom to her own too-well-known tact was to reach its climax in those five years at the appalling Hanoverian Court.

Has Mr. Tourtellot fitted some of his facts rather arbitrarily into his moral pattern? Few lives display quite so clearly cause and effect. Also, though he states Fanny's importance, he does not make it palpable; Miss Burney's dignity does not appear enough. Few people squander their gifts—alas! things are not so simple—they mis-invest what they have. And Fanny Burney's investments must have seemed sound enough. She saw illustrious days. *Were* those evenings, those long afternoons, those capacious

H

dinners enthralling without a break? Did no one feel the fatigues
of that society bristling with personal issues, in which topics were
hammered flat, in which everything mattered, in which rooms
must have been hot and many people splenetic? Conversation
was at its zenith. All the same, the charm of the conversation
picture resides, for some, in its silence, its glassy air of being set
back out of earshot, in time. As to what *was* said, we remain documented quite relentlessly well. There are periods which, even
while they were still the present, were being architected to make
an imposing past, and Fanny Burney enjoyed the hey-day of one
of these. And she never fell; she was never discredited; she trans-
ferred herself from allegiance to allegiance with unspotted loyalty.
Only, the past became always a little brighter behind her, the
future a little darker ahead. The obscurity of her last years had
tragic sources—bereavement, exile, poverty. But obscurity could
be kind; it at least hid her completely, no one could point and say
'*She* was Fanny Burney; you might not think so, but she once had
a marvellous time.'

The New Statesman and Nation.

LADY BURTON*

1942

Isabel Burton, *née* Isabel Arundell, appears to have had the character that goes with a specific physical type. The type can only be
a feminine one. Her full ovoid face, hare's eyes of a dilated intensity, high-bridged nose, small mouth with sharply indented
upper lip, placed high and blandly above an extent of chin—this
combination rings bells in my memory. I must have several
times met her, and always suffered from her. I fancy I am not alone
in my irritation. This Isabel must be the prototype of the unpopular woman who forges ahead in the world—narcissistic, complacent, egregious, but possessed of either heroic or sub-human
resistance and of an energy, quite simply, heroic.

Miss Jean Burton's biography of the lady owes debts that it
frankly acknowledges. As an overhaul of given material, with

---

* 'Sir Richard Burton's Wife.' By JEAN BURTON. (*Harrap.*)

some perspicacious additions, it is interesting. The Burton marriage was, in every sense, successful. It may be said that all successful marriages present cases of interlocking egotisms, but this case is major and makes a story that can afford to be retold. The story was first told as it went along: the Burtons were their own adequate commentators—they talked indefatigably about themselves, and their friends (well-chosen as they were numerous; it was Isabel's business to see to that) talked and wrote to each other about them. The dark tiger-man, explorer, expert on erotology, with his blonde, Junoesque, well-connected wife caravaned, during their visits to England, through the higher ranges of Victorian society. In the course of their just not continuous absences from Trieste they came across almost everyone at Continental spas.

For years together, however, they really were out of reach. Isabel was to realize her adolescent dream of being not only the mate of a superman but of facing dangers alongside him in the wilds. At steamy Santos (São Paolo, Brazil) and in the suburbs of Damascus—if the dangers were not acute, the discomforts were. And all these Isabel overrode with an insouciance one must admire in her. She did not depart from those seventeen rules 'For My Guidance as a Wife' that, on the eve of her marriage, she had laid down for herself. No one can question that she supported Richard with indomitable understanding and courage. She saw him off on his expeditions and waited through sickening silences for his returns. She continued to see to it that there should be no place like home. Their domesticity was not only as idyllic as Richard's temperament would allow; it was made more interesting by an occult tinge. They both encouraged psychic phenomena, and he had hypnotized her on their honeymoon.

The bringing off of her marriage to Richard Burton had been in itself a *tour de force*. Isabel was the eldest child of a younger branch of the Arundells; as Roman Catholics they had sustained considerable losses; they had a distinguished history but their fortunes to make. She had been born in Bayswater in 1831. The Emancipation Act, of two years before, for some time rather heightened anti-Catholic prejudice, and things had barely improved when she was a débutante. Her schoolroom days were spent in the country where she rambled and dreamed. A gypsy named Hagar Burton gave stuff to her dreams by a definite prophecy—this so influenced Isabel that during her one season in

London (though she was, by her own showing, a brilliant success) she disdained young men. Having put all they had into Isabel's London season, the Arundells moved to Boulogne, 'city of debtors.' Here, on the ramparts, Isabel first met Richard. Boulogne, that year, put out a few muted balls, and she kept the sash and the gloves in which she once waltzed with him. He was her preconceived idea of the only possible mate—but after Boulogne for years she did not see him again. When they did next meet, they quite soon became engaged. Their marriage—a blameless elopement—did not take place till she was thirty. He had no money, already some reputation but a decidedly doubtful name.

It was she who put him across, in a big way. On his behalf she became a brilliant, hypnotic bore. The Foreign Office dreaded her. She obtained for him a series of consulships, and during his prolonged absences did his work. She knew not respite till he became Sir Richard. She failed only in one thing—he did not die a Catholic, though she was to persuade herself he had lived as one. Their sunset—she with her blonde wig, he with his dyed black hair—had its own magnificence. It was financed by the proceeds of *The Arabian Nights*. In a more honest age they would have been lovable crooks. One salutes that singleness of the will that made Isabel realize her life-dream. It is a pity thât about lives in which dreams are realized there should cling, like a sort of vestigial remnant, the meretricious unreality of all dreams.

The Observer.

MYSELF WHEN YOUNG*

1948

Myself When Young is the first half of an autobiography Henry Handel Richardson did not live to complete. These chapters were written during her last years, in the Sussex house to which she had

* 'Myself When Young.' By HENRY HANDEL RICHARDSON. (*Heinemann*.)

retired after her husband's death. As it stands, the self-told story ends with her marriage to J. G. Robertson in Dublin, in 1895: she had, we learn, intended that it should cover the early years of the married life in Germany, and close with the migration to London in 1903, when Professor Robertson was appointed to the Chair of German language and literature. On from the point where Henry Handel Richardson breaks off—and the last lines here are the last she ever wrote—events are supplied by Miss Olga Roncoroni, drawing on the material (letters, notes and diaries) to which her friend had expected to have recourse. At the end of the book is placed Professor Robertson's essay: 'The Art of Henry Handel Richardson.'

This autobiography is not a work of art. The style in which it is written is bluff, pedestrian; it could be the style of some honest, natural person who had not written before. At a first glance, the object of the author might seem to be nothing more than to forge forward, at a steady pace, page by page, through time. Almost no passage directly illuminates the imagination of the reader; the selection of words would seem to have been, if not careless, utilitarian. The effect is domestic. And, in the matter of content, as to what has been set down, there could have been little discrimination other than memory's.

This was probably so. Henry Handel Richardson must have accepted that one remembers nothing that is not, somehow, important; that memory is the editor of one's sense of life. In that case, she submitted herself, when writing *Myself When Young*, to an inner, arbitrary dictation. To do this was an abnegation on the part of the artist, for whom creativeness means, most of all, choice. She may have begun writing with no design, no intention other than that of letting the submerged design of her life, like something hitherto written in invisible ink, appear. This could account for her abandonment, now that it was a matter of autobiography, of the whole illusory element comprehended in our idea of style: style in that sense notably served her when she wrote the novels—without that they could not have had their force. What she must have understood was, that in writing *Myself When Young* she was not creating, but, rather, contemplating what had created her. Her object, now, was not to set up illusion but to penetrate to its early source: she must, therefore, have fought shy of the magic that for any writer cannot but emanate from words. With the undiscriminating patience of a stenographer, she 'took down.'

The result is, an objectivity rare in autobiography—rarest of all in the autobiography of a novelist, for whom it is exceedingly difficult not to select, place, evaluate, dramatize and, thereby, virtually, invent. Few novelists of stature are, it may be granted, narcissistic, being saved from that not so much by moral grace as by a sort of boredom with the character they know too well. Few novelists, therefore, willingly contemplate themselves: their own susceptibilities, having been professionalized, have lost mystery for them. Trollope's Autobiography, for instance, shows a disinfected, total loss of self-interest after the evaporation of the miseries of youth. The novelist tends to be tempted into autobiography less by the *ignis fatuus* of his nature than by a fascination with experience (any experience, even his own) for its own sake. The introduction, essential to autobiography, of himself is only made congenial to his imagination by a series of touchings-up, of effective 'placings' of his own figure down perspectives of time or against backgrounds spectacular in themselves. Not dishonesty but sheer avoidance of boredom transmutes the majority of novelists' biographies into works of art. The novelist arrives at seeing himself by seeing himself as a character in one more novel.

Henry Handel Richardson's attitude to herself must, on the other hand, have remained unexplored and pure. The child, the girl, who take form out of these pages seem to be making their first impact upon the woman they have become. The out-going child became the out-going artist: something clean and immediate was in both the earlier and the later temperament; emotional costiveness, broodingness were in neither. An Australian-reared doctor's daughter, surname Richardson, christened Ethel Florence but known as 'Et' or 'Ettie,' lived with zest, rode the waves, missed nothing of what was round her. This was a rough society, in which no wind was tempered: the lively likeable brown-eyed child with the long nose wore bravado, suffered sharply, gave as good as she got. As a family, the Richardsons, always in pursuit of more stable fortunes, shifted about the Australia of the 1870's; adapting themselves, in every new place, to yet another community, harsh, human, outspoken and insecure. Dr. Richardson (acknowledged origin of Richard Mahony) was adventurous, but did not prosper: in the home there was perpetually an atmosphere of strain and makeshift. After his death, Mrs. Richardson, whose temperament leaves the strongest possible imprint on this her daughter's book, rode full tilt against Victorian-Australian convention by going to work—as a post-mistress. The reward for her struggle was, her two little girls continued to have their hair curled and were kept nice in speech. Intellectually, there could only be poor nutrition; socially, solitude.

No new books coming in [says Henry Handel Richardson] I took to making up stories for myself. To the accompaniment of a ball bounced against a wall. For I was a very active, not to say restless child, and never sat still if I could help it. As I spoke my stories aloud, the noise I made was considerable, and I don't wonder that I was often shoo'ed off by my mother from where she was sitting.—This method of 'making up' by word of mouth continued till I was sent to boarding-school at the age of twelve. Given a ball and a wall to bounce it against, I needed no other amusement. Nor did I feel the lack of companions to which our somewhat ambiguous position condemned us.

This was as well; for my sister and I were at this time a very solitary pair of children. Of course having each other we were never exactly lonely; but there could be no question of games that called for more than two; and we undoubtedly lost by not knowing the rough-and-tumble of group-playing. My mother, however, saw things differently. Hating the place and everything to do with it, she hotly declared that there wasn't a child of our own age fit for us to associate with. . . . And we did not rebel, for we had been early imbued with the notion that we were rather better than the people we lived amongst. . . .

In that one passage stand out obvious reasons why Ettie Richardson should have become a writer—solitude, the habit of self-amusement, the sensation of having been set apart, the instilled idea that one must be either superior or nothing, the wish to first draw abreast with, then overshoot life. It is not enough, however, to diagnose why she became a writer: what made her Henry Handel Richardson? She had a temperament formed to receive experience not only deeply but in a certain way, a temperament that profited while it suffered. Childhood, in which may be counted the first adolescent years, was evidently the time of her greatest intake: after that, some imperceptible gate closed— emotionally, the experiences of her adult life, friendships, courtship and marriage, strike one as being more exterior. The thin little girl with the long nose was not girlish; she had a young-masculine streak; she was positive, physically daring, inadvertently cruel, aggressive, impatient under the hair-curling. The successive objects of her affection were, generically, delicate and gentle. In no aspect is *Myself When Young* a love story: continuously, it is the story of a capacity for love. The first high point is the fourteen-year-old passion for the young clergyman, who, in the downright society of Maldon had not only the spirituality but the gaiety of a visitant from another world.

Within [she recounts] a number of years he was gone from Maldon for good and all.

On this night a few of his intimate friends were invited to the parsonage. After supper, some of us younger ones stretched ourselves on the steps leading up to the verandah, he among us. He was in his duck coat, I in a white dress, and Grace, looking down on us from above, said casually: 'In the moonlight Jack and E. look as though they were one.' The words were like a fresh dagger-thrust at my bleeding heart. I winced, and may have made some impulsive movement to draw back; for here he took my hand and held it, and went on holding it, patting it and stroking it. Why he did this only he knew. But the remembrance of it, the one ghost of a caress that ever passed between us, sustained me through many a bleak and empty month to come.

Once he left Maldon I never saw him again. . . .

Another memory went with that love: adventure—Jack and E. in the high trap, out driving; it was she who mastered the runaway horse. Later, with Melbourne schooldays, came the devotion to the elder girl—elegant, pretty, lovingly scolding the rough Ettie. This time, the end again came with a departure: Ethel's own departure to England with her mother and sister. Twice now she had experienced the agony of being torn away. Years later, she was exclaiming to her husband that she wondered how she, 'a poor ignorant little colonial,' could ever have come to have written *Maurice Guest*. 'My husband glanced up from his writing-table, and said in his wise, quiet way: "But emotionally very experienced." '

She was to have been a musician. High hopes were entertained, work and money had been invested already; it was for the sake of her elder daughter's career that Mrs. Richardson risked the move to England and, later, Germany. The time in the home country was depressing; there was always a semi-dependance upon relations; anxiety, calculation attended every step. Leipzig the family loved: they lived in exiguous student pensions, but life' was rewarding, exhilerating, full of music, ambition, friends. Through it all, the girl remained obsessed with the idea that she must make good: when her friendship with J. G. Robertson culminated in an engagement to marry, she could not fail to feel that she was defaulting. *This*, her mother made her feel, was the end of all the hopes, a making futile of all the sacrifices! The young Scot was a student, with as yet no future; and that marriage must mean the abandonment of Ethel's career in music was, at that epoch, to be assumed. How good a musician she might have made is not to be gathered from this book. She took, as it was, to writing as a second resort.

Ultimately, the marriage was made with Mrs. Richardson's good will. Yet it seems possible that Henry Handel Richardson may have kept, with regard to her mother, some sense of an unpaid debt. The marriage itself, as a sympathy, as a companionship, was ideal: it would appear that for more than thirty years Henry Handel Richardson was not again to know the intellectual loneliness which had so much oppressed her. It was in that atmosphere that the creative artist flowered into being; her latent powers developed through being understood. How dispassionately they were understood, how perceptively honoured, Professor Robertson's essay on his wife's art shows.

In the evolution of this novelist, countries played their part. The grit of Australia was to transmute itself into the Richard Mahony trilogy; though not until the German musical years had crystallized in the masterpiece *Maurice Guest*. The Melbourne school yielded *The Getting of Wisdom*. It was Henry Handel Richardson's destiny to feel claimed, entirely, by no one country: as a child in Australia she had hugged her Britishness to herself; the return to England had made her, inwardly, angularly Australian; her Irish blood had given her little more than an uneasy susceptibility to things Irish; in Germany she was student, traveller, inhabitant of a happy personal world, but outsider always.

There may be felt in her novels the challenge of an everlasting strangeness, a strangeness that the imagination must penetrate. She took nothing for granted.

The Times Literary Supplement.

BLIND ALLEYS*

1938

Brought Up and Brought Out is a brilliantly naïve book, essay on the discomforts of being young. Lady Mary Pakenham's childhood was spent in surroundings which, though correct, the family genius of a large and highly individualized family managed to make sufficiently fantastic. Fierce children—or rather, children blameless in public but tigers amongst themselves—Lady Mary and her brothers and sisters occupied that underworld set apart for its children by Society. They terrorized fellow-travellers on the Irish Mail, and at inappropriate moments slid on crimson carpets. These children were not 'brought out' shortly after birth; nothing was done to make them socially precocious; they felt isolated from other children by having to wear unaccommodating clothes. The Irish Question made itself known to them through a series of inconveniences and alarms. It is no doubt from being Anglo-Irish, or having been Anglo-Irish at one period, that Lady Mary has learnt something of her ironic immunity.

I was born knowing the difference between the Protestant Church and the Church of Rome. There wasn't a time when I was not aware that Protestants were respectable but dull, while Catholics were dirty but amusing. I was likewise born conscious of the Irish Question, and a terrible tedious question I thought it. My family did not share my opinion about this, though I have since met a remarkable number of people who do.
Considering how much I heard it talked about, I learnt very few details of this eternal question. I suppose I automatically shut off my brain whenever politics turned up in the conversation.

From living, or spending much time in Ireland, one learns that everything matters but nothing matters much. Fatalism is increased by a childhood during the War, and by playing a débutante's part in the General Strike. Children moved in numbers

* 'Brought Up and Brought Out.' By MARY PAKENHAM. (*Cobden-Sanderson.*)

from place to place also acquire a quizzical attitude. There is a nice picture of the family, some of them adolescent, some childish, putting in an economical summer in appalling hotels abroad. Foreign travel in more picturesque places, such as Italy, comes in well: the family spent what must have amounted to years in trains, and, with always equal tension and sense of drama, individual members were or were not sick. The fascination of this book consists in its presenting a series of pictures of life under very exacting conditions from the point of view of someone who may be sick in the train. Even animals did not provide a purely jolly world: Lady Mary has no sooner picked up a rather pampered kitten met near Florence than it dies in her hands.

This book does so much to expose the débutante racket that one wonders why it has not been burned by the social columnist. The mortifications and dullness of Lady So-and-So's girl, squeezing up a packed staircase to meet men hired by the stone, are exposed unshrinkingly. *Brought Up and Brought Out* should be, in common fairness, kept from the hands of non-débutantes of all ages who are happy leading this dream life. Lady Mary, cruelly well equipped, later explored the expensive illusion to its source by joining the staff of a well-known evening paper. Thus she has Society taped inside and out.

Nothing is more telling than to under-write one's experiences. Lady Mary is not out to expose anything, however many idols she shatters by the way. She seems merely to wonder why life is so funny and why nothing, however portentous, ever quite comes off. She gives important notes on fighting, and on why one feels so artificial with people whom one knows one can neither hit nor kick. Much of the spleen that goes to make us so touchy and treacherous no doubt arises from the suppression of violence. . . . The art of apparently saying everything and at the same time giving nothing away is completely commanded by Lady Mary. She respects institutions without asking anything of them; she has an acute distaste for seediness and decay, and for Bohemia's anxious conventionalities. The art school, the newspaper office, philanthropy all whittle down under her sharp knife. *Brought Up and Brought Out* could, apart from its content, be read for its at once adept and negligent style, and for its analysis of the nature of the blind alley.

The New Statesman and Nation.

KINDNESS TO WOMEN*

1937

Here is a translation of the first two novels—*Les Jeunes Filles* and *Pitié pour les Femmes*—in what is to be, in all, a sequence of four. *Le Démon du Bien* is still to be translated, *Au Bord de l'Abîme* still to come. In France, where the intelligent novel goes far, these books about women (women in love) have been widely enough read to rouse excitement and anger. Montherlant has been, I understand, accused of indecency on a rather subtle plane. He gets nearer the nerve of a matter—in fact, 'our women'—than people, even in France, like. Now that translation is to widen his English public, what, I wonder, will be the reactions to him here? Very mixed; in some quarters, possibly, hostile. He is likely to displease women, to unnerve men. He has a ruthless touch on a good many illusions. But his drive, his clarity, his magnetic style are unlikely to be forgotten. Above all, he arouses intellectual amazement. Messrs. Routledge are to be thanked for making Montherlant more accessible. Another foreign power touches the English shore.

The central character in *Pity for Women* is Pierre Costa, or Costals, a novelist. (In the earlier French editions he was Costa, then trouble arose with an actual M. Pierre Costa, so he became Costals, in succeeding editions: some confusion results.) He is, by popular reckoning, a selfish man. His novels draw in on him an immense volume of correspondence from women—youngish, susceptible, 'superior,' lonely in the provinces. The bulk of his fan-mail is to be inferred: two only, and no doubt the two most untiring, of his correspondents emerge in *Les Jeunes Filles*— Thérèse, the little country girl, the mystic, and Andrée (a much more difficult proposition) of Saint-Léonard, Loiret. Unhappily, Costals detests cerebral women, and *exaltées* are not his type at all. His young mistresses are natural, naïve and gay—or, at least,

* 'Pity for Women.' By HENRI DE MONTHERLANT. Translated by Thomas McGreevy and John Rodker. (*Routledge*.)
* 'The Young Girls.' By HENRI DE MONTHERLANT. Translated by Thomas McGreevy and John Rodker. (*Routledge*.)

placid. So is, or so appears to be, Solange, who half-way through *Les Jeunes Filles* rivets his desire. Solange's parents, with whom she lives, play a small part in the story. Otherwise the two novels comprising *Pity for Women* are built round four characters only—Costals, Thérèse, Andrée and Solange.

Les Jeunes Filles is a miracle of construction. Letters from and to women, an extract from a matrimonial gazette, leaves from notebooks, a cutting from one of Costals' articles are assembled to make the novel—apparently at random. Straight narrative only starts towards the end. *Pitié pour les Femmes* has, also, letters and extracts, but narrative predominates here.

This method—random assemblage—is for Montherlant's purpose brilliantly chosen. No fact appears without its effect of almost painful relevance. Statements are to be taken at their personal value. Emotion is progressive, cumulative, not checked or deflected by outside scenes. So much speed has each character gathered in its solitary course that each of the few encounters become collisions. Crisis is self-explanatory. Each of the three women exist only, and exist intensively, in one orbit: Costals'. All three, even the positive Andrée, are shown as behaving under compulsion: to an extent, their behaviour is involuntary. Solange keeps, for these two volumes—she is to lose it later—her mystery for Costals: the mystery of an animal. Thérèse (who remains 'off') exposes in her letters, step by step, her journey towards insanity. Andrée gathers a force as that dreadful and honest figure, the woman out to supply a felt want. The siege she lays to Costals surrounds his enjoyment of Solange. Her letters are heroic and fatuous: she is convinced he loves her, that they are held apart by his dread of the strength of his own feeling for her. She wields her intelligence in a fury of self-deception. She says: 'I understand you'—that final mistake, that final impertinence. Her mistrust of platonics becomes stronger: she offers herself to him repeatedly. She neglects to wash her arms, and gets stuck (when he takes her out in Paris) in a revolving door. She refuses to recognize what she is up against: the artist's dread of intrusive companionship. Only the second-rate artist is looking round for a soul mate. Costals, the absolute writer, is invulnerable. She has what he has classified as Reflex 227 B:

That well-known, established reflex, according to which a woman, because she is unhappy, tries to convince the man she loves that he is unhappy himself. Not only because she wants to comfort and 'mother' him, but because it exasperates her to see the man happy, and happy without deriving his happiness from her.

It is well within Costals' power to get rid of Andrée. She persecutes him; she fatigues him; she repels him physically. Yet, up to the final cruel scene in the studio, he lets the affair drag out its grotesque length. Why? Out of sympathy for her, out of a smothered *liking*, most of all, out of pity. He is one of those people, called cruel most often, who cannot be wholly, and so effectively, cruel: they are more than half located in the objects of their unkindness; they hesitate to deliver the *coup de grâce*. This complexity of the nature, this dread of cutting across a situation already exacerbatingly painful, is to appear more stongly in *Le Démon du Bien*. Here Costals not only cannot rid himself of Solange when he learns she intends to marry him (which he dreads) but cannot rid himself of the idea of marrying her. Hence his revengeful cruelty; hence the tears at Genoa. His peace with Solange ends in long, fruitless, claustrophobic quarrels. Women —at least the women in Costals' experience—remain ignorant of the one source of their power:

Women always refuse to consider how much falsehood, calculation, weariness and charity may enter into the love men testify towards them.

Cut away, therefore, from love its first and saving element of desire, and what but pity—exacting and potentially cruel—remains? Suppress the angry manifestations and you get ingrowing pity, generic, sublime and morbid. 'The heart infects everything.' Only with his son, Brunet, and with the earlier Solange does Costals feel either honest or pure. At the same time, something is lacking: some exaction which is the core of love. In theory, Costals is unassailable, with his work, his cheerful son, his string of young mistresses. But he is a man doomed to pity, doomed to attract its objects. To an extent, his calling accounts for this:

'It does one good to be with you again' (he says, returning to Solange after the break with Andrée). 'To be with a woman who lives among the realities. It's a fact: you are one of the few women I've ever known with any sanity. Literary men attract crazy women exactly as bits of meat attract the flies. We get the benefit of all their repressions, their feelings of not being wanted: what don't they expect from us in their dreams? . . .'

'But then, why do you reply to them?'

'What would you have? When I see flies on a bit of meat I say to myself, "Everyone has the right to eat." '

Not prettily put, but unwilling charity prompts it. . . . It may be argued that Costals as the realized artist, a man with nothing to gain from the affections, is a special figure, not possible to generalize, that his conclusions are special, not material generally. But he exists, enlarged and, in spite of everything, generalized, in an element that is Montherlant's own mind. The books, therefore, have implications that go beyond him. *Pity for Women* is a pitiless examination of the whole nature of pity—its range, its variations, it powers and its abuses. The examination is conducted in the light of a ruthless, disabused and exceedingly stern morality: a morality no sentiment can deflect.

The character of a vigorous and magnetic style is well kept in Mr. Rodker's translation of the second volume: *Pitié pour les Femmes*. Mr. McGreevy's rendering of *Les Jeunes Filles* is less happy.

New Statesman and Nation.

DRESS*

1937

Dress has never been at all a straightforward business: so much subterranean interest and complex feeling attaches to it. As a topic, it is popular because it is dangerous—it has a flowery head but deep roots in the passions. On the subject of dress almost no one, for one or another reason, feels truly indifferent: if their own clothes do not concern them, somebody else's do. In talk, this is an area of floating mines—tabus, *idées fixes*, snobberies, unadmitted frustrations. Ten minutes talk about clothes (except between perfect friends) tends to make everyone present either overbearing, guarded or touchy. The specialist speaks his own language, and gives nothing away; the intolerable person takes what he takes to be the informed view; while those who believe

* 'English Women's Clothing in the Nineteenth Century.' By C. WILLETT CUN-NINGTON. (*Faber.*)

indirect aspersions are being cast on their own way of dressing retreat into hurt silence. This apparently frivolous topic has led to much ill-feeling—love, food, politics, art or money are all very much safer. Clothes never remain a question of pure æsthetics; far too much personal feeling is involved in them. They play such an intimate part in the delicate business of getting oneself across that it seems impossible to discuss them, for long, objectively.

In theory, dress is an art. The architecture of textiles ought to rank only less high than the architecture of stone in so far as textiles are less durable—also, of course, the form created in textiles is less civic in purpose and less widely beheld. The great *couturiers* hold, and do impose on their clients, the great, abstract and architectural view. In their French houses the approach to dress is chastened and impersonal: where dress *is* an art, not only the stuff but the body become the art's matter. This approach to dress on the part of the wearer implies a sort of discipline—personal fads and sentiments have to be overcome: unselfconsciousness, loftiness are put on with the great dress. But this discipline, or release from a range of petty obsessions, is, unhappily, in nine out of ten cases, one of those good things that only money can buy. The great designer should and must be deferred to—but one buys the right to defer at a pretty substantial price. Fail to command this price, and dress drops at one from the psychological altitude: you are thrown back among your anxieties, your fixations, your will-o'-the-wispish personal fantasies, and are more than apt to be tricked by your false view of yourself. With most people of moderate income, bad, or at least uneasy, tentative dressing is the result of being delivered into their own hands. An unsuccessful appearance is more than a pity; it is a pathological document.

The artist, of any kind, is a person enough disengaged from his own personality to be able to objectify himself or it. Dressing is the one art the unqualified must practise. To present an appearance, a whole, that shall be not only pleasing but significant (which is, after all, the aim, however imperfectly realized, of the woman buying a hat or man buying a tie) is at least as difficult technically, requires as close a grip by the imagination, as disabused an attitude, as the writing of a book that should be fit to be published, or the painting of a picture that is to be seen. In the other arts, something relentless divides the aspirant from the professional: in dress, the aspirant is constantly on the streets. Consciousness of the failure of an effect to which the whole nature lent itself (or which, at least, it obstructed in the best of faith) makes many faces discouraged or evasive. Determination to brazen the thing out gives many faces an air of solid, piglike defiance.

Does fashion help? Such-and-such is worn this year; such-and-such ought to be 'safe.' Yes, fashion does give a line—but only a general one. It gives a general bent to the aspirations. And nothing is more restful than conformity. But fashion seems to exist for an abstract person who is not you or me. The complaint of non-combatants, the elderly and the old, is that everyone, nowadays, looks exactly the same as everyone else. The truth, probably, is, that everybody would like to look like one preconceived person, a figure suggested to them by the propaganda of fashion: they believe the figure to be their private ideal and do not realize how general the figure is. Stenographers with good figures, quick eyes and uncomplex natures approximate to this ideal most nearly. More pretentious or more difficult people are torn between the desire to express themselves (through fashion) and the hope of assuming, in fashion, an effective disguise. Exhibitionism and a nervous wish for concealment, for anonymity, thus battle inside the buyer of any piece of clothing. There is also the element of fetichism: certain colours, textures or objects exercise an unholy fascination that reason cannot combat, economy cannot check. Is the magnetic object a symbol? One cannot say. By departing at all widely from the current fashion, we are likely to give our fantasies unlimited play.

Even fanciful dressing follows its own order—or conforms, shall we say, to its own ruling obsession. The woman who decides to override fashion, 'to be her own fashion,' as she expresses it, and looks year in year out like a high altar, a Siennese angel, a Watteau, an artist's mistress in *Punch* or a person who breeds dogs, is relentlessly driven through her London shopping by the exactions of her particular whim. Her reward is small: among ordinary people the fanciful dresser is generally avoided, as likely to be either tendentious or fey. Overt self-dramatization is both dull and embarrassing: most of us agree to observe a certain caution in this.

Generally, up to a point, we are prone to accept fashion. We treat with it, and like to believe that we let it qualify our own personal taste (or fancy) to just the becoming degree. The middle reaches of England, the middle-classes, are the stronghold of free-conventional, in fact of compromise, dressing. We consider the *mondaine* slavish; actually, we find her frigid. Pure style in clothes is as intimidating as pure style in anything else. 'Keep an eye on the fashion, dear, but always know your own type. Don't ever look unnatural. If you can't wear a hard fashion, soften it off: a bow or a bunch of flowers will do wonders.' This has been the general line. We are not ones for effrontery. (Or, at least, we were not, until we saw it in play. Hollywood, within the last twenty years, has imposed itself more widely on English dress than Paris has in centuries. American clothes speak a more emotional language. The Hollywood type has stamped herself everywhere; she is found in remote villages, in Ireland, in Italy. She is one more great leveller.) We have also the tendency to oppose fashion, as something arbitrary. We are so romantic, so Protestant, that we each believe our own personal taste, or fancy, to be unique, independent, perhaps divinely implanted. Whereas fashion appears coercive, *voulu*.

But the fact is (as Mr. Willett Cunnington shows in his Preface to *English Women's Clothing in the Nineteenth Century*, and continues to show throughout his analysis) that fashion is not an order but a response. A new fashion is something we have precipitated, unconsciously. It is the fruit of fancies, tendencies, wishes, reactions to events that are our own, but that we do not recognize when we see them expressed in hats, dresses, 'accessories.' We take, more than we own, to new fashions because we have preconceived them. Fashion expresses us more truly (sometimes, to the eye of posterity, more cruelly) than we can, by individual effort, express ourselves. As individuals, we hardly exist at all; as unique beings we are very little effective. Any force that we exercise is a mass force. It is the general part of us—foggy and unrealized—that is powerful, that precipitates events, and with events, fashions. In a new season's hat or the new cut of a dress we have our unrealized tendencies served up cold. We may think we will or will not follow fashion, but fashion has been closely following us. We are first gently interpreted, then travestied. . . . Holding this view, Mr. Willett Cunnington has seen the history of the English nineteenth century as written in fashion jargon, depicted in fashion plates.

His work has been both meticulous and imaginative. He has

given each decade a reasoned interpretation. He groups fashions
under the Vertical (or Classic) and the Gothic. About the significance of the changing line there is, as he shows it, something fateful and sinister. The licentious gay days, in which women
plastered themselves into wet dresses, passed only too early, like
a pretty dawn. After that began the monstrous swell of the skirt,
and women were dog-toothed over like church porches. High
tiered hats like pagodas, and a fine triangular, rigged effect of the
figure went out with Victoria, whose youthful accession brought
in the girlish droop. This gave place to a gorgeous, embattled,
suggestive modesty. (Mr. Willett Cunnington shows how sexual
taste governs fashion.) The skirt reached its greatest circumference just past the mid-century. Woman then reached her height
as one kind of woman—select, immobile, fertile. Then the
Grecian Bend cleft the line of the back profile, and tilted the bust.
The tie-back (an exhibitionist fashion) followed. Æstheticism
made felt its sickly presences; emancipation began to blow rather
cold. Women, by bursting out of tailor-mades, grasping handlebars, looking pop-eyed under sailor hats, advised the world that
their interests were other than purely sexual. Harsh ridges
appeared along the hip-line.

Aniline dyes produced a revolution in colour, and the sewing
machine made mass-production possible. The taking-off of the
paper-tax made for the wide circulation of fashion journals. Thus
the mode began to lose its esoteric mystery, and to go more
quickly down in the world. Soon the proletariat dressed, instead
of clothing itself. The Empress Eugénie's shadow grew very
long, then diminished. Wars, reforms and literary revivals made
themselves felt in hats. . . . Mr. Willett Cunnington proposes to
cover, in a further volume, the few but important decades of *this*
century. It is to be hoped he will do so. His method and manner
are excellent. This present book of his is generously illustrated
with coloured plates of dresses in his own collection, clear linedrawings and contemporary fashion-plates. He appends a glossary of materials, also a glossary of technical terms. This is a
specialist's book with a hold on the common reader. It is large
(and handsome), but should be read as well as looked at: it
exercises a sort of charnel charm.

The New Statesman and Nation.

BEN JONSON *

1937

There has been, in regard to Ben Jonson, just the slightest campaign of intimidation; taste seemed to have formed round him a close borough. Intellect (in its most knotty, male and forbidding sense) has been stressed in the plays, by the critics in exaltation, at the expense of nearer, sensuous qualities. His lovers like so well to find him recondite that his plays have been set apart, for the common reader, as special, abstruse and cold, the cognoscenti's pleasure. The plays have not, by reputation, that enlarging, heroic extravagance to which, in Tourneur, Ford, Webster, the common fancy turns, these days, for release—they have been made to sound like the first note of fancy's knell. As compensation-literature they promise little. Other Elizabethans' god-like infantilism makes them rank high for comfort; their violent world corresponds to that of most private fantasy, which the emotions, with their *espagnolisme*, govern, in which the fanatic is supreme. To the child's-eye view, brought more and more to poetry, Jonson shows disconcertingly adult, at once recondite and *terre à terre*. His morality, an austere note, is emphasized.

Morality is a strong form of perception: as such, at its strongest, it blunts or bends on the muddle nowadays. It has come, in practical life, to stand for little more than an ineffective comment. Art, however, still needs to use it; it may be implicit but it has to be strong. By the plumb-straightness of lines and trueness of angles any work of the mind is, ultimately, judged: fancy may diverge from the upright, but there must be an upright. There must be, in literature, the mind's disengaged comment on enraged emotion—this *is* the work's morality. In this sense, morality is more than inherent in, it is the very nature of, the Ben Jonson plays' superb competence. What has been, possibly, overlooked

---

* 'Ben Jonson.' Vol. V: 'Volpone, or The Fox,' 'Epicœne, or The Silent Woman,' 'The Alchemist,' 'Catiline.' Edited by C. H. HERFORD and PERCY SIMPSON. (*Oxford University Press.*)
* 'Drama and Society in the Age of Ben Jonson.' By L. C. KNIGHTS. (*Chatto and Windus.*)

in the plays is, how much the moral-intellect has been given to feed on—or, in other terms, through what depths it drops a plumbline. The sensuous element is immense. This is Renaissance theatre: in those days one had a world at the fingertips, and the fingertips had not thickened. Immediacy of sensation comes through the language—concrete, and with an exact touch. The boom was at its height; wealth came in at every port. Magnetic new precious objects were on the market; each brought a world with it; luxury meant sublimation, not just dull expenditure. Learning, with its range of subtle experience, Latin elegance, outlandish mystery all struck the English shore. The world was not yet mapped; experience had no limits; a new mistress was an America. Intellect quickened love. The table soared into art, above the levels of subsistence or gluttony.

> . . . we will eate our mullets,
> Sous'd in high-countrey wines, sup phesants egges,
> And haue our cockles, boild in siluer shells,
> Our shrimps to swim againe, as when they liu'd
> In a rare butter, made of dolphins milke,
> Whose creame do's look like opalls.

Mammon's 'I will haue all my beds, blowne vp; not stuft: Downe is too hard—etc.,' Volpone's speech to Celia over the jewels, and a dozen more passages all show a lyrical freshness in greed itself, that first innocent flush of pleasure in the palace hotel —however much the context lowered the dream. Desire of objects, representations of pleasure offered their full bloom to Jonson's scalpel. He cut just deep enough to show the melancholy, the corruption beneath.

The force and speed of intellect going through these four plays —three major comedies and the tragedy *Catiline*—generates their first quality: dramatic excitement. The tension of the language, its oppositions, the play of concrete images make every page theatre. *Volpone* is, apart from everything else, social comedy at its cruellest height, and *The Alchemist*, with its crookish hilarity, its double crossings, its show-downs, is ready made, the first-rate scenario. *Catiline*, for all its menacing *longueurs*, comes back and back to the close-up: it never fatally soars off into a wordy void. Each play, spherical, revolves fast and steadily on the axis of its idea. Plot spins the passion.

These four plays have one subject: the obsessed person, the person of one idea. From the vantage point that obsession gives, he perceives in others the greeds, delusions and vanities that are exploitable, that are to serve his ends. The megalomaniac is curiously empowered. One dominating and single view or purpose gives each of these plays unity. They are areas mapped in the specialist's own terms. Morose, in *The Silent Woman*, is an exception: his desire is negative, so he is a negative figure, outwitted before he enters—the comedy, embroidering his defeat, is accordingly more complex, less centralized than the others. But Volpone, Subtle, Catiline, are positive and effective; they work with tools they despise—tools, sub-passions, whose very shoddiness makes them splinter and cut the user's hand. The divagations of greed—avarice, lust, snobbishness—are pressed flat, like horrid ferns, between every page of the plays. Was Jonson really anti-acquisitive, or was he magnetized to the instinct by what it offered his art?

Here are fine, fertile, extraverted crooks, not wasting a moment, not eating themselves like Bosola. They have no metaphysical worries; even ghosts are imperious: 'Do'st thou not know me, Rome?' Hilarious complicity, the confederate spirit, never got better play. There is the grand alliance of Dol and Face:

> DOL: Yes, say lord *Generall,* how fares our campe?
> FACE: As, with the few, that had entrench'd themselues
> Safe, by their discipline against a world, Dol:
> And laugh'd, within those trenches, and grew fat
> With thinking on the booties, Dol, brought in
> Daily, by their small parties. This dear houre,
> A doughtie *Don* is taken, with my Dol;
> And thou maist make his ransome, what thou wilt,
> My *Dousabell:* He shall be brought here, fetter'd
> With thy faire lookes, before he sees thee; and throwne
> In a downe-bed, as darke as any dungeon;
> Where thou shalt keepe him waking, with thy drum;
> Thy drum, my Dol; thy drum.

There are stampedes, but no demoralization; the master crook deserves well, like a good whip.

Mr. Knights' study, which should be read, relates the age that made food for these plays to our own age in terms of social and economic ideas. He discusses the sixteenth-century boom, with the unrest and flood of greed it let in, the break up of the simpler order, the thrust up of the *rentier* class, upheaving the values that kept it down, the complexity, vitality and uneasiness the up-thrust gave society, the distress below, the abuse of nobility. He dates back the connection between hard money and subtle sense, and shows how gold from America fostered the humanities. He shows the seedling, then, of the modern evil, now grown to its height. His work fills in the plays' background, gives further point to illusions, lights up the texture.

For the Herford and Simpson editorship of this Volume V of Ben Jonson, the accessibility and pertinence of the notes, the excellence of the type, we have once more to be grateful.

The New Statesman and Nation.

E. M. FORSTER*

1936   I

In an age when novelists hum like factories, keeping up to date with themselves, Mr. E. M. Forster's output has been, in bulk, small. The novels which, with their 'new standard of truth,' create an absolute world are five, only, in number. It is over thirty years now since the first; *Where Angels Fear to Tread* was short, and contained in embryo all the other books. The authority with which the novels are written, the power they have to expand inside the mind account, perhaps, for the patience with which his silences are received—he has never been mistrusted and has never declined. An artist does not rank somewhere between entertainer and tradesman for nothing; he is expected to ring up the curtain again promptly, punctually to deliver the goods. Silence is undue, and makes the public suspicious. But a quality in all Mr. Forster's work makes peremptoriness of this kind impossible. The books are so clearly more than efforts of his intelligence; when they do come they have so clearly imposed themselves that it is impossible to demand them when they do not come.

Actually, he has not been so silent. Two collections of stories,

* 'Abinger Harvest.' By E. M. FORSTER. (*Arnold.*)
* 'The Writings of E. M. Forster.' By ROSE MACAULAY. (*Hogarth Press.*)

Pharos and Pharillon, Anonymity, Aspects of the Novel, the Lowes
Dickinson biography have been landmarks down the last twenty
years. And the eighty or so 'articles, essays, reviews, poems, etc.'
reprinted in *Abinger Harvest* have been appearing since 1904. If
they were nothing more—and they are much more—they would
be notes on his so-called silences: the absorption and rapture of
travel, the exploration of books. That he has been prevailed upon
to assemble and republish them is a matter for gratitude.

Too often, collections are to be dreaded. They are the severest
test a writer can face. Tricks of mind, prejudices, an overworking
of privilege, an iota too much of accomplishment in the writing
stick out in the short essay, the *tour de force*: cumulatively the
effect may be desolating, show up unsuspected weakness in other
work. Too many collections are scrapheaps from well-known
shops—shavings, filings no doubt of excellent wood or metal, but
the dismal topicality of decades ago sits on them like dust, or a
journalistic smartness tarnishes them. Too few writers are right
in throwing nothing away. Mr. Forster is one great exception:
Abinger Harvest comes with harvest richness and timeliness.

The essays have been assembled in four groups—The Present,
Books, The Past, The East—and the scenario, which is beautiful,
of the Abinger Pageant stands alone at the end. The order is vital
and should, I feel, be followed—though it is tempting to keep
darting backwards and forwards, attracted by titles or opening
paragraphs. The collector's desire to be read in this order is more
than a whim; it gives the book a form, unity and intention rare in
its kind. The dates, startlingly various, of the essays play no part
in their arrangement, and should not: there has never been any
question of Mr. Forster's *development*; there never seems to have
been any early work. The age factor with him must have stayed
outside and arbitrary; his maturity is innate. That so many of the
essays should be so short, too short, seems less a fault in them than
in circumstance. (Many appeared in weeklies.) This tantalizing
briefness, whatever its first object, is the one trying element in the
book—the Greek beauty-box, the physician Cardan, the Doll
Souse, the Emperor Babur, the rational Indian wedding, Cnidus in
the rain, the Jodhpur dragon, the Scallies pass for moments into
the light and disappear too soon. But, for all one's own regrets and
disruptions, the book has its own, an extraordinary continuous-
ness. Perhaps because Mr. Forster has changed so little, perhaps

because his mind does not flick on and off—it must impregnate not only his writing but all his conscious moments; its abeyances, even, must have their colour. What is remarkable, in these essays as in the novels, is his power of having access to the whole of himself, to what he has called 'the lower personality': the obscure, the involuntary, the general that is, in us all, the stuff of dreams and art, the source of perception, the arbiter of memory. Few intellects so active are less isolated from the whole of the being. Mr. Forster does not make a doctrine of spontaneity; 'intuition,' he even says, 'makes dancing dervishes of us.' He must have come to terms with his intuition: happen to him what may, he remains, or appears to remain, at once the most active and the governing factor in his own experience. If the perfectly adjusted person does not suffer, Mr. Forster is not the perfectly adjusted person: the perfectly adjusted writer I feel he is. With him intellect not so much controls susceptibility as balances it: many of us have not the wits to feel. Given this highly sensitive equanimity, the effect of this quick succession of essays is, his not so much pitching upon a series of subjects as momentarily enclosing and then releasing them, added to.

To criticism he brings the make-up of the artist. He perceives in another man's work what he himself knows—which accords with his theory of the deep down, giant part of us being general. In his own novels the sense of conscious life's being built up over a somehow august vault of horror, that rings under the foot, that exhales coldly through cracks, is constantly palpable. Of *The Waste Land* he says: 'the horror is so intense that the poet has an inhibition and cannot state it openly.' And, later in the same essay: 'In respect of the horror that they find in life men may be divided into three classes.' . . . He finds the romantic in Ibsen, in Proust the adventurer. If he is hard on a writer it is in the manner of one accustomed to being hard on himself; he has none of the critic's godlike non-participation. He detects the finest fatal crack in the bowl. He sees Conrad's 'central obscurity.' 'The secret casket of his genius contains a vapour rather than a jewel.' Love for Jane Austen steels him against Miss Austen who forgot the nobility of Anne, the wise wit of Elizabeth, when she wrote letters. In some of the critical essays his own image more nearly appears than elsewhere; they are the least, in his own sense, anonymous of his work.

The prose throughout *Abinger Harvest* is the prose of the novels; not a word he uses ever obstructs the mind—prose which makes objects appear brighter than themselves, as in very clear morning light, instead of darkening behind a mesh of words. Like Flaubert's, though so unlike, here is a style made perfect by being subject to purpose, and beautiful with vitality. Its rhythm is so inherent in its content that one cannot detect it without analysis. The least frigid of writing, it is the most impersonal; he is enemy to all those lovable little tricks. 'Literature,' he says elsewhere, 'tries to be unsigned,' and as far as manner goes he approaches anonymity. But in prose the point of view is inevitable; every sentence must bear, however lightly, the stamp of the mind, its governing quality. Behind his irony, his impersonality, his gentleness, Mr. Forster is passionately civilized. The novels are manifestos, these essays ring with a note that is startling because it is rare. Passion will out, however much, however wisely irony may temper it. Beliefs that root in the nature cannot be silenced: his give him an unmistakable touch on a page.

The Spectator.

1938   II

'Let us suppose that of the hundred thousand people living in this town . . . there are only three of your sort. It goes without saying that you cannot conquer the mass of darkness round you; little by little, as you go on living, you will be lost in the crowd. You will have to give in to it. Life will get the better of you, but still you will not disappear without a trace. After you there may appear perhaps six like you, then twelve and so on until you form a majority. In two or three hundred years life will be unimaginably beautiful, marvellous. Man needs such a life . . .' exclaims Vershinin, in *The Three Sisters*, to Masha, who takes off her hat and decides to stay for lunch. This is optimism, liberal optimism, with a delay-action of several hundred years. *The Three Sisters* was written when, though they did not know it, the tide of civilization was full in: since then, the tide has turned and is steadily going out. Chehov did not live to see the present complete set-back. Mr. E. M. Forster's place, not in time but in feeling, is still at that recent high-water mark. He is the civilized man who had got to watch a decline. He has Chehov's perception of 'the mass of darkness,' of its encroaching power; he is aware of darkness chiefly as opposition, opposition to the possible light. This fixed belief in light, light somewhere, gives him a fixed position: he belongs to an order rather than to a time.

Time has not been a great factor in Mr. Forster's development. Few artists attain to his stature without some dynamic change in their point of view. Their susceptibility not widening with their expressive power, they must reject as much as they take in. Trial and error in the man himself lasts longer than trial and error in the artist, who may have come to early perfection while the man himself is still unresolved. With some artists the attempt at self-discovery is, itself, the art. But Mr. Forster, though his first novels were published when he was in the twenties, seems to have been adult when he began to write. Then he took up without hesitation, in fact with evident certainty, the position with regard to life that he has occupied since. Nothing has budged him from it. It took no term of years to show what would be inevitable. He may have had the power to anticipate experience; for though experience must have deepened, it has not altered him. At all events, he went with that first book direct to his personal maturity —and in an artist that is more than a private matter. The thirty-three years since *Where Angels Fear to Tread* have given him further data, but have not changed his conclusions. In those years his scope and power have widened naturally: the novels describe enlarging circles round a fixed, and essential, centre point. His 'development' has been a matter of equipping himself more fully, and with wider and wider reference, to express what he has from the first felt. His susceptibility, in those two early novels so near together in time, was a young susceptibility, in its depth and pain-fulness—in that sense, it is a young susceptibility still. His visual detachment from the scenes in his mind was from the first, and is, perfect: his emotional detachment is incomplete.

Intellect gives the five novels their structure, and edits feeling—the novels' source is emotion, and their matter is purely emotional. The fine mind is needed to translate his intuitions, whose direct-ness makes them foreign and unfamiliar on the pages of novels. For some rather muddled reason he has been called a high-brow by people who find the term suspicious: in fact, he is not abstruse; he does not write from an altitude; his novels are as concrete as Jane Austen's. What is intimidating? Possibly the absence of *idées reçues*—especially *idées reçues* on the subject of sex—possibly the unambiguousness, possibly the fact that, though he deals in feeling, like the popular novelists, and with the relations between people, the feeling is stamped with a particular quality, the relations are disabusedly examined. What gives his feeling, or his characters' feelings, that particular quality? A sort of frightening control: the control of someone who says nothing when he has just witnessed an accident, who not only does not give way but smiles and talks about something else. The novels, even the almost unbearable *Longest Journey*, do all smile, and their smile is genuine. Taken down from the shelf and opened at random, few novels could be more inviting than any of these five—the dialogue, the set-out, the quick-moving, equable passages, the delightful *contretemps*, the absence of a single clot or turgidity at once invite one to diversion and pleasure. Here is sheer *story*: one cannot fail to read on. All the same, through all this runs vehemence, like the power-charged wire through the pretty coloured cord of the flex. . . . The politeness (in the great sense) of Mr. Forster's writing alienates from him violently minded people, who feel he does not make enough fuss.

In fact, Mr. Forster's voice is pitched on that one note that goes on being heard under an uproar. He is not rhetorical; he is not a 'prophetic' writer (in his own sense in *Aspects of the Novel*). His position has always been, austerely, a personal position: there is therefore no question of his becoming isolated. Though still read by a minority, he was not intended to be a minority writer: the majority for him does not yet exist. He has been mistaken for an over-moderate man. He is not a moderate man; he is one kind of fanatic—the fanatic inside his own control. He is a leading menace to the forts of folly—his art does not merely tilt at things, it undermines them surely. He uses an irony which is seldom gentle, and is in the long run deadly to what it attacks—for instance, the Wilcoxes. His ruthlessness of expression is checked only by his austere style. No, no one could call him moderate: a fairer charge against him is the charge of unfairness—brought up by his treatment of half his cast in *A Passage to India*. This novel, because of its popular-controversial subject, drew the attention of a public for whom the earlier novels remained sealed—in fact, of a public whose perplexity or inattention had let them go out of print. *A Passage to India* started with one advantage: it was clear

to everyone what it was about. No doubt the Anglo-Indians did
not get a perfectly fair deal—no more, for the matter of that, did
the Wilcoxes, Agnes, Cecil Vyse or Mrs. and Miss Herriton. In
all Mr. Forster's novels disinterested unfairness is, in fact, generic.
The observation seems to be: what of it? A novelist is not an
umpire. Mr. Forster does not exist to compile documents; he is
an artist, with the right to be arbitrary. In the moral war he depicts
there is not private justice; individual fates count for nothing.

His bad, his recalcitrant characters are the Enemy. For the
most part they are flat characters (again, in his own sense), they
do not expand or suffer; they seem to have no problems; they are
opaque. Though they do not generate evil they do, like blocked
gutters, receive, store and exhale it. These bad ones are simplified
characters, used dramatically. The good characters are anti-
heroic. They travel steadily, always painfully towards the light;
they expose themselves; they suffer humiliations. At their greatest
—Margaret Schlegel, Fielding—they are very positive. Then
there is the neutral character, who is the battle-ground—Philip
Herriton in *Where Angels Fear to Tread*, Rickie in *The Longest
Journey*, Lucy in *A Room with a View*, Mr. Wilcox in *Howard's End*,
Adela in *A Passage to India*. A fourth group of people are the
direct, the non-moral, the naturalistic—Gino, Stephen Wonham,
George Emerson, Helen Schlegel, Aziz. These people behave
intuitively; they suffer (with the exception of Stephen) but do not
suffer morally. Conducting nature to the more complex characters,
they have the importance of Italy, Wiltshire, the Indian scene.

The world of the novels opens a vast light landscape, in which
every feature is dramatic, in which every object is not only
sentient, living, but sends a current direct to the human nerves.
This is a world of beauty which is intimidating. Its creatures, Mr.
Forster's characters, dread, and rightly dread, the forces behind
each other: chasms may open for them—and often do. But it is
untrue to say these characters are intimidated by life: they are pug-
nacious; they stand up to what is dreadful in a queer mood, at
once exalted and tough. They oppose the mass of darkness.
Are these Forster people on the retreat now, or are they the fore-
runners of Vershinin's triumphant majority?

Mr. Forster is, first of all, our great novelist: all his other work
is stamped with his fine mind, but is subsidiary to those five books.
It was, however, high time that his work should be related into

a body and its importance considered as a *whole*. A study of him was wanted, and had to be undertaken by someone whose range was wide, who could appreciate his range. Miss Rose Macaulay's study, *The Writings of E. M. Forster*, has been looked forward to, and now fulfils its promise. This is an outstanding piece of critical work. To begin with, Miss Macaulay has succeeded in writing both for those already familiar with Mr. Forster's writings and for those who still hardly know them at all. For the first, what she says will have the fascinating aspect of a discussion; to the second it will be at once invitation and guide. The structure of her book—which might be a difficult problem—is excellent: here is an intellectual portrait, with its background, and a comprehensive study of all Mr. Forster's work, with a simultaneous running analysis. His writings are considered from two points of view—as pure art and as the exposition of his feeling for life.

The analysis of the novels is brilliantly done: it cannot have been easy, in a few pages, to give the outline, the character, and above all the import of each. Besides this, there is an examination of the critical writings, the essays, the work on the novel, the prefaces, the biography and the guide book. Perhaps not enough is said about the short stories, whose technical interest is immense. In some of her most valuable chapters Miss Macaulay suggests the passing of time in those spaces between the too rare appearances of the books. Mr. Forster's intervals of silence have been a perplexity, as well as a deprivation. Silences, in a man from whom we have exorbitant expectations, take on a sort of positive character. Miss Macaulay has sketched something into the silences, described travel, touched in preoccupations. The greatest achievement of her book is that she has strung the works—from the longest novel down to the shortest essay—on what seems to be a line of personal continuity, so that the appearance of each, in its time, appears inevitable. Sympathy, admiration and unobtrusive perception have made her achievement possible. Her own style, pointed and lucid, and covering ground in a few and well-chosen words, her avoidance of constricting generalizations, and the smiling detachment with which criticisms are levelled, not only give *The Writings of E. M. Forster* a distinction worthy of its subject, but make it an important addition to the body of Miss Macaulay's work.

The New Statesman and Nation.

MANCHESTER*

1937

In a series of city biographies, Lady Longford's *Dublin* has been followed by Mrs. Ryan's *Manchester*. The succession seems natural: Dublin's great phase ended about the time that Manchester's was beginning. Dublin's past is panoramic and violent, Manchester's short, complex and, conventionally, prosaic—she was the coming era grubbily crystallized. Her beginning was, it is true, fairly grandiose: she was Brave New World once; pride of the old age of a heroic century. In the last decades of the seventeen-hundreds, society marvelled at the Duke of Bridgewater's hanging canal; visitors poured in to see the functional city.

No wonder . . . that the feelings of writers about Manchester burst the bonds of prose and exploded into rhymed epigrams and dream-drawings—fleets of ships sailing in a stiff breeze along aerial canals, or allegorical frontispieces like the one which stands at the beginning of Dr. Aikin's Description of the country from thirty to forty miles round Manchester, and which the author himself has described for us. 'The group of females in the frontispiece represents Agriculture, Industry, Plenty of Commerce, allegorical personages peculiarly connected with the district which forms the subject of this work. The ship in the background alludes to the port of Liverpool. The Cupids sporting above express the joy and satisfaction resulting from such an association.'

But there was less time for polite fancy when Manchester made her grim growth, darkened with smoke, and ringed herself with satellite towns. Her vast built-over areas, their mounting population, faced her with problems with which, for a long time, she had no means to deal. Prosperity cast a shadow. Her local government system remained parochial: the abominable housing, undrained squalor, disease, poverty, ignorance known to prevail in this city of soaring fortunes got her a bad name. The South found her ruthless and self-regarding, progressive in her own terms only: one learned to titter at her provincialities. The city had to have enemies; she had come to stand for a new ethic, a new pressure, a new political force. Manchester men, from their villas

---

* 'Manchester.' By RACHEL RYAN. (*Methuen.*)

round the black city, posted to business as men ride to hounds: a stern excitement commanded them. Nonconformists, Liberals and Free Traders—these vigorous men, England's Yankees, undermined instead of attacking landed society; power came more and more into their hands. They could not have been such a force had their standards been purely material; the world saw the rude flank of a strong natural integrity. They had neither time nor taste for the amenities—all the same, when they wanted to they could 'do' art: in 1857 Manchester threw open a superlative Exhibition of Art Treasures, from all over the place. Visitors, headed by the Prince Consort, once more made in crowds for Manchester during a brilliant summer, and the general view of her had to be modified. This signalized the beginning of the city's cultural life: museums, galleries, libraries came into being (she had always had music), then culture pointed the way to the civic decencies. Attacks on slum housing were delivered, and slowly but far-reachingly took effect. The Corporation enlarged its aims with its powers. Architecture did not do well, but times were not good for that anywhere. Impressiveness (Gothic or otherwise) was the object; money became stone and smoke settled on that.

What Manchester lacks in style she makes up in character; her short, dense past is an active part of her present; there must be something about her you could cut with a knife. She gives off something that the newcomer savours eagerly and consciously (if not always with relish) and that seeps in under the consciousness of the busy inhabitant. To the number of books on Manchester already to hand, Mrs. Ryan has added her book not only on but about it, about its particular quality, or Manchesterness. She resumes the past of the city in an exceedingly clear and able preface. But her book is outstanding, because it does for a city what criticism should do for a work of art: it relates it to other experience, and also adds something to it. Soberly documented at the outset, she has made an experiment, and I think an advance, in the technique of writing about places. Daughter of C. E. Montague, granddaughter of C. P. Scott, her childhood was spent in Manchester: she has used a child's impressions to re-create the city. A child's feeling for the imposing or the mysterious, its *flair* for the curious, its dread of the sinister, its reaction to volume in form or sound are spontaneous, unliterary and true. Nothing was banal then, and one's aspirations and snobberies were at least one's own.

Mrs. Ryan came of a family with a strong family character, nucleus of a society of its own, breathing what she soon found was
'a highly conditioned air and by no means the native Manchester
atmosphere.' Outside lay Manchester, rich with that atmosphere.
Her own friendships and visits had thus the delightful nature of
explorations: the little girl learned a candid perspicacity.

Her portraiture is, accordingly, excellent, and there are several
fascinating interiors—days spent in friends' homes. The great
figure of C. P. Scott is alive in some of her pages, and there is a
child's-eye, stereoscopic view of The Firs. Eccentrics, foreigners,
tradespeople keep that importance that is theirs in their own right
and that they have for the young. The social texture seems very
truly given. There is a Hallé concert, a glimpse of Blackpool and
of an industrial hill town. Manchester with its dark ring on ring
of growth materializes on a tram-ride into Town from the quiet
suburb. 'Town' comes across well, with its height, gloom, clang
and pressure, and Mrs. Ryan gives each quarter its character. Her
writing throughout is quiet, accomplished, vivid; a detached affection for her subject informs it, and sympathetic fancy has been
ably balanced with staid fact.

The New Statesman and Nation.

GRACE*

1938

Selection is always present in any act of the memory; it cannot but
be continuously present in the attempt to re-create one's own life.
One cannot surprise one's past: the very quickest look back makes
everything fall into order—if only into a momentary order, the
order of a mood. The long look back compels one's years into
form. This may be because before any deliberate retrospection
starts one has already rejected, with an unconscious violence,
what is untoward, what might not fit in the pattern. For that
pattern, whatever may be its nature, is an intimate part of one's
self-esteem, and one's idea of survival is closely bound up in it.
Having always in view the pattern one must not lose, one's sense

* 'Unforgotten Years.' By LOGAN PEARSALL SMITH. (*Constable.*)

K

of relevance, in reviewing one's own life, becomes as strict, as immovable as a law of art. Ultimately, one's own emotional taste must be the censor of memory. Thus the memoir, the reminiscence takes its place half-way æsthetics and pathology.

When a writer writes his own life the wish to give form is doubled; the wish is conscious as well as necessitous. His past is to serve his book; it is no more than so much matter. He is not strange to himself; he has lived in his own presence; he can write of himself with a cold familiarity. He looks back at a life lived entirely consciously; there is no question, here, of harvesting naïve and unknowing years. Before he could hold a pen, perhaps, he has been Trigorin, secreting prose round moments even while they were living. To an extent, he has made his experience. He has noted life from an angle; what he has not noted does not, for him, exist. His very pains and pleasures have been largely *selected*, even at times when they seemed most deeply felt. Scenes had a memory-value even while they were lived. Disciplined, automatic, his memory works to plan. The writer's memory is like a tidy cupboard: he knows exactly what he will find inside. What he cannot assimilate, he has already rejected. He has thrown out all bulky untoward objects, objects on which the cupboard might not shut.

Mr. Logan Pearsall Smith wrote his reminiscences during a cruise on Mrs. Wharton's yacht. On this cruise, nothing untoward happened, except a misunderstanding with the skipper about a boat, and a rather vigorous argument about peonies. He has titled those reminiscences with what seems, at the first glance, a happy banality. *Unforgotten Years* could be a sort of generic title for memoirs; it epitomizes the names of a hundred volumes, very often of social interest only, that sit in libraries on the memoir shelves. At the first glance, it seems odd that such a title should not already have been hit on—by some lady of fashion at her wobbly, frail *escritoire*. It could be no more than nostalgic, ambiguous, mellow, safe. But that this choice should have been Mr. Pearsall Smith's gives the title a sinister exactitude. There is no ambiguity here. He knows that years' survival is more than a touching accident. Years do not stand in the memory by sheer virtue of having been once lived. Years are turned away or recalled exactly as one wishes. Those years one accepts are the unforgotten years.

An intensive censorship of experience underlies Mr. Pearsall

Smith's perfected prose. No dust has collected on the years, the moments that were once so analytically lived; they are in perfect condition, ready to be assembled into what is, for a memoir, a faultless form. His style shows his distinguished wilful precision; it has no rough matter to cope with, for nothing that he records as having happened has not already been assimilated by him. From seven (when he attained the state of sanctification) he undeviatingly chose his experience. He was the child of a Philadelphian Quaker houshold dominated by a magnificent, zealous faith. In such a household, life was a crucible. As a very small child, Mr. Pearsall Smith was agonizedly conscious of the untoward. There was much that he did not like; he was 'a gorilla for screaming.' When he was four, the reconciliation, at first in itself painful, began. Two little girls prayed aloud for him in his presence, prayed that he might be given a new heart. Between four and seven his struggles intensified.

In vain were his efforts to keep good by the force of his own will alone; and it was only after three years of spiritual struggle . . . that he renounced these Pelagian attempts to conquer Sin and Satan by his own carnal struggles, and realised that only by Grace, and unmerited Grace alone, and by no 'deadly doing' could he attain the conquest that he sought.

By seven, he had won through.

I may do, I have undoubtedly done, things that were foolish, tactless and dishonest, and what the world would consider wrong, but since I attained the state of Sanctification at the age of seven I have never felt the slightest twinge of conscience, never experienced for a moment the sense of sin.

These passages from the early life are important because they explain, I think, Mr. Pearsall Smith's persisting attitude to life— an attitude, above all, of immunity. His taste, his nature, his gifts, his susceptibilities seem to have been able to ripen and to perfect themselves inside a small, separate and unthreatened world. There can have been no more upheavals; his piety has veered quietly from religion to art. Those delicious sensations that surrounded religious experience surround æsthetic experience. He belongs to the generation of the Chosen—and how far the Chosen are from us now—their leisure, their grace, their subtleties and, above all, their immunity. They enjoyed Grace—Grace tempered with irony.

And what a prose Grace produced! Emerson was the earliest influence, then came Pater, then the nobler aspects of Flaubert. (Were the passages about the sweating and the hysterics also copied into Mr. Pearsall Smith's commonplace book?) And there was always Sir Thomas Browne. Over all this book about inner experience there extends a levelling irony. He writes—this perfected prose, adamant, unechoing, unevocative, prose like a fortification, prose without any belfry to hold a bat. In this prose are embedded once-living creatures and moments. As though overtaken by lava, forever immobilized, scenes, gestures, hopes, fears, illusions, traditions, fanaticisms are here to be marvelled at. Philadelphia, the Quaker traditions, Evangelical English house parties, Harvard, Balliol, Paris, the house in Sussex with its terrace and talks . . . Walt Whitman and Mrs. Wharton. . . .

Mr. Pearsall Smith writes best—that is to say, most feelingly—in the early chapters, in which his lovely, dignified and unaccountable mother appears, and in the last chapter but one, about manuscript-hunting—a chapter the sportsman dominates. The rest of *Unforgotten Years* reads like an ordered dream, a dream explored to its limits, with no cold shadow of to-morrow morning ahead.

The New Statesman and Nation.

A STRAIGHT NOVEL*

1937

Mr. Somerset Maugham still writes the classic, or straight, novel: there is nothing tricky about his construction; he does not make telling cuts, shoot from unlikely angles or vary his distance from the object in view. *Theatre* is straight narrative, not photography: he has an almost hypnotic command of narrative style; not a sen-

* 'Theatre.' By W. SOMERSET MAUGHAM. (*Heinemann.*)

tence stops the mind and each leads on to another in a rapid overlap. This is a style that is neutral, functional, and fully efficient,
the servant not the mistress of the writer's invention, a method
perfected (within its own limits) not a preoccupation. Not a
phrase is there for its own sake; transparency to meaning is the
object, not colour; not a phrase obtrudes romantic complexity.
For its activity, Mr. Maugham's style is stripped: there is no
atmosphere, no American cuteness, no attempted poetry: it is
professional writing, without a touch of amateur privilege—and
this is pretty rare now. Rare also—a good deal too rare—is a
novel not setting up to be anything but a novel, not made the
parade-ground of indignation or fantasy. It might not be well to
make Mr. Maugham a model, but he should set a precept: he
might correct our tendencies to maunder, to exhibit or to
denounce. With first-rate ability, but without high-class fuss, he
drops a plumb-line into the subject. Here is a personality so
positive, so pickled in experience it attracted, that it can use style
impersonally. The professional has not time for stunts.

Theatre is a story told from one point of view—that of the
actress heroine, Julia Lambert. This centralizing of the story in
one person, a person at the same time visible to the reader, makes
for emotional unity and brings the other characters into scale so
satisfactorily that one wonders why the method has, lately, lapsed.
It is possible that only the accomplished writer can hope to
sustain what might be monotony. Julia's values—assessed by the
author with satirical coldness or, still more coldly, made to assess
themselves—alone give the action significance, and so make the
plot. Her blunders and limitations are used (like *Emma's*) to let
counterplot appear: her shrewdness is at fault when emotion
twists it, or vanity. That a good deal is going on that she does
not, cannot or will not see, is obvious: the reader, at an impassive
glance from the author, picks up inferences, signals she overlooks.
Hence the excitement of this exciting book: it is like a film in
which someone will not see what is coming. But the element of
surprise is always present: you were not so much in on the joke
as you had thought.

This is comedy on a rather painful plane, with a few bad
moments, some grand ones, and embarrassments that bring the
heart to the mouth. Julia Lambert, in private life Mrs. Michael
Gosselyn, portrayed with good-tempered malice, some sympathy

and an occasional tightening of Mr. Maugham's cruelty, is a force-
ful, engaging, never romantic figure. Her interior monologue,
some of her conversation, is energetic and bawdy; she has a touch
of the trouper; her behaviour in love or society is controlled,
languid, artful in the exact sense—it may be said to be dictated, as
a religious person's behaviour is dictated. Success and massage
have preserved her youth for her up to forty-six: her heart, when
she meets Tom—a dim young man from an office brought to
lunch by her husband—is both young and free. She brings her
life to her acting, on one occasion, with what looked like being
fatal results for a play, but she can always borrow her acting for
her life, save her face, bluff in impossible situations or retrieve
some dangerous spontaneity. In her naivety, her ruthlessness,
her coarseness, her impatience with her own suffering, the major
artist appears: she hates (though abides by) dieting, and likes love.
Her duplicity is natural and automatic—she is two people: seldom
are both present. It is possible that the profession of acting may
sublimate in the female the falsity, insatiable monomania and anti-
human vanity that Mr. Maugham so detests: at all events, Julia is
one of his most agreeable heroines.

Theatre is not a documentary novel of back-stage life, an analysis
of its glamour or of its hopes and fears. This is theatre life at its
suavest, most settled and least Bohemian—for which I, for one,
am thankful. The cast of the novel are already successful people,
full of shrewdness and energy, without waste emotion, subject in
one case only to the aberrations of love. Massage and the siesta,
dressing-room comforts, cutlets and creamed spinach, costly respectable pleasures, photographers and reposing riverside week-
ends are the routine. Julia (except once in her lover's arms) seldom
thinks of the theatre: she *is* the theatre. Outside that intense
existence, never quite interrupted, life is a mesh of detail through
which her placid husband, her disconcerting son, her dresser, her
rich woman friend, her platonic lover appear. Only Tom, or her
passion for him, cuts near the quick of her life and begins to
impinge on art.

Julia's first and last stage appearances inside the bounds of the
novel, before and after the love-affair, have the same calm:

Having addressed the envelope she threw the card in the wastepaper
basket and was ready to slip into her first-act dress. The call-boy came
round knocking at the dressing-room doors.

'Beginners, please.'

Those words, though heaven only knew how often she had heard them, still gave her a thrill. They braced her like a tonic. Life acquired significance. She was about to step from the world of make-believe into the world of reality.

The mature woman's infatuation for a young lover, the distinguished person's obsession with a nonentity, sounds a stale enough subject: here it takes new irony and—by Julia's control of the situation from her disadvantageous position—a curious bold grace. Julia's eagerness for love and royal high-handedness expose her to a string of humiliations from the recalcitrant, muddled and common Tom, avid for luxury but suspicious of being bought up. He hurts her a little deliberately, but—as with most objects of misguided affection—his main power to hurt is in his stupidity. Every degree of that torture inflicted by stupid beloveds on highly organized lovers is noted by Mr. Maugham. Julia is not on the Proust scale, but her suffering, her ironic sense of the falseness of the position, is in the Swann and Charlus tradition. By making Julia something more than a woman, giving her the artist's bisexuality, Mr. Maugham has been able to generalize her love. Julia is so far masculine in that love with her has an æsthetic element: she fell out of love with her husband when his beauty was over; Tom's extreme youth, with its particular attributes, is a strong factor in her feeling for him. Her lack of bunk about this, her unreflecting pleasure at the affair's outset, and her personal greatness—as much greatness at least as Mr. Maugham will allow her—make her affair with Tom, for all its humiliations, grandiose and unsordid. Her doubleness, the Phœnix vitality of the actress side of her nature make it impossible for her to be wholly trapped: at the same time, these contribute to Tom's uneasiness. The situation between them, its phases and variations, is magnificently realized—and generalized.

The sum of *Theatre* is: an astringent tragi-comedy, with twin subjects, love and art. Mr. Maugham anatomizes emotion without emotion; he handles without pity a world where he finds no pity. His disabused clearness and hardness do, it is true, diminish any subject a little. If great art has to have an inherent kindness, his is not great art. But what a writer he is!

The New Statesman and Nation.

THE SHADOW ACROSS THE PAGE*

1937

'*What I detest about nearly all essays and novels is that they take their tone from those connecting-links, bridge-passages or what you like, which form nine-tenths of the work and are not individual to the author. The only literary sin of any importance is to dilute one's originality. And that dilution, in some graceful and accepted form, is the aim of nine hundred writers out of a thousand. These are the anti-artists. . . .*' Mr. Stonier himself is not guilty of that dilution: his *Shadow Across the Page* has no forced or false continuity. His paragraphs, parted by spaces and hard stars, read like extracts: they are in fact extracts from a progressive silence. Like islands that are the high points of a submarine range, they have a submerged connection with one another. These are pure impressions (in Proust's sense), impressions not utilized, given whole for their own sake. Impressions used, placed or given slavish justification in what we have to pass as art are very often deformed. Mr. Stonier keeps his outside the tyranny of relevance—or, at least, of false relevance. 'Prose literature,' he says, 'should be immediate, like poetry or music, and not always "about" something.' True relevance, the entirety of the nature, lies so deep down that it is difficult, though perhaps not impossible, to expose it: every artist adds year by year to a major unwritten work—like Flaubert's book about nothing that should stay itself on itself by the inner force of its style. Mr. Stonier chooses to leave his written paragraphs unbridged—it is hard to know if he has begged a question or posed one. The pen stops where fusion of feeling and thought stops. Such moments of fusion being intermittent, how far should prose attempt the unnatural bridge?

Superficially, *The Shadow Across the Page* is a note-book, or a sketch-book. Scraps of talk, silhouettes human or animal, apprehensions of seasons changing, the lucidities of insomnia, perspectives of dreams (like streets going off at an angle), phrases from that inner dialogue of the lover and self-distorted mirror-views of the author fill it. There are notes on an æsthetic, on 'the

* 'The Shadow Across the Page.' By G. W. Stonier. (*The Cresset Press.*)

griefs of timidity,' on the phases of accidie. Sensations here enjoy, or suffer, democracy: none are on promotion. 'Be thankful,' says Mr. Stonier, 'for one writer who does not dwell among the immensities.' In fact, he has a cult for the monstrous behind the trivial; he, too, lines up *idées reçues*—note by note he assembles those toppling figures, Mr. and Mrs. Samson and Miss Wilkins. Mr. Samson's gate blows down and then dogs foul his lawn; Mr. Samson is accosted, is always furious on the telephone, has the insincerity of all good-natured men, snips his hedge in the moonlight, sheds his coat in summer, peers from behind the blind, will not have swedes in the house, believes the churches have failed, crushes moths as he talks, has honeymooned in Naples— but Mrs. Samson was never really keen on it. Mrs. Samson, through whom brandy passes quickly, would not appeal to Miss Wilkins's God. Miss Wilkins undresses in the dark; she always awaits a letter. . . . These people magnetize one's sense of the terrible.

Mr. Stonier, 'poet by instinct, satirist by circumstance,' is also journalist of the sensations. He reports crises, menace and pressure in that world we each inhabit alone; also, impartially, its unstable markets, intermissions and silly seasons, He has a flair for 'story' on the plane of the nerves. There is rumour, an intimation in the stir of a tree, the first breath of a season, the stopped escalator, the silhouette at the bar, the vague, emphatic, gesture sketched in the street. *The Shadow Across the Page* is pasted with headlines, from an unprinted newspaper, which score the imagination. His notation is exact: there is panic in the half-thought. 'In some moods we see the sunlight in a minor, in an infernal key. . . .' And here is news of the *beau monde*.

The clouds part: it might be curtains giving a last glimpse of some great reception. Everything there is bright and stately. The palest of blue skies, clouds faintly lit, cloud confections like drapery in a painting. How far away it seems, the opening of a fan, a landscape of music, yesterday's afternoon. Then the rain descends.

And of the home:

As the days draw in we find a new comfort in the evenings. The midges haunt a corner of the lawn where they have been all the summer, hung apparently in a glass bowl. It is almost dark before small birds cease from the geometry of their flight. We watch the smoke rising from a chimney and it changes from mauve to ghostly grey. A window rattles, in a treble voice a man cries 'Puss, puss, puss.' To-night, perhaps, we may sleep with easy consciences.

The Shadow Across the Page has an independence, a voluntary abruptness and remoteness that make it seem to forbid praise. Such a premium is rightly set on the word beauty that it is hard to find an adjective for this prose. Mr. Stonier has, to an almost unnerving degree, the power to communicate obliquely, to show thought in *déshabille*, to crystallize what is half-conscious and fluid in general experience, to perpetuate what is fleeting. Impersonally, he exposes his personality, as one might show an instrument. To do this without bourgeois coyness is, I take it, to be an artist. He says: 'Literature. The romantic impulse, the classic consideration.' Consideration here has not post-dated the impulse. It becomes owing to us that Mr. Stonier should attempt those bridges, which ought not to be detestable—or rather, show those connections, geologically existent, and let the whole range emerge in an entire work.

The New Statesman and Nation.

VAN DOREN ON SHAKESPEARE*

1941

Mr. Van Doren is an intuitional critic. Punctiliously, he admits in his introduction debts to the accepted writers on Shakespeare. But I feel that he still owes a debt to himself: if he has read much, he has discarded much. In the main, he appears to start from scratch, and this gives his observations a virtue one must respect. His style, plain, concrete, innocent of inflations, seems equally innocent of derived thought. His *Shakespeare* arrives from America at precisely the moment when our part of the Old World hopes to hope most of the New, and the Van Doren human directness and lack of nonsense appears to warrant and to confirm the hope. The impression of freshness is so strong, one might say that the plays of Shakespeare, for the first time published, had reached a reviewer working in good faith. 'Reviewer'

* 'Shakespeare.' By MARK VAN DOREN. (*Allen and Unwin.*)

is perhaps misleading: Mr. Van Doren shows the poet's traditional sensibility—a sensibility that does not function to order, whose only imperative is experience. That the reading and rereading of Shakespeare plays has done something to Mr. Van Doren one cannot doubt. His impressions—as he says in his Introduction—are of the study rather than of the theatre and possibly, in some of his friendly quarrels with Shakespeare, he ignores the enormous x of theatre-craft. The 100 per cent. playability of almost all of the plays most account for elements in them that seem to this critic adverse or forced, or even (though he does not use the word) on the phoney side. Actually, I believe it is impossible to see Shakespeare played without some sort of shock, some disruption of the subjective image that had already formed in the reader's mind. The unread audience—for whom the plays were intended—are less liable to the effects of blast.

Mr. Van Doren's preoccupation is with the poet. His introduction advances no governing theory, and the succeeding discussions are, in consequence, free. They are so free as to give, at their less fortunate moments, the impression of being random and *ad hoc*. The reader is left to assemble Mr. Van Doren's conclusions, and inevitably, by the end of the book, much that was of too independent merit tends to drop from the mind. The accepted chronology of the plays has been followed: the criticism attempts to describe an arc inside the arc of the poet's powers. The suggestion towards the end is not of decline, but that Shakespeare re-entered, after the height of the tragedies, a second, now adult, phase of superb virtuosity in the writing of the 'romantic' plays. The by now almost careless perfection of the sheer play-form permitted, according to Mr. Van Doren, a finer, more personal point to the poetry. Human probability—he contends—lessened, as though in the tragedies it had exhausted itself.

Throughout, there is the approach to the timeless phenomenon. If Shakespeare's Elizabethanism is not, to Mr. Van Doren, wholly irrelevant, it is, as he says at the outset, immaterial enough to discount. The contribution of Shakespeare's own time and its manners towards the creation of Shakespeare's absolute world was, in Mr. Van Doren's view, superficial. And he rules out, as an element, social thought—in fact, thought in almost any deliberate sense. 'The great and central virtue of Shakespeare was not achieved by taking thought, for thought cannot create a world.'

The suggestion is, that Shakespeare was more tentative than he knew, and that he was feeling his way towards inherent perfection by a not conscious process of hit-and-miss. In the poems (the subject of the first essay), Mr. Van Doren points out, the subjects are constantly overshot; the drop to the context—he instances weak closing couplets of sonnets—seems at once reluctant and arbitrary: in effect, the sonnets consume themselves. The Shakespeare of the sonnets, says Mr. Van Doren, never more than departed from the idea of personal love: he had only one love, his own poetry. And the critic's reading of the first seven plays shows Shakespeare not yet abreast of his own power. There is a conception of genius as possible enemy—so that the picture of Jacob wrestling with the Angel is brought immediately to the mind. It is, by this showing, from *Romeo and Juliet* onwards that the plays assimilate, as well as generate, poetry. From then on, Shakespeare more than lights up his successive subjects; he penetrates, and is penetrated, by them. It is from then on that Mr. Van Doren traces the steady, though not uninterrupted, ascent. The plays would appear, to this critic, to differ in quality not in their mould or colour but from their having been fired in a furnace of varying heat.

If Mr. Van Doren denies Shakespeare thought (in the sense of effort) he does not deny him method. But the method is little, and then unacademically, discussed. It is the extant, achieved Shakespearean world that interests him, even when, at the start, the world shows lacunæ and pits and mists. Once this main attachment of the critic's interest appears, the essays gain value through continuity. There are recurrences to the themes of will and pride, also, to conflict, social as much as spiritual, to the position of characters at odds with what, in the essay on *The Two Gentlemen of Verona*, Mr. Van Doren first calls 'the gentlemen's world' of the comedies—sweet surfeit, imperturbable stylishness, inherited ruthless gracefulness. Malvolio, Shylock, in his own way Angelo—this gentlemen's world creates its buffoons and victims, but such people are its disturbers, too. Their defeats are not conclusive; after their exits they are found to have acted like death's little pin. Though, only with *Othello* is this particular conflict elevated to tragedy. Apart from these figures, Mr. Van Doren emphasizes the enormous power of mistrust, the check on action, the sinister inverse of the apparently sound will. Above all, he is to show that this is a world of mirrors—active or impotent, sane

or mad, its giant characters are at every moment self-seen. As
for Shakespeare's women (other than the 'wailing women') Mr.
Van Doren chiefly commends the shrewdness behind their *jeux
d'esprit*.

Sir Hugh Walpole, in his Foreword, says he considers Mr. Van
Doren is at his best when writing of the less well-known plays.
Clearly these give more scope. At the same time, the essays on
Othello and *Antony and Cleopatra* seem to me outstanding: they
show feeling and force.

The New Statesman and Nation.

OPEN TO THE PUBLIC*

1937

On the white wrapper of *Helen's Tower* there is a small but distinct,
pretty vignette of the Tower itself, which sets the note of the book
—intimate charm. Inside the wrapper, the publisher says:'Harold
Nicolson has conceived the idea of writing his memoirs in an
original form. He hopes to produce a series of volumes under the
general title of "In Search of the Past." Each of the volumes will
centre around some interesting figure whom Harold Nicolson has
known personally and whose character and career will be treated,
partly in narrative form, and partly in terms of his own memory
and states of mind.'

The project is interesting. There are two pasts. There is one's
own—largely subjective, private, an annexe of one's identity, a
past whose value shifts and is constantly modified, a past for which
one can only search in oneself. This is the past one *calls* up. Then
there is the past one *looks* up—the outside or public past, which is
static, official. One may reinterpret this, but one must be objective
in writing it down. Mr. Nicolson has undertaken, in *Helen's
Tower*, to make these two different pasts interact. He is to regard
at once history and feeling. He is to write a book that shall be at
once informative and a work of art. He must suffuse the book in
personal colour, and at the same time keep facts clear of distorting
memory. He must make it equally palpable that he is writing
about Lord Dufferin because Lord Dufferin was his uncle, and, at

* 'Helen's Tower.' By HAROLD NICOLSON. (*Constable.*)

the same time, that he knows how to write about him as though he were not his uncle.

Lord Dufferin, thus, appears alternately in two theatres: public life, family memory. He is judged by two standards—so far as judgment appears in the obliqueness, the irony of Mr. Nicolson's style. As the uncle, he appears throughout impeccable: he was gracious to Miss Plimsoll, tipped, patted or simply suffered his nephew at what may have been some crisis in his career. As the public man, the now adult Mr. Nicolson must re-examine him. To the child, the grown-up person is impassible. To the grown-up, the fellow grown-up is a mosaic of weaknesses—glazed over, perhaps by an impermeable moral excellence, or by persisting charm.

Was Lord Dufferin a great man? Miss Plimsoll failed to allay Mr. Nicolson's first doubts. It is the continuance of the doubt—always tender, never quite unfriendly—that is likely to make *Helen's Tower* so sympathetic. Lord Dufferin's career, at Court, on missions, as Governor-General, Viceroy, Ambassador, is related with excellent clearness, only blurred here and there by patches of speculation. The man, what went to make him, the ruling ideas behind his policy stand out well. Pertinent incidents are both well found and well pictured. At its best, Mr. Nicolson's writing is succinct and businesslike. At its worst, it is far too agreeable. Then, what he has to say goes down like a pill in butter.

This is a picture of an aristocrat. Lord Dufferin combined stern honour with luxuriant fancies. In taste, he indulged his imagination; in conduct, he was wholly ruled by his conscience. He appears to have been romantic, upright, sensitive, tenacious, astute. He loved pomp with the simplicity of a pious man. His good judgment and a succession of crises made him an opportunist *malgré lui*—his mobility may have been a factor in this: he was always on the spot just before anyone else. Protestantism focused his mariolatry on his mother, then on her memory—Helen's Tower itself, at Clandeboye, is the shrine to this. He was a Liberal who disbelieved in Home Rule. Was he a man always at work, with infinite moral care, on a self-portrait? His kindness and charm were—and will remain, till the last of a generation dies off—bywords. Possibly there is no absolute in greatness. He was great in his context. His behaviour was in a tradition he honoured; he served a system he saw no reason to question; each decision he made—Imperial, international or domestic—must have been made in the light of his entire morality. Rightly to make one's effect is a great part of one's duty. His most glorious appointment was India, his most difficult Paris. Miss Plimsoll thought him the greatest man in the world.

But what is all this about Miss Plimsoll? What sort of counter-poise is she meant to make? She must be where the 'states of mind' come in. But Mr. Nicolson has not established her relevance. As a biography of Lord Dufferin, the main parts of *Helen's Tower* are ably architected. But are the personal lunettes functional, or just pretty? Is one meant to look through them, or just at them? Do they, in any important sense, approach Lord Dufferin, or his age, to us? Yes, they do afford a domestic view of him. But do they offer, even from the most oblique angle, further insight into the problems of being Lord Dufferin? They have little time-colour. These are pictures of any child in any great house. The easy conclusion is, that the Plimsoll interludes were fun for Mr. Nicolson (to write about, not to live through) and ought to be fun for us. *Helen's Tower* may, of course, beg questions as to relevance by its claim to a new form. But, however new the form, everything must integrate. Deeper thinking than seems to have gone to it was necessary, to justify Miss Plimsoll. The newer the form, the more clearly it has to show its own artistic necessities. Fun is nice, but it has to be necessary.

Mr. Nicolson's own experience is valuable: he writes of the setting, the family, with inside knowledge. Some of the Clande-boye passages are excellent. A few are over-written. Let Mr. Nicolson not be the prey of his own good writing. There is a frighteningly fine line between accomplishment and facility. Here is a writer who is unusual in his command of both matter and manner. His readers, in honour to him, can hardly be too exact-ing. *How* he tells what he has to tell is vital. Privacy is on the retreat now; curiosity has things its own way. At least, then, let us try to civilize curiosity.

More and more great houses are having glass fronts fitted, numbers of great families are recruited for literature. To the insatiable public, almost nothing remains inaccessible. This is democracy realized. Is it to be a pity? *Helen's Tower*, and its successors, are likely to be important in determining this.

The New Statesman and Nation.

CHILDREN'S PLAY*

1941

Web of Childhood suggests answers to a number of questions, not only about the Brontës but about art. How much does creative imagination owe to its domination by a first fantasy? One fantasy —sometimes simple, sometimes complex in form—may be found at the root of any one artist's art. The greater—that is to say, the more vital, powerful and expansive—the art, the more ingrowing, in most cases, the fantasy. Often the fantasy is a private dream, to which the imagination returns and attaches itself with an almost voluptuous energy. Almost all people have had such dreams, or day-dreams, and with each person the dream, though remaining the same in essence, is capable of a number of variations—in childish friendships such dreams are pooled, shared and developed, and 'imagination-games' are the result. With adolescence, the dream begins to be surrounded by a new kind of disturbing emotion; it is defended by a sort of *pudeur*, and is not communicated except in cases of emotional intimacy, or as part of the attempt to create an intimacy. In the non-artist nature the dream appears, with maturity, to reach the end of its power: it is more than exhausted, it really dies, or if it does not die it remains, like an awkwardness, in some part of the nature, to reappear perhaps in certain phases of love. At any rate, the non-artist does tend to denounce his dream (or fantasy) with his intelligence, or only to remember it with a smile. Of the artist, it may be said that the dream not only does not exhaust itself, but continues at once to feed on and to condition the man's or woman's experience. It occupies its own area, just on or just over the edge of the consciousness; it demands to be expressed, and to express itself it recruits the intelligence.

The Brontë dream, or fantasy, was unique in being a group-dream: it was not only shared but generated by four children at once. It was unique, also, in not being physically ephemeral—the young Brontës not only played, they wrote their play down. So

* 'The Brontës Web of Childhood.' By FANNIE ELIZABETH RATCHFORD. (*Columbia University Press. Humphrey Milford.*)

144

Web of Childhood provides the only documentation, so far as I know, of an entire childish domain of fantasy. Had nothing more been ever heard of the Brontës the value of the book would remain great—as a key to the Brontë genius its value is inestimable. Miss Ratchford, its compiler and analyst, has searched through, transcribed and closely studied the tiny notebooks in print hand and scraps of paper of which the Brontë juvenilia consist. Kingdoms, cities, administrations, campaigns and, above all, a highly dramatic pattern of highly individualized figures are opened up to our eyes. Miss Ratchford's research is so important that one wonders why, given the increasing interest in the phenomena of childhood and of genius, it has not been undertaken before.

The game began with a dozen toy-soldiers given to Branwell Brontë one evening, on the Rev. Mr. Brontë's return from town. Commandeered by the family, these twelve soldiers became the Twelve Young Men, in whose adventures the masculine spirit latent in Charlotte and Emily had full play. Upon them followed the islands, carefully mapped, then the city of Glass Town, which, destroyed by a cataclysm when Charlotte had to leave Haworth for school, was to rise again as Verdopolis. Over these brooded, dynamically, the four named Genii who were the four Brontë minds. The high-passioned aristocracy of this region enjoyed the titles and names of the Wellesley family—the Byronic Duke of Zamorna, of whom we have portraits from Charlotte's accomplished pencil, was to be the peak. In the affairs of Verdopolis, Charlotte and Branwell were the moving spirits; Emily, with Anne as ally, seceded to devote herself to the creation of Gondal. But Verdopolis and Gondal make evident the same radical fantasy.

The Brontës' continuous childish creative act passed over from childhood into their young maturity. It may be said that Branwell succumbed to it—it completely held him back from maturity. The sisters' attempts to detach themselves from the dream-world caused them accesses of racking pain—it was *not* for the four walls of Haworth parsonage that the young governesses felt nostalgia. Charlotte, adult, beheld its dangers. 'I long,' she writes, 'to quit for a while that burning clime where we have sojourned too long —its skies aflame, the glow of sunset always upon it—the mind would cease from excitement and turn now to a cooler region where the dawn breaks grey and sober, and the coming day is at

L

least obscured by clouds. . . .' Emily attempted no such renuncia-
tion: she passed from Gondal to *Wuthering Heights*.

As notes on the genesis of the Brontë novels—the evolution of
Zamorna into Rochester, for instance—much of *Web of Childhood*
is interesting. Miss Ratchford holds that her material disposes of
two major fallacies of the Brontë legend—Branwell's influence
over Emily and the infatuation (past a degree) of Charlotte for
M. Héger in Brussels. She has certainly thrown on the Brontë
psychology a not unexpected but very revealing light.

The Spectator.

MR. HUXLEY'S ESSAYS*

1936

Mr. Huxley has been the alarming young man for a long time, a
sort of perpetual clever nephew who can be relied on to flutter the
lunch-party. Whatever will he say next? How does he think of
these things? He has been deplored once or twice, but feeling is in
his favour: he is steadily read. He is at once the truly clever person
and the stupid person's idea of the clever person; he is expected
to be relentless, to administer intellectual shocks. This attitude
to Mr. Huxley, to which his early work may have given credit,
has been maintained, and strengthened, for about twenty years.
Actually, he is now at an age which in any other profession would
be considered sober: he is well into middle age—or maturity.
This is a statement which may be considered slighting in a country
that dreads maturity for its artists, in which there is a deep and
horrific gap between the bright young fellow and the good
old bustard, in which the dream-child and the prodigy dominate literature. Shocks apart, the growing pressure, behind
Mr. Huxley's work, of adult seriousness may give his public unforeseen offence: he threatens to break a pact by which the clever
person is not permitted to be in earnest right through. Whereas,
if you are moral, to be clever is superfluous, even unbecoming.
Happily for this country—while she makes this distinction—she

* 'The Olive Tree and Other Essays.' By ALDOUS HUXLEY. (*Chatto and Windus.*)

has few grown-up writers, fewer grown-up æsthetes; Mr. Huxley is both. As a novelist, it is true, he still gives his readers pleasure by adolescent harshness, a dashing cynicism, the depiction of excruciating scenes and what are called 'unnecessary' incidents— like the dog on the roof in *Eyeless in Gaza*, or the moron's death in *Those Barren Leaves*. (Strictly, those two incidents are necessary; they are the moral pivots of the two books.) As a novelist, he still has a touch of the prodigy: in a great glare of intellectual hilarity his characters dangle rather too jerkily; they are morality characters with horrified puppet-faces. His novels, however, have it over his best collections of essays in one important particular: they are continuous. And Mr. Huxley's continuity—the transitions he makes, the positions he abandons, the connexions he underlines —is very important.

The Olive Tree is another collection of essays, written, with two exceptions, within the last few years. The piece (placed last) which gives the book its pretty and concrete name is pure reflection, a running-on of the mind. The quickness and limpidity of its flow remind one that Aldous Huxley was labelled a writers' writer—which meant, presumably, that he writes better than lay people are expected to understand. Few readers now are as dumb as the critics thought: we know technique when we see it. The vitality, aptness, structure and inherent beauty of Mr. Huxley's style is plain to, more or less, anyone. He is occupied, now, with something beyond this—though real style, it is true, cannot be involuntary. His analysis of T. H. Huxley's prose is instructive.

The preface to the D. H. Lawrence letters reappears, and is given context and fresh point by some of the other essays. The juxtaposition of subjects, in this collection, is telling; they lend one another interest and gain collective importance. One would gladly have the links that form in one's own mind tested by Mr. Huxley, and associations, however idle, explored. If he would write one long, embracing essay—those different sofas, for instance: Crebillon's and the sofa in the Spaxton billiard-room-chapel on which Brother Prince, the Beloved, redeemed the flesh. (*Justifications* is brilliant.) Exactly what divided D. H. Lawrence from Laurence Oliphant of the *Sympneumata*? What would Crebillon have made of *Lady Chatterley*? Again, there was Lawrence's 'Art for my sake' and there was poor B. R. Haydon's piteous arrogance: should one, in fact, like Lawrence, stand by one's genius if, like Haydon, one really has not got any? We should like this gone into.

Learning and frivolity polish all these essays, but there is something more. *Writers and Readers* and *Words and Behaviour* are as overtly serious as parts of *Eyeless in Gaza*. The foundations of the ivory tower are shaken; there are no longer untouchable palaces for the mind. Intellect cannot withdraw; it must go into the battle. Mr. Huxley is out to combat, with mathematical coldness, with chemical deadliness, the forces of unreason he sees destroying us. Actually, he can never write—can anyone?—without emotion: his statements are often given colour by horror. He sees us as hypnotized by abstractions, morbidly passive, herdable, driven on to our fate. Morality, a morality of the mind, is all we have against ruin. So he writes:

'In a fictitious world of symbols and personified abstractions, rulers find that they can rule more effectively, and the ruled, that they can gratify instincts which the conventions of good manners and the imperatives of morality demand that they should repress. To think correctly is the condition of behaving well. It is also in itself a moral act; those who would think correctly must resist considerable temptations.'

In fact, he is preaching a new asceticism: if he presses this point further he will not be popular. Meanwhile, he has done, in this collection as ever, a great deal to amuse us: dug up the Perfectionist Bundlers, reclaimed Haydon and quoted his anecdotes, shown the way to Crebillon, painted an oasis, and given some notes on snobbery, examinations, fetichism and time. *The Olive Tree* goes to its place in that lengthening row on his shelf—perhaps he was born versatile: did he make himself diligent?

The Spectator.

BARRIE*

1941

The life story of Sir James Barrie has been written by Mr. Mackail with an exacting evenness that is interesting. The thoroughness

---

* 'The Story of J. M. B. Sir James Barrie, Bart., O.M.' By DENIS MACKAIL. (*Peter Davies.*)

BARRIE   149

of the biographer is evident: almost every detail seems to have
been supplied—in fact, after the early years of the childhood, the
story moves literally from month to month. The biography,
which, necessarily, is long, is impossible to read with a passive
mind: Mr. Mackail, with the concealed art of the novelist, invites
one to draw conclusions he does not authorize. This would
appear to be a biography fraught with pitfalls, but by which—and
surely this is a triumph?—no one can be offended, no one hurt.
It is apparent that Barrie existed in a hyper-personal, highly
charged atmosphere of charm and pain, and that with every year
of his life the temperature round him rose; that to inspire him was
to become his victim, and, at the same time, to be unwilling
assistant at his tortuous victimization of himself. For actors in
Barrie's personal drama there was only one possible exit: death.
The drama had the mysterious compulsions, the subjectivity, and,
to an extent, the pathology of a dream.

One might divide the biography—for, as I said, Mr. Mackail
has been too wise to give any arbitrary frame—into the dream's
genesis and its workings-out. James Barrie was the third son and
ninth child of a weaver in Kirriemuir. The early circumstances
of his family were bleak, strenuous, austere and devoid, in the
ordinary sense, of charm. His mother, Margaret *née* Ogilvy, had
a brother who was already a minister, and one would take her to
be the motive force in the steady upward trend of the Barries if
such a trend were not evident in, apparently, every representative
Scotch home. (Mr. Mackail, by the way, has disposed, at least
for the duration of the biography, of the question as to whether to
say Scots, Scottish or Scotch: Barrie said Scotch; one is glad to
leave it at that.) Even when not inspired by hero-mothers, the
young Scotch do not seem to relax their unsmiling determination
to make good in the world. In real life admirable rather than
attractive, it seems the fate of this race to be put across, in a big
way, by those few of its sons whose imagination fostered itself
on romantic art. The child James Barrie never, in deed, revolted
against the strenuous atmosphere—but his imagination steadily
moved South. Warmth was necessary, so his childish-unchildish
rapacious emotion fed on the Kirriemuir family scene, till the
natural affections grew unnaturally deep. Death, the death of a
brother, entering his life early, went to intensify all this: the dead
boy perhaps froze that image of childhood that was to appear

forever in his art. Barrie went to a succession of schools, then
to Edinburgh University, where he did modestly but obtained a
degree. The small pale anxious student with the remarkable eyes
already made his personality felt. But, 'Grind . . . Humbug . . .'
alternate in his diary. The determination to be a writer crystallized, was announced to his family.

The first real move South was no further than Nottingham.
Existence, on the staff of the *Nottingham Journal*, continued narrow, intensive. However, he worked at theatre-criticism and met,
and went for a drive with, his first actress here. He wrote middles,
on which his still anonymous fancy could give itself fairly free
rein. Then the *Journal* cut down its staff, and for the Kirriemuir
young man there was nothing but the anti-climax of return. Free-
lance writing at home, with, always behind it, a tautening certainty of his destination; then the big plunge—London. There,
tentative pauses, a few rebuffs, the early struggles—not desperate.
Quite soon began the crescendo towards success. Almost before
he was middle-aged the laurels had begun to heap themselves up.
Life expanded as far as life can expand—which is not, as Barrie
found, very far. First nights, dinners, majestic houses, romantic
intimacies, academic acclaim. . . . The more success assumes
dream-proportions the more life shows itself inferior to the dream.
One gets the picture of a small figure committed to an outsize
fate. No wonder Barrie liked Chaplin.

One cannot add any more comments to the phenomenon of
success. Barrie was spared the final ironic tragedy: he never
ceased to believe in the worth of his own work. But he continued
through his life to be subject to devastating silences, melan-
cholies. His emotional make-up was so odd that if he could man-
age to live at all (as he did), one feels that he could have sustained
almost any conditions. With people he seems to have avoided
any relationship that his imagination, under the rule of symbols,
could not in its turn rule, mould and inform. The failure of his
marriage—as to which Mr. Mackail's reticence is to be respected—
went in deep: this was something worse than a death. I am convinced there was not a trick in his art: not only did technical hard
work go to the output of it, but he was innocent of, at least, the
wish to exploit. He wrote of his own nostrums. Children, big
dogs, beautiful mothers, strong hearts, weak wills, great wishes,
mild realizations—he wrote for an age to which these were dear.

From an urbane London his imagination turned back to float Kirriemuir and its pious ones in a world-illusion. But to that shrine of illusion he himself rendered his yearly pilgrimage North. Barrie's art was art of the kind that is overflow, superfluity from a man's person; an affectable man's art for an affectable age. Minor art, if you like, for minor men. But it has a strength out of one kind of suffering. And who shall say any suffering is unreal?

The Spectator.

CONRAD*

1936

Mr. Crankshaw's book on Conrad is well-timed. For the moment —a moment in literary consciousness being something at once immediate and extensive—Conrad is in abeyance. We are not clear yet how to rank him; there is an uncertain pause. It would be inexact to say that his reputation has declined; his popularity has, at the most, contracted; he is still steadily if not widely read. But he was a writer great, above all, in his power to command the imagination: for the moment, this power of his has not its old grip. The change must be in us, in the nature of our susceptibilities, in the directions that our excitement takes. When a writer has been brought to a halt by death, one kind of activity in him has to replace another: he can no longer cover more ground, like a tractor; he has to work upon us with a static persistence, like an electric drill. Expectation of more to come and æsthetic topicality are two large elements in a living writer's hold on the public mind. With death, the sense of immediate communication slackens; the man with whom we were sharing the present day, who while acting upon us was being acted upon, is gone: his books come under the shadow of mortality and, if they are to live, have to reinstate themselves with us. To live, they must be either classics or curiosities—and curiosities have not much life. Their particular, personal element tells, for a time, against them— possibly we are more estranged from the lately dead than we know

* ' Joseph Conrad. Some Aspects of the Art of the Novel.' By EDWARD CRANK- SHAW. (*The Bodley Head.*)

—they have to stand on their general, major qualities. The entertainer has now to become a monument, outside our own variations of taste and fancy. If his books are to outlive him, we expect them to outlive us.

Conrad is suspect for the very magnificence that had us under its spell: we resist verbal magic now. His novels are, in the grand sense, heroic: now we like our heroics better muffled—the terse tough heroics of the Hemingway school. His dramatic, ironic sense of fate is out of accord with our fatalism. Most vital of all, perhaps, he seems to be over-concerned with the individual: with conscience, with inner drama, with isolated endeavour. Romantic individualism is at a discount now. 'You may take it,' says Conrad, through the mouth of Mills in *The Arrow of Gold*—'you may take it from a man who has lived a rough life, a very rough life, that it is the subtleties of personality, and contacts, and events, that count for interest and memory—and pretty well nothing else.' This we no longer feel—or do not admit.

Only perversity or smallness of spirit could deny Conrad's stature. But he has, lately, been slighted as an artist. Mr. Crankshaw sets out not only to reinstate him but to give his work its place in art as a whole. Conrad was not just a brilliant phenomenon, but a practitioner. He practised the most difficult, because to the untaught eye the most straightforward, of the arts, in which nine-tenths of everything that offers itself to the imagination has to be rejected, in which questions to which there is no definite answer constantly pose themselves, in which there is no straight going—the artist's course being deflected by rock-like impossibilities up to his very last page. To what degree the difficulties which confronted Conrad were general, inherent in the writing of any major novel, to what degree they were particular, Conrad's own, Mr. Crankshaw has set himself to find out. Parallel with his study of Conrad's method—or, better, making a frame for the study—its author has given us an analysis of the novelist's art in general, having reference to Flaubert and to James.

Mr. Crankshaw has been temperate and discerning. 'We have here,' he says of Conrad, at the outset, 'genius, which consists of an original and passionate spirit, hard work and calculation (calculation . . . conscious, unconscious or somewhere between the two). The spirit is an everlasting mystery; the rest we can study with some detachment and objectiveness.' He shows that, of Conrad's particular difficulties, some were inherent in his make-up, immovable limitations—such as his lack of 'objective precision,' and of style (which cannot be learnt) in the classic sense—others his own exactingness forced him to create. Did not Henry James say of *Chance*: 'It places Mr. Conrad absolutely alone as a votary of the way to do a thing that shall make it undergo most doing'? Conrad, he shows further, could not invent; he has therefore to take an incident, remembered or recounted, and steep and steep it again in his imagination till it comes out crystallized over, almost frighteningly luminous but still, sometimes, unclear. He lacked the vital precision of the inventive mind.

It is hard to give a summary of Mr. Crankshaw's book. He appears to make his points a shade over-deliberately, but his method justifies himself. His discussion of Conrad's lack of style is provocative and interesting. This ranks high, too, as a general book on the novel.

The Spectator.

GORKI STORIES*

1939

Short story writers form a sort of democracy: when a man engages himself in this special field his stories stand to be judged first of all on their merits *as* stories, only later in their relation to the rest of his work. The more imposing the signature, the more this applies. The craft (it may be no more) of the short story has special criteria; its limitations are narrow and definite. It is in the building-up of the short story that the craftsman side of the artist has to appear. Very close demands on the writer's judgment are made; the short story is not a mere ease for the passing fancy; it offers no place for the unobjectified sentiment, for the impulsive start that could not be followed through. It must have implications which will continue when the story is done. It may be a *tour de force*, but it must not be a by-product; if it reads like a

---

* 'A Book of Short Stories.' By MAXIM GORKI. Edited by Avrahim Yarmolinsky and Moura Budberg. With a Foreword by Aldous Huxley. (*Cape.*)

by-product it is so much waste. Its disadvantages are, an emotional narrowness that the writer would not permit himself in a longer work, a necessary over-simplification of characters, and a rather theatrical tensing-up of the dialogue—if there be dialogue. The writer who rates above all things verisimilitude and the all-round view, or who cannot sustain one mood till the writing rounds itself off, does better to leave the short story alone. It must be recognized that even in the short story of the greatest integrity there has to be a sort of concealed trick.

Serious writers have failed in the short story through either disdaining or failing to learn the trick. Gorki did not make this mistake. The stories in this collection show a virtuosity on a scale with his seriousness. Written over a period of thirty years, they have been arranged in chronological order; each shows an increase of pointedness and of velocity. In the later stories there is less action but a much greater tautness of mood: *Chelkash* (the first, 1894) deals wholly with action but loses some power through being diffuse and slack; *Karamora* (the last, 1924) concentrates what might be formless, a life-mood, into a miraculous piece of hard irony. It took high ability to get away with *Karamora*. Gorki's aim in the short story seems to have been philosophic portraiture: to this he made action subordinate. In the earlier stories, either from lack of craft or imperfectly realized purpose, he lets action get in his way, and at the same time overcasts, muddles or checks it. Later, he makes action perfectly illustrative. From, roughly speaking, 1900 on, the stories have at once movement and depth. Their apparent spareness allows a greater complexity. Gorki becomes a stricter artist as he becomes a more wide-natured man.

These are all hard-case stories, treated with a prevailing austerity of mood. Enough distinction cannot, these days, be made between austerity and 'toughness.' Toughness has a wet inverse, a maudlin streak; it is adolescent—austerity is adult. Gorki writes to invite judgment, and judgment is the bone and muscle of pity. The reaction to human suffering must be awe, first, not simply the good cry. Almost all the stories here show the deformation of major natural feelings by impossible circumstances: *Notch*, *Chums*, *Twenty-six Men and a Girl*, and *Lullaby* are outstanding examples of this. But they show, too, the strong tortuous upward growth of the spirit of man, that will not stay down—

there is that other aspect of the magnificent *Lullaby*; there is *One Autumn Evening* and the last pages of *Red*. Again, in *One Autumn Evening*, *Birth of a Man* and *The Hermit*, the triumphant, however brief, summer or high tide of the spirit in the realization of sexual love appears. Gorki identifies happiness, purity, dignity with the *generalized* moment, when man rises clear of his cramping individual consciousness to the full of his human height, forgetting himself. The individual, *qua* individual, only suffers, and suffers meanly enough. Any passion (including the passion of pity) is not a release merely, it is an apotheosis.

The attitude to power is, in these stories, unexpectedly neutral. Consciousness of power is a predicament, its misuse a catastrophe for the misuser. Power looms large in *Chelkash*, *Notch*, *Cain and Artyom*: its first victim is, the man who is wielding it. (Its more evident victims, down to the prison kitten, bow to oppression as to a natural force; the down-and-outs of the doss-house stiffen their backs beneath it: one of them says in a hoarse voice: 'I am a man'). The predicament of the empowered person, in this Gorki underworld, is more closely examined than are the ethics of power. Petunikoff the merchant, in *Creatures that Once Were Men*, is the only instance of power from wealth; elsewhere, it is a matter of personality (as with the compelling *Chelkash* or the playboy convict *Notch*) or of disorientated brute strength (as with *Red* or with *Artyom*). Accident, in *Evil-Doers*, puts the complacent charcoal-burner in a key position that is fatal to him: he gets murdered for moralizing to desperate men. Only *The Hermit* exercises power as painlessly, naturally as he sweats: this animal mystic, a sublime, very old man, who has been an incestuous father, unties neurotics by simply saying 'My dear . . .' But he has to live alone. The implication throughout is, that the powerful person lives among his fellows in a torment of strained will.

In *Karamora*, renegade and police spy, the man with the double nature, we get, probably, Gorki's final exposition of crooked innocence. Karamora has vision, with one blind spot. He awaits death puzzled but not ashamed. Here the Russian genius is under analysis.

Gorki's descriptive passages are charged with emotion. At their best they have a poetic force; at their less happy they sag, weakening the form. Weather, with Gorki, is anthropomorphic, temperamentally part of the human scene. Mr. Aldous Huxley points out, in his Foreword, how much the limited flexibility of translators' English, the incurable lack of approximation in sound and the finer sense, must blur some effects at which Gorki aimed, on which, for these stories, he must have often relied. The sensuous, super-rational elements in one language cannot but be lost in a transposition. Much of the writer's private magic goes. Actually, these translations (by different hands) read well; they are not guilty of quaintnesses or embarrassing slang. Inevitably, they drop, in sustained passages, into that sing-song that haunts translated Russian. The complexion of Gorki's prose is, in fact, lost, though its harder features appear. And this loss of sensuous bloom brings tricks—legitimate tricks—into prominence. After a few experiments, Gorki hit on a structure he used again and again. He over-used repetitions, he over-strained analogies. He is too quick on the heavily struck chord. Almost all the stories fade out into empty, dusk-ridden scenes: his endings comply with a formula. His sureness appears, in places, unsympathetic; it becomes too clear that he knows how to play his hand. But his faults are a master's faults. His limitations are those of a man who has learnt a technique too well: his greatness remains evident, for his vision is always ahead of his technique. He is more than adept, he is profoundly disciplined. These fifteen short stories rank high.

The New Statesman and Nation.

D. H. LAWRENCE*

1947

In view of Lawrence's unique interest, the condition of his literary reputation requires explanation. For between his achievement and his fate as a writer there is certainly a serious disproportion. Even while he lived, Lawrence met great popular and critical resistance. He was never read as widely as he deserved and seldom read properly. And since his death, his fate has become even worse. A literary position that was never secure seems to be steadily weakening. In the short space of a decade and a half, a writer of the first rank gives evidence of

* 'The Portable D. H. Lawrence.' Selected and with an Introduction by Diana Trilling. (*Viking Press.*)

becoming a peripheral figure—someone whom the younger readers among us neither know nor feel they need know and whom the elder readers among us remember with a touch of awkward indulgence for their own youth.

So, at a point in her Introduction to *The Portable D. H. Lawrence* says Mrs. Trilling, rightly. In making her selection she has been guided as by a diviner's rod to what was most vital in Lawrence: the real springs—we are given not necessarily the 'best' of Lawrence, but necessarily the most relevant. Relevant to what? To his genius: to the tensions and conflicts thrust up out of his nature into his art: to his relation to time. This book may or may not reinstate Lawrence; it should ensure his being freshly and fairly judged—and indeed, one may ask, in the very freshness, is, fairness not likely to be inherent? Oblivion of or indifference to D. H. Lawrence during the decade and a half has been, I believe, more really a loss to us than an injustice to him; not to read Lawrence is to suspend some faculty. To him (to the art which is him) it may be that this winter sleep has done no harm—do literary reputations, in their cycles, perhaps follow some beneficial, restorative natural law? Judgment has rested; the controversies, the oscillations set up by first violent impact have had time to die down.

It is misleading to speak of 'the real Lawrence': one can discuss only the Lawrence real to oneself. For my own part, in returning to Lawrence I find myself in the presence of a contemporary—not merely my *own* contemporary but the present day's. This means, to be face to face with the fact that it is Lawrence's critics, rather than he, who have 'dated.' One as I am of the older group of readers, I find that it is the *surround* of Lawrence's work—the heated, for-or-against reception we in our youth, in the first place, gave it—that I recall with embarrassment; never the work itself. It is, if anything, my own psychopathic history which seems to haunt the pages I now reread. Very quickly, however, that subjective mist dissolves: there is a midday solidity and clearness about the print . . . Can one, I question, indeed *return* to whatever—be it a place or person—has been never totally left behind? Part of the strength of Lawrence is that what he saw (if not always what he said) sinks itself into the memory, deep down; his vision not only fuses with but permanently affects the vision of his reader. Lawrence forever crops up (I can think of no better term) in the consciousness, in the creative work of a generation who, having read him young, now come to maturity. He has been absorbed into the system, on and in which he continues to act. He wrote, and was read, before his day was yet come: now his day has (I believe) come, he is not, or is hardly at all, read. What a paradox, apparently!

I can speak, inevitably, chiefly for England. Here, I am told and can see, the young generation also do not read Lawrence. Of how much of his very real presence in the air round them the young English are conscious, I cannot say. Indirectly, he can but be reaching them through the writers they do admire and read— of these Joyce Cary comes most immediately to my mind, though I believe I could pick up the Lawrence trail across the work of most English novelists making their mark now. Most English of English writers, Lawrence will not be got out of the English blood stream: he has psychic ancestors, as he must have descendants—would it be quite fantastic to place the Richardson of *Clarissa* among the ancestors?

His day. We who read him young are now called upon to live out the day Lawrence foresaw. First the war; now the new raw personal social consciousness, with its lifting of the protective veil between individuals. Like the characters in a Lawrence novel, we are now in England thrust up against and into each other in a merciless, scorching propinquity. During the war for six years of extinguishing nights we moved towards, past and alongside each other in the acute sightless awareness of his 'The Blind Man' story. During the war in London Lawrence was the one artist whom I, for one, constantly had in mind. Originally, the prophetic side of him was perhaps ignored; the stress was all on the 'doctrine,' the salvationism, with its exciting and shocking (literally) accent on sex. We were then by twenty years or so nearer to the Victorian inhibited hush: nowadays, the incidents in his novels are among the commonplaces of experience. So much less is shocking; so much more is trite. The pattern he projected is being approximated to in 'real' life—how lifelessly, sometimes, only Lawrence could know! Perhaps that is one reason why the young now do not read Lawrence: they think, 'He cannot tell *us* anything!' His name reaches them only as a distorted rumour, or as news of yesterday.

None the less, I repeat that this is his day. He has outlived his denouncers: for instance, who cares now that Lawrence was an anti-intellectual? The intellectuals during the decade and a half of Lawrence's eclipse, have had time to prove themselves; but have they taken us very far? In writing, now, a sensuous concreteness is demanded—is this not already at its perfection in the Lawrence short stories, in the more mobile passages of the novels? We want the form of naturalism, with at the same time a kind of internal burning—in Lawrence, every bush burns. . . . I agree with Mrs. Trilling in finding the short stories better than, or, at least, æsthetically more satisfactory than, most of the novels, and 'The Fox' the best piece Lawrence ever wrote. The scene in the farmhouse parlour (the young soldier and the two restless girls) contains and sheds life as does the globe of a lamp light. In some of the novels, particular instance being *Women in Love*, individual characters may seem to split apart under a too great pressure— though, in the section of the *Rainbow* given in this anthology, mystical impulsive simplicity is intact. The artistry of D. H. Lawrence has maintained, however flickeringly, its reputation: what now, to the young generation, calls for study, and would repay study, is his craft.

New York Times Book Review.

THE MOORES*

1939

George Moore, the merchant of Alicante, built Moore Hall when he returned from Spain. The site, on the top of a wooded hill overlooking an inlet of Carra Lake, caught his eye—no doubt it embodied his Irish dreams. He had meant to improve, and to settle at, Ashbrook House, the more modest home of his family, but, like other Irishmen of his period, he could not but deviate into the grand idea. He had the means: he had more than made good during his term abroad—perhaps his ability came from his mother's side; she had been an Athy of Renville, and the Athys head the roll of the great Galway burgher families. Now, backed by a solid fortune, this first George Moore set out to buy up land at a time when land in Ireland cost more than it does now. He had a right, also, to his wish for the grand, for he had soared out of the Anglo-Irish ambiguity by taking out a patent of nobility in order to attend the court of Spain. He had established, as far as one knows rightly, descent from the Yorkshire family of the Blessed Thomas More. He and his wife (*née* Miss de Kilikelly, or Kelly, reared in Spain and married by him at Bilbao) had thus made part of the aristocratic society of Catholic *émigré* Irish that gathered at Catholic courts. The Catholicism of the Moores—as the fourth and last George Moore was not slow to point out—was recent, and on the whole unimpassioned: that Miss Athy, the merchant's mother, had been a Catholic and brought the religion in. Miss de Kilikelly confirmed the matter, of course. In the clement, propitious Spanish air, the George Moores got from their religious background advancement, poise. But back in Ireland, in Mayo, the position of Catholic gentry was not too good.

However, a chapel was built at the top of the new house, and the family practised its own religion in an easy, unbigoted way. Later, they were to attract Miss Edgeworth and her friend the Dean by their liberalism, their readiness to discuss. With the Moores, there were no mines in this area; their fanaticisms worked out in other ways. The last George Moore's abnegation of Rome

* 'The Moores of Moore Hall.' By JOSEPH HONE. (*Cape.*)

and rather wordy embracement of the Protestant faith was the first Moore act of religious fanaticism.

The woods at the top of Muckloon Hill were cleared, and Moore Hall went up. Begun in 1792, the bland Georgian house in its watchful position over the lake and islands was not to live much more than a hundred and thirty years. In 1923 it was burned down—victim, like other Senators' houses, of party violence. Mr. Hone shows a dreadful photograph of the shell—not the least indignity is the ivy. While it stood, classic and bare and strong, the house embodied that perfect idea of living that, in actual living, cannot realize itself. The inside, in proportion and decoration, was of Renaissance simplicity. It was (someone said) a house built for hot days; the ceilings must have reflected the lake light. On the first floor, 'the summer room' gave, through a Venetian window, on to balcony over the portico. Had George Moore the First forgotten the rains of the West, the isolation in acres of wet woods? His son, George Moore the Second, the historian, when recalled, to rule here, from London, from the pleasures of Holland House, added a notable library. But it was he who said, 'Beautiful as it is, much as I love it, I have not always been able to exclude ennui from its precincts.'

As the returned merchant found, and as his son the thinker found later, to dream of Ireland is one thing, to live there another. Ireland broke each of the Moores, in her oblique way. But being spirited people, they broke well.

George Moore the First created more than a house. By building Moore Hall, and by buying much land round it, he saddled his descendants with that something between a *raison d'être* and a predicament—an Irish estate. The hold is ghostly as well as material; there is a touch of 'I have, therefore I am.' And, from the outset, nothing went very well. The former Miss de Kilikelly moped for Spain and never quite settled down. The eldest son, John, gave trouble: reared abroad, he took his transplantation to Ireland in only too good faith. He detached himself from some squalid troubles in London to plunge into revolutionary politics. The Moores, already appalled, next learned that Citizen John Moore had been, immediately after the French landing, proclaimed President of the Republic of Connaught by General Humbert. John was arrested; tortuous and expensive litigation ended only with his obscure death. The unimpeachable Moores had the

M

neighbourhood's sympathy, but nothing was bad enough for poor John.

Thus, George Moore the Second became the heir; his father's death recalled him from London to Moore Hall. He married a Mayo lady, Louisa Browne. This Louisa Moore, with her hard, brilliant dark eyes and curled upper lip, was a *maîtresse femme*. Women like this, in every few generations, dominate, in all classes, Irish family life. Her husband's frail health and his pre-occupations made her master as well as mistress of Moore Hall. In her passionate dealings with people—most of all with her eldest son—Mrs. Moore stopped at nothing. Anything might be used to implement a quarrel. The letters she wrote George Henry were those of a thwarted mistress rather than of a mother. She took up an impossible position when, her second son John having been killed in a riding accident, she set herself against all horses, point blank. With George Henry, love for a faithless mistress cured itself (no thanks to the intervention of his aunt, Miss Browne) but horses continued to impassion and dominate him— as they dominated Mayo and most of Irish society. Augustus, the third son, precocious and disappointing mathematician, soon cared for nothing but horses, either. First with the Mayo squireens, then in England and with the Waterford set (who jumped their horses in halls) the two brothers showed indomitable courage and silliness—and George Henry ran up horsey debts. Mrs. Louisa Moore lived in that sort of dread that does seem able to magnetize tragedy—Augustus *was* killed, riding at Liverpool. Life for George Henry took a serious turn—he turned to the heartbreak of politics.

It was Mrs. Louisa Moore who maintained, on behalf first of her husband, then of her sons, the friendship with Miss Edgeworth. Interchanges of visits and letters between the two households were lively, affectionate, fruitful. In Miss Edgeworth's conversation, in her power to put him back into touch with what should have been his own world, the historian found real solace. Unable to keep back ennui, shanghaied in this world of rain and intensive family feeling, with Miss Edgeworth he breathed astringent air. This man wrote, in an unfinished Preface:

I have had no celebrity in my life. But a prospect of posthumous fame pleases me at this moment . . . we are so made that while we are still living we like to think that we shall not be forgotten after our deaths.

He referred to the promise, solemnly given, that his family were to see through the press his *Historical Memoir of the French Revolution*. For this purpose, £500 was set aside; in this was to lie his posthumous fame. It was good that he found the prospect worth so much. For his *Historical Memoir* was never published, though Miss Edgeworth brought up her failing powers and Louisa and the already distracted George Henry did what they could. It was left to the last George, in an access of family spleen, to bring up the fate of the manuscript.

George Henry Moore's problems as landlord and politician occupy later chapters of Mr. Hone's book. *An Irish Gentleman* was the title of George Henry's biography, by Colonel Maurice Moore, his second son. Their father's death left George Moore the Fourth, the writer, and Maurice Moore, the soldier, heirs to the family predicament—and to more, to the family *sense* of predicament. The keen British officer and the Catholic patriot ceaselessly struggled inside Colonel Moore's breast. Also, Colonel Moore loved Moore Hall with passion, his wife had lived there, his children were bred to love it—but Colonel Moore was only the second son and George had broken the entail and could do what he liked—a position George did not fail to make more than clear. George himself was martyrized by a divided wish—to be the free artist, to be the *grand seigneur*. He was plagued by Moore Hall worries wherever he went—fateful letters in dogged handwriting, sure to begin inside, 'Sir, I am sorry to tell you . . .' Letters that make the absentee's heart sink at an Irish stamp. Such letters had harried every reigning Moore; they followed George to Paris, to Ebury Street. The debts, the debts, the roof, the tenants, the drains, the trees. . . . How continue the page of unmarred prose with the Irish stamp sticking out under the manuscript? If George's mincing shoes and town clothes looked funny to his employees, he was none the less a just landlord; he rackrented Moore Hall for sensations only—the lake gave him two books. In essence, he wished to return—the Ely Place years had disabused him of Ireland, but he kept the physical feeling for Moore Hall— his ashes repose on one of the lake islands now. His cruelty—an unnerving sprightly sadism—to his over-sincere brother was, I think, neurotic, fruit not only of their over-intensive childhood but of generations of life before them rank with the family myth.

Mr. Hone's *The Moores of Moore Hall* covers much ground, in years and experiences, and is at the same time admirably compressed. He has dealt temperately with his material. He quotes just fully enough from letters—family letters, letters from stewards, trainers, debtors, neighbours and friends. Small momentous incidents come out—there was the cook, for instance, who could no longer stand heat. The racing chapters could not be livelier, and seem to me well-informed; the sticky political passages are done with clearness and calm. Here is not only a very welcome pendant to Mr. Hone's existing *Life of George Moore*, but a picture, put in perspective and generalized, of an Irish landed family's scope and fate.

The New Statesman and Nation.

HAMILTON ROWAN*

1943

At the end of July, 1806, Hamilton Rowan came home in style. Killyleagh was *en fête*. 'The bells of the church,' says his agent, Archibald Hamilton, 'which had lately tolled his father's funeral, now rang for joy at the son's arrival.' Spectators, waiting for miles along the road, were gratified by the length of the cavalcade. The four elegant bays were removed from the shafts of the carriage, and townspeople competed to take their place, so that 'the carriage and all the family were drawn triumphantly into the town —except Mrs. Hamilton Rowan, who very sensibly observed that she would not be drawn by human creatures who could debase themselves to the rank of beasts.' There were, in fact, demonstrations of just that kind against which Mr. Hamilton Rowan had been advised by his cousin and neighbour, Lord Dufferin. Himself, he was out to discourage nothing: all this was exactly after his own heart. He became, upon approaching the Castle, 'very much affected indeed. The scene was impressive to an extreme. After so long an absence—an absence which but a short time ago he thought was to be for ever—after so many years of exile and misfortune—once more to enter the seat of his ancestors and to enter

---

* 'The Desire to Please.' A Story of Hamilton Rowan and the United Irishmen. By HAROLD NICOLSON. (*Constable.*)

it as its proprietor and lord-absolved-restored-renewed-trium-
phant—'twas not easily to be borne. He melted into tears.'

The end of the exile—which had been, from the start, one long
slow graduation in disenchantment—marked the official end of
Hamilton Rowan as rebel, hero and patriot. It was the inconvenience of a long-standing death sentence—this only remitted in
Dublin the other day—that had kept the master of Killyleagh from
home. As for the 'misfortune'—you could trace the use of that
word to the agent's typical tactful Irish obliqueness, but actually
it goes pretty near the mark. There *had* been one consistent misfortune: temperament. From this had sprung (as the world saw
it) aberrations of every possible size. Hamilton Rowan, whose
mother had made a special journey to London that her child
should not see the light on Irish soil, had been born, in 1751, to an
age and into a society in which the moon was the enthusiast's only
proper friend. His parents' marriage had been of the kind that
is unpropitious most of all for the children: the English Rowans
deplored the Ulster Hamiltons; in Rathbone Place the boy was
reared with a bullying sternness intended to weed out every
Hamilton trait. Could Ireland fail to become the magnetic alternative to the detestable, daily English regime? Could nobility
fail to be queered into silliness, daydreams into obsessions, courage into bravado, in a youth made heir to his English grandfather's
fortune on condition he changed his father's name for his mother's
and not visit Ireland at younger than twenty-five? Apparently, he
both had his cake and ate it: while drawing, to meet his Cambridge
and other debts, on his expectations under the Rowan will, he
paid secret flying visits to his father and Killyleagh. But if this
duplicity kept both parties quiet it aggravated the conflict inside
the man.

Hamilton Rowan (whose surname at birth was Hamilton, and
whose children reverted to that name) was Mr. Harold Nicolson's
great-great-grandfather; *The Desire to Please* is Hamilton Rowan's
story. The book has a sort of double structure: there is direct
biography and there is speculation. The biography covers the
years and scenes—Ireland, London, Ireland, France, America,
Ireland again—at an even pace; the speculation is static and works
down, like a drill. The action is very clear, being part of history,
but the actor is, at times, a blurred, looming close-up, made more
rather than less mysterious by being almost too near the eye. This

placing of Hamilton Rowan just out of focus I take to be not a failure but a deliberate intention of Mr. Nicolson's art. The underlying subject of *The Desire to Please* is the feeling of a descendant towards an ancestor. The suspicion of being implicated, the over-susceptibility to certain traits, the sense of guilt, the touches of harshness (such as one might feel towards oneself), the wary search for the ulterior motive—all are there. That this analysis of the sense of being descended is fascinating, I need not say. It might, however, seem to the outside person that Mr. Nicolson has overshot the strong latent naïvety in Hamilton Rowan, and that he has either ignored, or abandoned as too simple, explanations of his character and his conduct that might be clear to another eye.

The story of Hamilton Rowan, as told in *The Desire to Please*, begins, not with his birth in Rathbone Place in 1751, but with his emergence—out of the family past, out of a disregarding silence and awkwardness—into his great-great-grandson's youthful consciousness. Mr. Nicolson, as a boy on visits to relations in Ireland, became aware of an ancestor who for some reason had not been quite the thing. This was the man whose face came to be printed, together with faces of other patriots, on handkerchiefs into which the Dublin crowd wept, outside a prison, during a 1920 political execution. How was he to be reconciled with the great houses? The child's first wish to drag anything awkward up gave place to intellectual curiosity, to the will to assimilate Hamilton Rowan, even though this might mean having to know the worst.

The worst does not seem so very bad. Hamilton Rowan's behaviour was impolitic. The failure of the projects he espoused made him appear mistaken. He threw his personal weight— and through everything he remains an impressive man—behind causes without enough calculation. The American Revolution and the French Revolution were two dawns that, for him, lost their colour late. He identified England with oppression, as he had had reason to do in youth. The sobriety and the vehemence of the Ulster Whigs, of the United Irishmen, rallied in him all those faculties that he had always, really, hated to dissipate. Acting with the United Irishmen, he conspired with France against England, in Ireland's interest. His adventures were, on the whole, ignominious; his troubled life held not one explicit heroic moment. His tastes were simple: he loved dogs and boating and his on the whole rather bleak wife. *Did* anything so consistent, so calculating, so fundamentally cold as 'the desire to please' really dominate him and determine the course he took? I see in him rather the desire to *be* pleased, to believe in masters, to release the waiting floods of his admiration. The ideas to which he had sacrificed, from which he recanted in order to return as master to Killyleagh, no longer drew any force from his nature: it was his tragedy that they had died in him. He was the principal sufferer from his own guilelessness.

The New Statesman and Nation.

WEEPING EARL*

1943

Hugh O'Neill was the second Earl of Tyrone. The title had first, in 1542, been granted by English patent to his grandfather, the limping Conn, who, with the formalities proper to 'The O'Neill's' person and to centuries of O'Neill independence behind him, came to Greenwich Palace to make formal (time was to show how purely formal) obeisance to the ruling English monarch, Henry VIII. Conn's predecessor in this act, thirty-one years before, had been his Ulster neighbour and kinsman by marriage, Young Hugh O'Donnell (son of Red Hugh, that 'full moon of the hospitality and nobility of the north') who left the presence at Whitehall as Sir Hugh. What had preceded, what was to follow, what was the motive for and who profited by the interchange of these equivocal courtesies? That lesser Gael, O'Conner Sligo, who deemed it wise to come in more or less entirely under Henry VIII's system of 'Surrender and Regrant,' was to provide a warning sinister enough to stick in the O'Neill and O'Donnell minds. The weak Earl of Desmond, after miserable years in London, still had his apotheosis—the Munster rising—ahead of him; he had been back again where his forefathers started before his head was hacked off in the wet woods. From Desmond the second Earl of Tyrone, who rode Munster with the English who rode him down,

---

* 'The Great O'Neill.' A Biography of Hugh O'Neill, Earl of Tyrone, 1550–1616. By SEAN O'FAOLAIN. (*Longmans.*)

had also something to learn. Ultimately, it was Tyrone (Hugh O'Neill) and Red Hugh O'Donnell the second who were the double kernel of the resistance to English expansion in Ireland in Elizabeth's reign.

Mr. O'Faolain's *The Great O'Neill* is a study of the man and his time—a time of which he was considerably ahead. As a character, Hugh O'Neill was and is inscrutable; he gave away little and left little behind. As general, as statesman with no defined State behind him, he was recognized by his contemporaries abroad. At home, patriotic myth has not only blurred but falsified his figure: from these however heroic mists it becomes his biographer's purpose to rescue him. As uncertain successor to the O'Neill lordship, he was occupied, till well on into maturity, with playing his own hand—and it was to the English interest that he should continue to be so occupied; hence the English flirtation with his successive rivals. The Elizabethans, as Mr. O'Faolain shows, were adept at giving slight tips to the rocking stone. The Anglo-Gaelic lord's lust for personal power looked like making him an amenable man—but were power once acquired, it could not fail to spell trouble. It was acquired, and did. O'Neill knew how to play up to the English idea that he was being kept banked down. He used years of quiescence to extend his domination and to multiply and to build up his men. Increasingly reluctant to fight the English, he became increasingly able to do so at any time. It took the climax of a series of English blunders to make Hugh O'Neill a patriot *malgré lui*.

Elizabethan England had instructed O'Neill, if it had not—or had it at all?—impressed him. For seven years of his boyhood he was allowed to view, from close up, the more august side of that civilization to be imposed on his own country, soon, by fire and sword. Sir Henry Sydney's taking of the boy of uncertain future back with him to his home in England may have been either an act of private compassion, or, equally, an experiment in policy. The English wish to civilize Ireland was as keenly felt as the Spanish wish to civilize Mexico, and was at least no less disinterested. Each Gaelic lord, on his brief appearance in London, looked shocking, with his air of contrary hauteur, 'his escort of gallowglasses, armed with battle-axes, bareheaded, their curls long, their shirts bright saffron, their sleeves flowing, and their tunics brief beneath their furry cloaks,' and rumour found him

worse than he looked. Each was the apex of his own tribal
system, into which, since Strongbow, the Anglo-Norman feudalism had seeped. Carew was to write to Cecil of 'the great desire
of the Irish lords to keep justice out that they may tyrannize with
absolute power, confiscating both goods and lives at pleasure.'
As for the creatures tyrannized over, they were savages by such
unmistakable showing that their reclamation would not have been
worth the gesture had it not excused the annexation of land. . . .
To civilize young O'Neill, to return to a place of power in Ulster
a perfected Elizabethan gentleman, would not be a bad idea—if
that *were* Sydney's. The lad knew Ludlow Castle, Penshurst,
where he was allowed to play with young Philip Sydney, London
(on a leash) and—under Leicester's patronage (which was to prove
more enduring than Sydney's)—Kenilworth.

Here, however, was a Renaissance character with whom
Elizabethanism did not take. For one thing, the subject was
glowering with a strong sense of family wrong: his uncle Sean,
'The Proud,' had successfully murdered his (Hugh's) father,
Matthew—beloved bastard and named heir of Conn O'Neill.
Over there in Ulster, Sean the usurper had now the field to himself. Pleached alleys, fishponds and graceful converse would,
under the circumstances, seem very unreal. To tolerate them
could be no more than a policy. Hugh O'Neill, upon his return to
Ireland at seventeen, had already begun to embrace those humiliations attendant on playing for English support. He was Baron of
Dungannon, but not, for years more, Tyrone. The satisfaction of
seeing his uncle's head on a pike was to be mitigated for him, too
soon, by the emergence of his second cousin Turlough, who not
unfavourably caught the English eye.

Hugh O'Neill was a man who knew how to behave—but knew
when not to. His public tears and his bawlings may have been
unstrategic: their effects could not have been bettered by calculation—they embarrassed his English peers; they gained time. He
had the knack of setting a scene his way: one crucial interview had
to be shouted across a stream; his talk with the second Essex (a
turning-point) took place with O'Neill on horseback in a river,
water up to the horse's neck, Essex high and dry on the bank.
Mr. O'Faolain's study must stand or fall by the importance he
succeeds in giving its subject—and to my mind it stands triumphantly: shrewdness and a perception on the poetic level are

equally present in the interpretation. The art and the artfulness of the novelist have been both used and subdued here. As to the history—the point of view, with its here and there almost blighting detachment, gives the record, *qua* record, still more point. The Elizabethan campaigns in Ireland do not make pretty reading —though it still becomes evident, in some contexts, that they are reading to recommend. Mr. O'Faolain, as an Irishman, shows unusual power to photograph this country's attitude to his own. Evidently it is the extra-Europeanism of Ireland, the lack of common memories based on Roman rule, that has been and still may be found repugnant. All the same, O'Neill, the 'savage,' could reach round England to entertain lively relations with Rome and Spain. He spoke a language, he acted in a tradition that Europe, if not England, was able to understand. He was not only Catholic and patriot; and not only as Catholic and patriot has he been studied here. He was the last of the barons—across the water, in England, the Tudor new order, raised over the fall of the barons, could still not be indifferent to his threat. In England, the overt Shakespearean tussle, the threat to the throne, was over: power-politics kept men jockeying outside the Queen's door. Is one to wonder that this last of the barons—this red-eyelashed, peering Gael, this salmon-fisher, this honeymooner disdaining the gallant word—tried Elizabeth's temper to frenzy, and, in the end, finished her? He was the fly in the ointment, the crack in the mirror, the thorn in the flesh. When he made his final submission to her Deputy, Mountjoy, O'Neill had not yet been told that she lay dead.

The New Statesman and Nation.

ONE IRELAND*

1937

Lord Dunsany, perhaps a little disorientated by the largeness of his publisher's invitation, halts and hovers rather over his opening chapters, then drops into his swing and writes an engaging book. High-handed, whimsical, bland, touchy, reactionary, and impossible to pin down to any point, here he has it all his own way— and what a way it is. *My Ireland* has, throughout, a sort of contrary

* 'My Ireland.' By LORD DUNSANY. (*Jarrolds.*)

soundness. It is written to please himself and, please God, in-
furiate others. The merit of the completely personal book is that
it often captures, or rather blunders upon, that general quality
that makes literature. This title (not his own choice) with its
possessive smugness is certainly putting-off; one is led to expect
some more of those whimsical retrospections to which the country
have been too prone lately. 'I shall never forget how the mountains looked as I hacked home, etc.' But here the relation felt
between the man and his land is profound, subtle and reticent.
The retrospections are pungent, and are so defiantly mustered that
they escape sentiment. Here is, for Ireland, more than sheltered
affection: this goes back further than Eton, a turn for the twilight
of history, or the Kildare Street Club. And here is, for this author,
a refreshing absence of mystic experience. What dominates the
book is satisfied love of a country, body and spirit—love which
the too apt pen, by making articulate, has too often denatured or
falsified: here it is not falsified.

In these pages, Lord Dunsany may be tendentious—in fact, he
is clearly out to be tendentious, with his *Sackville* Street, his
pouncing inverted commas, his little digs at the new Ireland that
are about as playful as would be the nudges of a surviving bog
moose—but he is not phoney. His feelings are too furious to
exploit. The finest part of his book, written in Ireland last winter,
is more or less of a journal and is about shooting. Turgenev,
Tolstoi, stake no claim on this as a subject; Lord Dunsany's experiences and reflections are his own. Art these days shows signs
of decamping from enlightened Metroland, where it has lodged so
uneasily; Horseback Hall is coming into its own again; we have
had quite enough, for a bit, about the country from the kind
hiker's angle; kindness to huntable animals is once more at a discount: art shows a re-mellowed attitude to sport. In fact, there is
now in sight rather too much extraversion and blood. But at this
still apposite moment comes Lord Dunsany, squelching about
Irish midland bogs with his gun, full of bloodthirsty tenderness
and of rude poetry either unselfconscious or raised to the hyper-
consciousness of art. He is authentic, full of tips (care of shooting
boots) and of plain facts:

The outwitting of golden plover depends, in one of its branches, on
going to the right spot in a hedge, while another man goes round to
the far side of a field and drives them over. But I did not go to the

right spot in the hedge, and only got one. Then I drew a small snipe-bog blank because it had been drained. But my gamekeeper pointed out that there was no harm in that, for it would be just the same again in two or three years. And this is undoubtedly true, for soil and air in Ireland seem to be at one in bringing back the bog to its own, wherever man has lifted the spade against it. The soil seems to work for the bog, while the damp air fights against man. And so the spade is laid by, and the bog steals softly back; and in a few years there it is again, as though man had never troubled its ancient stillness . . . Memorials to this struggle may be found all over Ireland, and they mostly seem memorials to the victors, the wind and the weather.

All through: the romantic, endemic feeling for ruin:

One does not fully understand Ireland if one overlooks the pace at which ruin floats on the gentle wind, and the grudge that the Irish soil seems to bear to civilization. Earth seems to triumph in the end over civilization everywhere, but a few decades in Ireland seem to have powers to bring down to oblivion, such as only comes with a thousand years to Egypt.

There is more, of course, to a book like this than shooting—there are personalities, hunts, legends, gossip, landscape and extinct cricket fields, now in pasture. Nostalgic and measured prose, which is at the same time vigorous, hangs over all this an iridescent veil. The book is not very happily illustrated by photographs of a Come-to-Ireland nature: these have little relation to Lord Dunsany's prose.

Lord Dunsany's turn of mind is his own, but his nature, his habit of living, are generic, inherited. The old regime throws out from time to time its artists, sports like this, minds that show degrees of creative, sometimes poetic, power—overbearing fantasists. Oddly enough—or is it odd?—lordly art has almost always a rude, sometimes not far from vulgar, and somehow saving quality: it may be orchidaceous, but it is rooted. Too cerebral bourgeois art, with its lack of attachments, is on the whole more often brittle, and so, ephemeral. There exists in one kind of art a touch of the peasant toughness that Proust saw in the Guermantes. For pages together in *My Ireland,* Lord Dunsany chooses to show himself as a quite impossible person—complacently dream-bound, overbearingly blind. Many might wish to displace him. But he has gone to the making of his Ireland, and his Ireland is valid—rich as peat with its memories, ignorant, but impossible to ignore.

The New Statesman and Nation.

DOUBTFUL SUBJECT*

1939

The past of Ireland is an uneasy subject: controversial, bloody and bitter, with no trappings, few uninterruptedly pleasant prospects down which the eye can run. To the English mind, that past is not even stirring—it is too full of defeats. The tragedy is too plain to permit analysis—and it is for analysis, inference or the picturesque that history is read now, as an exercise or another kind of escape. Peace-lovers seek the past because it is safely over—and nothing in Ireland is ever over. England's past is at present one of her chief assets; it must have only one adjective—'glorious.' And England's past in Ireland has not been glorious: its residue is a sort of embarrassment. When the Englishman looks at Ireland, something happens which is quite unbearable—the bottom drops out of his sense of right and wrong. That *méfiance* holds good in a generation: few Englishmen who served in His Majesty's Army in Ireland in those years that just preceded the Treaty care to be reminded of that country again.

So, ignorance of Irish history, in the English and most of the Anglo-Irish, has not been seen as a blot on culture—till now. The traveller finds few monuments. Till lately, a mist covered the centuries: sieges, risings, massacres, famines, forlorn hopes had been heard of; inevitably, Ireland appeared only in English popular history where the fates of the two countries most momentously touched. Her entity as a country, her continuous, underlying existence, her conditions were very little known of—except when conditions, through some access of misery, forced themselves on the English popular eye. Her native—as opposed to the Anglo-Irish—culture was, before the height of the Gaelic movement, ignored. In fact, Ireland was not objectified.

Lately, however, this ignorance—one might say this wish for ignorance—has begun to dissipate. What was at the most a sporadic sentimental interest in Ireland has given place to a demand for exact knowledge. This is to hand: Irish scholarship has never needed an outside impetus; for years it has been thorough and self-rewarding; to-day, simply, it meets with a

---

* 'Irish Life in the Seventeenth Century: After Cromwell.' By EDWARD MAC-LYSAGHT, M.A. (*Longmans*.)

* 'The Sword of Light.' By DESMOND RYAN. (*Arthur Barker*.)

wider recognition. Also, the output of semi-popular, but informed and temperate books on Irish subjects is on the increase. Ireland appears on the European map.

Here are two books which, in different manners, uncover tracts of the past, or the Irish scene. On *Irish Life in the Seventeenth Century* Mr. MacLysaght has done useful, thorough and extended research. This particular period in Ireland has been little touched by the social historian. Ireland just after Cromwell, with that influx of violently imposed settlers—the effects on her civilization, the confluence of temperaments, the unwilling adjustments, the repercussions of constitutional and temperamental changes in England—is a fruitful subject for study. Mr. MacLysaght has not aimed at a facile 'picture'; he has given no emotional colour. He has, more usefully, weighed and collated facts, then left the reader's judgment and imagination to work. He has drawn largely on letters and manuscripts—accounts by settlers, travellers and officials. One of his merits is, he examines every authority, allows, in any account he quotes from, for the writer's predispositions or temperament, and is as careful to warn against the hasty deduction as he is to avoid the hasty deduction himself. Especially where the matter is controversial (as in the chapter on the subject of 'Morals') he does not neglect to balance opposing views. At times this impartiality is carried almost too far: it becomes hard for the reader to draw any final inference—even so, one must commend his fullness and honesty.

As a result of this serious, dogged work a clear picture of seventeenth-century Ireland does come to form in the mind. The opening chapter on 'Characteristics and Traits' is general, but not blurred by generalizations. In 'The Gentry and their Dependants' appears the inevitable contrast between the unwelcome, enforced new upper class and their predecessors. There is an interesting note on the strong ties formed by the foster system. The absorption—in some happier cases—of the newcomers into the native background, the weathering-down of their foreign traits, is well shown; the idea that Ireland is predisposed to feudality is examined. Sports and recreations, within the period, life in Dublin and city life in general, 'The Clergy and the People,' amenities, culture, communications make the stuff of succeeding chapters. The writing, admirably concrete, is enlivened, though not overloaded, with anecdotes and quotations. Both for the initial

interest of its method and subject and for its promising value as
a book of reference, this solid, sufficiently graphic study of seventeenth-century Ireland should be recommended very highly indeed.

Mr Desmond Ryan's *The Sword of Light* treats a heroic subject
—the survival of Gaelic in Ireland—in a heroic manner. Mr.
Ryan's rather too highly dramatized style should not be allowed
to detract from the seriousness of his argument. Sub-titled *From
the Four Masters to Douglas Hyde,* the book begins with the early
seventeenth century, with the four Annalists of Donegal Bay and
their contemporary, the less exact Dr. Keating. Then there is
blind O'Calloran, the last of the Irish bards, who sang from house
to house in the eighteenth century, a chapter on the Ossian con-
troversy, and a picture of Miss Charlotte Brooke in Co. Cavan—
her ardour, her limitations, the impetus that she gave. The Gaelic
Society of 1808, the discouragement (stressed by Mr. Ryan) that
the Gaelic enthusiasts received from O'Connell, and the attempted
use of Gaelic for Protestant propaganda in the early nineteenth
century are the subjects of the middle part of the book. Philip
Barron's magnificent and abortive effort for Gaelic, sixty years too
soon, the brief life of his college on the Waterford coast, makes
one of the finest chapters. Mangan the poet, John O'Donovan
'the Fifth Master' are drawn with feeling—both as persons and
forces—and the Gaelic League, Dr. Hyde and the present-day
'victory' for the Irish language bring the book to its close as the
history of a culture (and something deeper than a culture) that
was threatened, ignored, persecuted, belittled but not lost.
Sources of the antagonism to Gaelic have been by turns political,
snobbish, religious. Mr. Ryan, with good will and a degree of
fairness, examines them all. His work is creditable; it may also be
popular.

The New Statesman and Nation.

DUBLIN*

1936   I

Dublin and New York are two standard examples of the grand
manner—the eighteenth century's and the twentieth's. Dublin

---

* 'Dublin Under the Georges, 1714-1830.' By CONSTANTIA MAXWELL. (*Harrap.*)
* 'A Biography of Dublin.' By CHRISTINE LONGFORD. (*Methuen.*)
* 'Dublin Old and New.' By STEPHEN GWYNN. (*Harrap.*)

exhales melancholy, the past and the sense of an obliterated purpose that no new world activity can exactly renew: an anticlimactic, possibly endless pause hangs over her large squares, long light streets and darkening Georgian façades. Meanwhile New York, congested on her narrow island, as beautifully brittle-looking as candy in the air, shoots higher yearly, throws out bridges across the Hudson and speedways across the State, tears herself down, re-piles herself in toppling masses and infuses the century with her nervous life. New York grew on a series of impulses; Dublin is rooted in political stubbornness: her great phase had the unity of a social idea.

Miss Maxwell has chronicled what remains—with every salutation of the new Ireland—Dublin's most fully vital, if not her most happy, phase. Under the Georges she was a European capital: as that she has still to find herself again. Strife and complexity, danger and bitter feeling have never released their grip on this unhappy town, but in the eighteenth century, under Grattan's Parliament, the Irish of the Ascendancy turned to them their most nearly unknowing face. Hemmed in by country trouble and shaken by city strife, the aristocratic dwellers each side of the Liffey maintained an almost Venetian level of gaiety. Entertainments were princely. Whatever else happened, they had a good time. Security may have bred, elsewhere, a sounder magnificence, but never magnificence at such fever pitch. Here the great were often shady, but few were shoddy. Trinity College threw out crabbed and mordant wits. The deaneries were head-quarters of good company. The Archibishop's wife drove round Dublin in one of the most dashing turnouts on record. The theatre, in spite of the difficulty of keeping the audience off the stage (on one occasion Sheridan had to clear the Smock Alley theatre with firearms), kept, at least to the time of the Union, a notably high form; concert rooms were packed with exacting audiences, and enthusiastic peers composed a private orchestra. The ladies' conversation was full-blooded and snappy, if not always informed. In clubs and drawing-rooms the rate of play was high; the consumption of drink and victuals at dinners was astounding. Elegance in the exact sense may have been rare: spleen and a tough, drink-pickled melancholy underlay much of the glitter: the glitter itself had a tarnish. The scandalous and infinitely regrettable Union struck all this fun in Dublin a fatal blow.

The conditions in which the poor lived were nauseating, even for the period. A certain amount of relief led to some grand building, though even the new Lying-in Hospital seems to have been open to criticism. The other hospitals, the prisons and orphanages were charnel-houses, with an immense mortality. Liffey floods increased the horrors of a very negative sanitation. English policy and foreign wars struck repeated blows at the Dublin industries: the city's distress-pressure was heightened by influxes of futureless, disaffected country workers. Protection— supported by bloodshed, sacked foreign-goods warehouses, burnt effigies and nocturnal howlings—did what it could. The fortunate classes, in so far as fashion and expediency allowed them, stood by what Irish industries there were. The charming and ill-fated Lord Edward Fitzgerald was not alone, though he was the most militant, in espousing a romantic nationalism. A curious and unspoken complicity of spirit between all classes must account for the fact of there not being, in a city of such extremes and such constant feverish pressure, more, or in fact any, sustained, class-hatred.

Miss Maxwell's book, which deals with many more, and more complex, aspects of eighteenth-century Dublin than I have given here, is the fruit of wide, thorough, unbiased and enterprising research. She is admirably documented as to the city's political, social, industrial, academic and artistic life during the period she covers, and she has set out her material most ably. Her style is unaffected, unemotional (though a curious, wry emotion exhales from its matter), concrete, and therefore, I think, excellent.

The New Statesman and Nation.

1936   II

Lady Longford's story of Dublin is tactful and spirited; it cannot displease the native, it will amuse the visitor. Her book—the first of a series of city biographies—had to be very short: she has done very well with it. She rushes through history with rapid discrimination, making pauses only for anecdote: rightly, for Irish history is a constellation of anecdotes glittering on a profound and untracked gloom. Briskness is essential to Lady Longford's manner and to the form of her book; only two subjects tempt her to potter—the Anglo-Irish (who first began to make trouble centuries back, while still called the Old English) and the Dublin theatre. It will be interesting to see whether other towns in the series—Jerusalem, Moscow, Los Angeles—offer as much as Dublin to common sense and fun. The Irish discussing themselves are often boring, long-winded and full of vanity: they have been given style recently by a new *désabusé* kind of English wit. It took an Englishwoman—and one with flair—to write this agreeable, vivid, smooth, un-bitter book. Her style and tone have their dangers: she comes in places a little too near smartness, but she gives tragedy place by respectful understatement, honours the fantastic and the heroic, and shows throughout a sober regard for fact. Dublin has loomed in art through a haze of native sentiment, often a tortured sentiment. But taste—of which so great a part is intelligent and voluntary—better qualifies the biographer. Lady Longford ably paints the city's portrait and summarizes its past.

Dublin, on the east, the Europe-regarding, coast of Ireland, owes her vitality and complexity as a city to a continuous influx of foreign life. The invader, the trader, the opportunist, the social visitor have all added strife or colour. The Norsemen found her a village—called Baile Atha Cliath, or Fort of the Hurdles—on the lowest ford of the Liffey. The river's mouth made a fine harbour, her position was strategic; since their day until lately she was garrisoned by invaders, whose ostentation has always been uneasy. Once her walls went up she became a capital, full of heady passions. The Normans, invited over, gave a bad deal, but got a worse deal than they had time to see. Prince John's Lordship of Ireland was not happy; he was frivolous, tactless and overbearing, offended the older Normans, who had been settling down, and gave early support to an Irish theory that when the English come over they go to bits. Richard II found enlightenment did not work. The Fitzgeralds, of Norman origin, made perpetual trouble; Lord Edward, finally, led a forlorn hope. Dublin, connected with Ireland by a system of nerves, registered and reacted to trouble throughout the country: the relation of Paris to France provides no analogy. She became the head-quarters of Protestant domination, of aristocratic pretension, of bourgeois power. A minority supported by theoretic authority fled to her at any crisis, to be fortified. Under Henry VIII, the Protestant aggression had its way in Dublin: George Browne, the Archbishop, found the greater part of Ireland unsatisfactory; he complained to Thomas Cromwell: 'The common people of this isle are more zealous in their blindness than the saints and martyrs were in the truth.' Puritanism, later, found the city slippery in its grip. Dublin has always been foreignly irresponsible; an uninformed enthusiasm commands it, and the Stuarts, attractive and kingly, were warmly supported there. The Restoration was signalized by a great burst of fun: the theatre (precious to Lady Longford) first came into evidence, and Roman Catholics were tolerated. In spite of defeat James II, owing to personal characteristics, became unpopular. Under William and Mary some hanky-panky over the linen industry brought capitalism into the open as a declared force. Longer lapses between violence made constitutional difficulties more apparent. 'The work of the Irish Parliament was very much obstructed by the fact that certain officials were English, and only came to Ireland in their spare time.'

Lady Longford makes place for portraits of Swift, Molyneux, Wolfe Tone, Grattan, Lord Edward Fitzgerald, Emmet, O'Connell and Parnell. Her desire, which is honourable, to place Swift in the gallery of enthusiast patriots makes her overlook, or ignore, the in-turning edge of his wit. To burn for Ireland is not to burn for truth: Swift never buried for Ireland the quality that he had. Lady Longford, referring to Swift's last charity—the leaving of his money to found a hospital for lunatics in Dublin—suppresses in her quotation his next couplet:

> He left the little Wealth he had
> To build a House for Fools and Mad;
> *And shew'd by one satiric Touch,*
> *No Nation wanted it so much.*

The anecdotes are well chosen, pleasant and pithy. There are pictures of pre-Union Dublin in redundant and crazy flower. The nineteenth century is summarized, there is a sympathetic family picture of the Wildes, a broad daylight photograph of the Celtic Twilight and a respectful résumé of 1916. Lady Longford does justice to Dublin's present urbanity: the startled and somehow not yet quite authentic glitter of cinemas and all-night cafés, the inexhaustible talk with its malice and unfocused uplift, the Grafton Street animation, the morning coffee, the theatre. Prolonged European disturbance offers Ireland an opening; she bids fair to

become for the English a more accessible Switzerland, an amiable,
rural country, now that the rifles have cooled there, poetry
with the sting drawn, a country with a decay-glamour, a touch of
the Old South. Dublin may make a bid to be Basle and Berne, the
clearing-house for the sensitive tripper, the intelligent pause on
the way to country house visits, the gateway to bay and bog. For
this her biography, informed and sophisticated, is exceedingly
well timed. But the city is not in tune yet; she is overcast like a
yesterday one remembers with no pleasure; her trams give her
away, they have no Continental brightness; they crawl through
the Georgian quarters with a rasping vibration and the red plush
inside gives out a dusty and charnel smell.

The New Statesman and Nation.

1936   III

At the first glance, Dublin nearly always delights the visitor by its
grand perspectives and large light squares, its at once airy and
mysterious look. Then there is a less happy phase in getting to
know the city—when it appears shut-up, faded and meaningless,
full of false starts and dead ends, the store plan of something that
never realized itself. The implacable flatness of the houses begins
to communicate a sort of apathy to the visitor: after her first smile
and her first grand effect, Dublin threatens to offer disappointingly
little. This stale phase in the stranger's relations with the city can
only be cut short by imagination and vigorous curiosity. Dublin
is so much more than purely spectacular; she is impregnated with
a past that never evaporates. Even the recent past, the nineteenth
century, leaves on some outlying quarters of the city a peculiar
time-colour. Every quarter—from where the two cathedrals
stand in the maze of side-streets, to the latest ring of growth,
where red villas straggle into the fields—has, in fact, got a character you could cut with a knife. The more you know, the more
you can savour this.

Unlike London, Paris, Edinburgh, the city, at each side of the
river, covers flat land. The earth under it forms no romantic contours, and does not thrust the buildings up into different levels:
from no point does one get a momentous view of the city. Her
position, between the sea and the mountains, is beautiful, but can

only be guessed at from her heart. Dublin's grandness, as a capital city, is anti-romantic; it lies in her plan, and her fine buildings, alone. Her interest lies in her contrasts, in the expression she gives to successive different ideas of living. Dublin does not represent Ireland; she is one aspect of it: she stands, or had stood, for wealth, for the imposition of power, for the generally European element that has made itself felt but never been quite absorbed. Not for nothing is she the capital of a country in which blood runs to the head: life here has been always lived at high pressure; everybody is highly articulate; this has always been a city of 'characters,' in which nothing gets done impersonally. Emotional memory, here, has so much power that the past and the present seem to be lived simultaneously. In Dublin, as in the rest of Ireland, if you do not know the past you only know the half of anyone's mind.

Mr. Stephen Gwynn's *Dublin Old and New* supplies that background which the stranger will need. This is not a guide book, and not a history—though it resumes those parts of the past always most present in the Dubliner's mind. There is information, but no bare information: what we learn is made palatable and given colour by Mr. Gwynn's smiling, unhurried style. To the Dublin-born person, this book rings true and is evocative; at the same time, Mr. Gwynn has known how to detach, from the web of Dublin's character, facts which will strike the stranger's imagination. He has, chiefly, traced the social growth of the city ; he relates its human history in the course of a tour through the streets themselves, picking out here a statue, here a tablet, here a building or corner dark with associations. He also gives, in words, such a vivid plan that the appended map is almost unnecessary.

He is at his best with portraits, and has great command of anecdote. His eighteenth-century Dublin has been knowingly touched in, but, wisely, he has given most of his space to the nineteenth century, assembling a good deal of unwritten history, filling in a tract between fact and gossip. He has taken aspects of Dublin of which he is most fully qualified to write. *Dublin Old and New* should endow the stranger with a sense of the city's continuous, vivid and far from placid life: the residential quarters, the university buildings will no longer present an obdurate mystery. The best of Mr. Gwynn's chapters have the spontaneity of talk, and follow the same compelling, zigzag line. A good deal of the traditional gloom of Dublin (which literature, lately, has reinforced) is relieved by his stories of witty lives. After the Union, Dublin declined from her aristocratic showiness: a good many families left and found their focus in London. But judges, divines, the great doctors, the Trinity College figures continued to enjoy, and to add to, the city's urbanity: there was less wildness, but there was wit, good living and dignity. In Ireland, the nineteenth century showed the best of its mellowness, without the industrial element. It had more grace here, though life was often tragic, never fully secure.

His chapter on the museums and galleries, touches the unhappy subject of the Lane bequest. Here, and elsewhere, something more natural than tact guides him through the complex history of a city in which almost every subject is controversial. The great quality of *Dublin Old and New* is its companionableness: it should be carried round with the guide book but not read in the street— its style is too retrospective and leisurely—read, rather, in the intervals of sight-seeing, or, best of all, in bed in the hotel. It should feed a taste for Dublin—and, also, bring to the notice those quiet and atmospheric quarters (along the canal, for instance) that the tourist often overlooks.

The New Statesman and Nation.

III

TWO PIECES

The Mulberry Tree

The Big House

THE MULBERRY TREE

1935   [Downe House]

The house with a shallow front lawn, swagged in July with Dorothy Perkins roses, stood back from a tarmac road outside the Kentish village of Downe. The main block, three stories high, had a white pillared portico and a dado of ivy, looking friendly and undistinguished. It contained classrooms and bedrooms for about sixty girls, the staff study and the dining-room. To the left facing the porch (as we seldom had time to do) was a stable-yard, to the right, a warren of painted iron buildings—gymnasium, music-rooms, wash-rooms—twisted off at an angle, parallel with the road. A low trellis of ivy concealed these windows.

The back of the house, one portion curving out in a deep bay, faced a lawn flanked each side by heavily treed paths, tunnels in summer. A bed of azaleas outside the senior study french window made the summer term exotic. Features of this lawn landscape were an old mulberry tree with an iron belt and a mound with a large ilex, backed by evergreen shrubs, on which Shakespeare plays were acted. It was usual during rehearsals to pluck and chew the leaves of the ilex tree. We girls were for ever masticating some foreign substance, leaves of any kind, grass from the playing fields, paper, india rubber, splinters from pencil-ends or the hems of handkerchiefs. In the course of my three years at school both the ilex and mulberry trees took on an emotional significance; under the mulberry a friend whose brother at that time captained the Winchester eleven, and who was herself our only overhand bowler, criticized my behaviour on an occasion, saying I had done something that was not cricket. The lawn gave on a meadow crossed by a path to the playing field: beyond the school boundary, meadows and copses rolled off into Kent pleasantly. In summer there was a great smell of hay. I remember also one June a cuckoo that used to flap round the school roof, stout, squawking and losing its mystery. It has taken years for me to reinstate cuckoos. The Cudham valley was said to be a great place for nightingales, but we girls can never have walked there at the right time. . . . From across country, features of this rather odd and imposing

185

back view of the house were its very white window-frames, a glass veranda on to which the drawing-room debouched and a modern addition, one side, in the form of a kind of chalet, from whose balcony I played Jezebel with a friend's teddy bear.

The survival of such childish inanimate pets was encouraged by fashion; several dormitory beds with their glacial white quilts were encumbered all day and shared nightly with rubbed thread-bare teddy bears, monkeys or in one case a blue plush elephant. Possibly this seemed a good way to travesty sentiment: we cannot really have been idiotic girls. A friend of mine wore a carved ivory Chinese dog round her neck on a gold cord for some days, then she was asked to wear this inside her djibbah. A good deal of innocent fetichism came to surround these animals; the mistress of the blue elephant used to walk the passages saying: 'You must kiss my elephant.' Photos of relatives, sometimes quite distant but chosen for their good appearance, the drawings of Dulac, Medici prints and portraits of Napoleon, Charles I, Rupert Brooke, Sir Roger Casement or Mozart lent advertising touches of personality to each cubicle's walls, slung on threads from the frieze-rail and flapping and tapping in an almost constant high wind from the open windows. The ever difficult business of getting oneself across was most pressing of all at this age: restricted possessions, a uniform dictated down to the last detail and a self-imposed but rigid emotional snobbishness shutting the more direct means of self-expression away. Foibles, mannerisms we therefore exaggerated most diligently.

If anyone said 'You are always so such-and-such' one felt one had formed a new intimacy and made one's mark. A good many young women were led to buffoon themselves. It seemed fatal not to be at least one thing to excess, and if I could not be out-standingly good at a thing I preferred to be outstandingly bad at it. Personality came out in patches, like damp through a wall.

The dormitories were called bedrooms, and we had little opinion of schools where the bedrooms were called dormitories. Ours were in fact the bedrooms of a fair-sized country house, divided into from four to six cubicles. The window cubicles went to the best people, who were sometimes terribly cold at nights; the door cubicle went to the youngest inhabitant, who could hold everyone up if her sense of decency were over-acute. 'You *can't* come through' she would shout; 'I am indecent.' The niceties of

curtain-drawing and of intrusion varied from bedroom to bedroom, according to temper, but we always closed our curtains to
say our prayers. No embarrassment surrounded the saying of
prayers at this school; in fact it would have been more embarrassing to have left them unsaid. Whom one sleeps with is always
rather important, and ill-assorted companions could cast a gloom
over the term. There was always one rather quiet girl who
patiently wished herself elsewhere, lurked a good deal behind her
curtains and was afraid to speak. As in a railway carriage, one
generally disliked one's companions less after some time. The
tone of a bedroom would be, of course, set by the noisiest girl,
who talked most freely about her private affairs. As one began to
realize that bedroom lists for a term were drawn up on a psychological basis, the whole thing became more interesting. Great
friends were not put together and we were not allowed into each
other's bedrooms, but it was always possible to stand and talk
in the door, with one toe outside. Assignations for serious or
emotional talks connected themselves with the filling of hot-
water-bottles and water cans at a tap outside the bathrooms, when
one was otherwise ready for bed. Girls of a roving disposition
with a talent for intimacy were always about this passage. A
radiator opposite this tap was in demand in winter; one could lean
while one talked and warm the spine through the dressing-gown.
The passage was dim-lit, with wobbly gas brackets, and it was
always exciting to see who had got there first. The radiator was
near the headmistress's door, and she would disperse any group
she came out and found. It irritated her to see us being girlish in
any way. We cannot really have been emotional girls; we were
not highly sexed and any attractions had an æsthetic, snobbish,
self-interested tinge. Conversations over the radiator were
generally about art, Roman Catholicism, suicide, or how impossible somebody else had been. At nine o'clock a bell rang from
the matron's room and we all darted back to our bedrooms and
said our prayers.

I first went to this school in September 1914. We unpacked
our trunks in a cement passage outside the gymnasium and carried
our things upstairs. The school must have re-assembled with an
elating sense of emergency, but as I was new I was not conscious
of this. Everything seemed so odd that the war was dwarfed, and
though one had been made to feel that one was now living in

history, one's own biography was naturally more interesting. I found my school-fellows rather terse and peremptory, their snubbing of me had a kind of nobility: whether this arose from the war's or my own newness I did not ask: as I had been told that this was a very good school it was what I had been led to expect. A squad of troops marching past in the dark on the tarmac road, whistling, pointed the headmistress's address to us in the gymnasium that first night of term. Wind kept flapping the window cords on their pulleys, the gas jets whistled and the girls drawn up by forms in resolute attitudes looked rather grim. The headmistress stated that it did not matter if we were happy so long as we were good. At my former school the headmistress had always said she knew we should be good as long as we were happy. That sounded sunnier. But in my three years at this school I learnt to define happiness as a kind of inner irrational exaltation having little to do with morals one way or the other. That night in the gymnasium I felt some apprehension that my character was to be lopped, or even forcibly moulded, in this place, but this came to be dispelled as the term wore on. The war having well outlasted my schooldays, I cannot imagine a girl's school without a war. The moral stress was appalling. We grew up under the intolerable obligation of being fought for, and could not fall short in character without recollecting that men were dying for us. During my second year, the *Daily Mail* came out with its headline about food-hogs, and it became impossible to eat as much as one wished, which was to over-eat, without self-consciousness. If the acutest food shortage had already set in, which it had not, meals would really have been easier. As it was, we *could* over-eat, but it became unfeeling to do so. The war dwarfed us and made us morally uncomfortable, and we could see no reason why it should ever stop. It was clear, however, that someone must have desired it, or it would not have begun. In my first term, we acted a pageant representing the Allies for the headmistress's birthday, and later sang songs of the epoch, such as 'We don't want to lose you, but . . .' at a concert in the village, in our white muslin Saturday evening frocks. Most eligible fighters had, however, by this time gone to the war and we can only have made their relatives more hysterical. An excellent bun supper was provided by the village committee, and some of us over-ate.

I do not remember ever discussing the war among ourselves at

school. Possibly some of the girls may have done so, but I had
a sense of inferiority owing to having no brothers and not taking
in a daily paper. Though, seated beside one of the staff at meals
one would say: 'Aren't the French doing splendidly?' or 'Isn't it
awful about the Russians?' The Danish music mistress, however,
had melancholia and we were not allowed to mention the war at
her table. I do not think it was so much the war that made her
melancholic as her unhappy friendship with the violin mistress;
any attempt to make conversation with her was the last straw.
She looked extraordinarily like Hamlet, and as she was a neutral I
always resented her taking up this attitude about the war.... If a
girl's brother were killed or wounded we were all too much embarrassed to speak of it. Though death became familiar, it never
became less awkward: if heroic feeling ran low in us I think this
was because the whole world's behaviour seemed to be travestying
our own: everywhere, everyone was behaving as we were all, at
our ages, most anxious not to behave. Things were being written
and said constantly that would have damned any one of us: the
world seemed to be bound up in a tragic attack of adolescence and
there seemed no reason why we should ever grow up, since
moderation in behaviour became impossible. So we became
in contradistinction violently precious, martyrized by our own
good taste. Our morbidity was ingrowing. I cannot, either,
remember discussing men. Possibly the whole sex had gloomy
associations. One or two of the girls fell in love in the holidays,
but something in the atmosphere made it impossible to talk
of this naturally without seeming at once to make copy of
it. All the same, I and my friends all intended to marry early,
partly because this appeared an achievement or way of making
one's mark, also from a feeling it would be difficult to settle to
anything else until this was done. (Like passing the School
Certificate.) Few of my friends anticipated maternity with either
interest or pleasure, and though some have since become mothers
it still seems inappropriate. Possibly, however, we were not
natural girls. We may have discussed love, but I do not remember how. The future remained very hazy and insecure. We
were not ambitious girls, though we all expected to distinguish
ourselves in some way. Not one of us intended to be L.O.P.H.
(Left On Pa's Hands). We lived, however, intensively in the
present; when the present became over-powering there was an

attic-loft over the bedroom ceilings in the main buildings, with
sacks and a cistern in it, where an enterprising person could go
and weep. Less fastidious people wept in their cubicles.

We were not in love with each other at all continuously, or, as
far as I know, with the staff at all. A certain amount of emotion
banked up in the holidays, when letters became important. During the school day we all looked violently plain: school uniform,
even djibbahs, cannot expect to suit everyone; red wrists stuck
out of our cuffs and our hair (short hair was not at that time the
prevailing fashion) was so skinned back that our eyes would hardly
shut. After games we charged indoors, stripped, rubbed down,
put on stays and private clothes, released our front hair and became a little more personable. On Saturday nights, in modified
evening dresses, quite a certain amount of glamour set in. In the
week, curvilinear good looks were naturally at a discount and a
swaggering, nonchalant air cut the most ice. If you were not good
at games the best way of creating an atmosphere was to be good at
acting. We acted a good deal. On Saturday afternoons, one or
two people who could play the piano emotionally had séances in
the music rooms. All this was the best we could put up in the way
of romance. All the same, one or two people contrived to keep
diaries, moon round the garden alone and be quite unhappy.

Competitive sociability and team spirit were rather well united
at my school by the custom of picking up tables. The first day of
term seven seniors shut themselves up and, by rotative bidding,
each picked up from the rest of the school a team of about eight
for her table at meals. Each team moved round each week to the
next of the seven dining-room tables, each table presided over by
one of the staff. The object of each team was to make the most
conversation possible, and to be a success: girls were therefore
picked with a view to chattiness, desirability, tact, table manners,
resource and charm. Certain unfortunate girls were never in
demand, and the screams of seniors repudiating them could sometimes be heard from the other end of the garden. It was a great
thing to be at the head of the most patently animated table in the
dining-room. Many of us have grown up to be good hostesses.
If a girl sat just eating on without saying anything the head of the
table would kick at her, if within reach. So that young nervous
girls got into a way of saying almost anything. The great thing
was to amuse the mistress whose table it was, and keep her smiling

constantly: each girl had to take it in turns to do this. There was a French table and a German table: the games mistress was usually difficult to talk to. The headmistress sometimes received our remarks with irony, and was inclined to say 'Quite . . .' The table rule bound us only for breakfast and dinner; at tea and supper we sat with whom we liked, few of the staff were present and very merry we were. Quarrels, if any, sometimes occurred at this time.

The other great social occasion was Saturday evening (as I have said). We danced (we thought) rather glamorously in the gymnasium to a piano, and dances were often booked up some days ahead. On summer Saturday evenings we walked round the garden between dances, feeling unlike ourselves. The garden was long, with lime trees and apple trees and long grass with cuckoo flowers in it: it looked very beautiful in the late evening light, with the sound of the piano coming out through the gymnasium door. On winter Saturday evenings we danced more heartily, in order to keep warm. The staff filed in in evening dresses and sat on a platform, watching the dancing, and occasionally being asked to dance, with expressions of animation which, now that I look back, command my respect.

Lessons must have occupied a good deal of our time, but I remember very little of this. What I learnt seems to have been absorbed into my system, which shows how well taught I was. I used to sit riveting, or trying to rivet, the mistress's eye, but must otherwise have been pretty passive. I spent an inordinate amount of time over the preparation for some lessons; the rest of my preparation time went by in reading poetry or the Bible or looking up more about the facts of life in the *Encyclopædia Britannica*. We were morbidly honourable girls and never spoke to each other at preparation or in our bedrooms after the lights were out. I often wonder whether in after life one has not suffered from an overstrained honour from having been too constantly put upon it in youth, and whether the espionage one hears of in foreign schools might not have kept one's sense of delinquency more enduringly active. In these ways, we were almost too good to last. We did not pass notes either, though one of my friends, just back from a day in London, once wrote on the margin of her rough note book, and pushed across to me, that Kitchener had been drowned. Perhaps the occasion may have excused the breach. I simply thought, however, that she was pulling my

leg. . . . Games were compulsory and took up the afternoon:
it did not matter being bad at them so long as you showed energy.
At lacrosse, girls who could run would pound up and down the
field; those who could not gripped their crosses fiercely and
stalked about. Lacrosse is such a fierce game that I wonder we
all lived through it. Hockey, though ungainly, is not nearly so
perilous. The only real farce was cricket, a humiliating performance for almost all. I never thought worse of anyone for
being good at games so long as she was not unattractive in other
ways; one or two of the games committee had, however, an air of
having no nonsense about them that was depressing. We were
anything but apathetic about matches: when a match was played
away the returning team would, if victorious, begin to cheer at a
given turn of the road; we all sat with straining ears; if the chara-
banc rolled up in silence we knew the worst. Our team so often
won that I should like to think we had given them moral support.

The literary society was presided over by the headmistress, of
whom I should like to place it on grateful record that she did
definitely teach me how not to write. There were gardens to
garden in, if you had nothing more personal to do in your spare
time, and, because of the war, there was haymaking in season.
Two or three of the girls who had formed the idea that they
wished to be engineers in after life spent a good deal of time
looking through the windows of the engine room at the light plant
and water-pumping machine; sometimes they were let in by the
geography mistress to help her oil the thing. The geography
mistress was a Pole, who had built the chapel as well as all the
other modern additions to the school. The chapel was put up
during my second year and dedicated by the Bishop of Rochester:
a friend of mine pointed out to me during the service that the
Bishop's sleeves were not white but of very pale pink lawn, and
I have had no opportunity since to correct this impression: perhaps it was not incorrect. The chapel was approached by a dark,
draughty and rather impressive arcade from the gymnasium.
There were no cases of religious mania or any other obsession
while I was at school.

Seeing *Mädchen in Uniform,* and reading more sensitive people's
impressions of their school life, makes me feel that either my old
school was prosaic or that I was insensitive. A toughish, thick
child, I did not in fact suffer in any way. My vanity would have

been mortified anywhere and my heart was at that age really all over the place. At my old school there was nothing particular to conform to, and the worst that can be said of it is that I got no kick out of not conforming to anything. I was only too well understood, and when I left school my relations complained that my personality had made rapid and rank growth. I talked too much with a desperate self-confidence induced perhaps by competitive talking at meals. I say with deference to the susceptibilities of possible other essayists in this book that I consider my old school an exceedingly good one. If girls ought really to be assembled and taught, I can think of no better way of assembling and teaching them. No one dragooned us; in the course of three years I never once heard the expression *esprit de corps* and we were never addressed as future mothers. The physical discomfort was often extreme but (I am prepared to believe now that its details escape mc) salutary. I regret that my palate has been blunted for life by being made to finish up everything on my plate, so that when I dine out with a gourmet my manner becomes exceedingly artificial. I was taught not only how not to write (though I still do not always write as I should) but how not, if possible, to behave, and how not to exhibit feeling. I have not much idea what more than ten people at my school were like, so cannot well generalize about our type or mentality. No one of my companions betrayed my affections, corrupted me, aggravated my inferiority complex, made me wish I had more money, gave me a warp for life or did anything that is supposed to happen at schools. There is nothing I like better than feeling one of a herd, and after a term or two I began to feel firmly stuck in.

Memory is, as Proust has it, so oblique and selective that no doubt I see my school days through a subjective haze. I cannot believe that those three years were idyllic: days and weeks were no doubt dreary and squalid on end. I recall the most thundering disappointments and baulked ambitions, but those keep repeating themselves throughout after life. I do not desire to live those three years again, but I should be exceedingly sorry to have them cut out of my past. Some years after I left, the house, after so much pounding and trampling, began to wear out; the school moved and the building has been reinstated as some kind of shrine, for Charles Darwin lived there for some years and died there, I believe, too. Our Morris wall-papers have been all stripped off

o

and the white woodwork grained: the place now rather seriously and unsatirically reconstructs a late Victorian epoch. Our modern additions have been pulled down; the geography mistress has re-erected the chapel, the gymnasium, the lavatories and the music-rooms elsewhere. When I revisited the place, only the indestructible cement flooring of these remained. To indulge sentiment became almost impossible. I have never liked scientific people very much, and it mortifies me to think of them trampling reverently around there on visiting days, thinking of Charles Darwin and ignorant of my own youth.

THE BIG HOUSE

1942

Big houses in Ireland are, I am told, very isolated. I say 'I am told' because the isolation, or loneliness, of my own house is only borne in on me, from time to time, by the exclamations of travellers when they arrive. 'Well,' they exclaim, with a hint of denunciation, '*you* are a long way from everywhere!' I suppose I see this the other way round: everywhere seems to have placed itself a long way from me—if 'everywhere' means shopping towns, railway stations or Ireland's principal through roads. But one's own point of departure always seems to one normal: I have grown up accustomed to seeing out of my windows nothing but grass, sky, tree, to being enclosed in a ring of almost complete silence and to making journeys for anything that I want. Actually, a main road passes my gates (though it is a main road not much travelled); my post village, which is fairly animated, is just a mile up the hill, and a daily bus, now, connects this village with Cork. The motor car demolishes distances, and the telephone and wireless keep the house knit up, perhaps too much, with the world. The loneliness of my house, as of many others, is more an effect than a reality. But it is the effect that is interesting.

When I visit other big houses I *am* struck by some quality that they all have—not so much isolation as mystery. Each house seems to live under its own spell, and that is the spell that falls on the visitor from the moment he passes in at the gates. The ring of woods inside the demesne wall conceals, at first, the whole demesne from the eye: this looks, from the road, like a *bois dormant*, with a great glade inside. Inside the gates the avenue often describes loops, to make itself of still more extravagant length; it is sometimes arched by beeches, sometimes silent with moss. On each side lie those tree-studded grass spaces we Anglo-Irish call lawns and English people puzzle us by speaking of as 'the park.' On these browse cattle, or there may be horses out on grass. A second gate—(generally white-painted, so that one may not drive into it in the dark)—keeps these away from the house in its inner circle of trees. Having shut this clanking white gate behind one, one takes the last reach of avenue and meets the faded, dark-windowed and somehow hypnotic stare of the big house. Often a line of mountains rises above it, or a river is seen through a break in woods. But the house, in its silence, seems to be contemplating the swell or fall of its own lawns.

The paradox of these big houses is that often they are not big at all. Those massive detached villas outside cities probably have a greater number of rooms. We have of course in Ireland the *great* houses—houses Renaissance Italy hardly rivals, houses with superb façades, colonnades, pavilions and, inside, chains of plastered, painted saloons. But the houses that I know best, and write of, would be only called 'big' in Ireland—in England they would be 'country houses,' no more. They are of adequate size for a family, its dependants, a modest number of guests. They have few annexes, they do not ramble; they are nearly always compactly square. Much of the space inside (and there is not so much space) has been sacrificed to airy halls and lobbies and to the elegant structure of staircases. Their façades (very often in the Italian manner) are not lengthy, though they may be high. Is it height—in this country of otherwise low buildings—that got these Anglo-Irish houses their 'big' name? Or have they been called 'big' with a slight inflection—that of hostility, irony? One may call a man 'big' with just that inflection because he seems to think the hell of himself.

These houses, however, are certainly not little. Let us say that their size, like their loneliness, is an effect rather than a reality. Perhaps the wide, private spaces they occupy throw a distending reflection on to their walls. And, they were planned for spacious living—for hospitality above all. Unlike the low, warm, ruddy French and English manors, they have made no natural growth from the soil—the idea that begot them was a purely social one. The functional parts of them—kitchens and offices, farm-buildings, outbuildings—were sunk underground, concealed by walls or by trees: only the stables (for horses ranked very highly) emerged to view, as suavely planned as the house. Yet, in another sense, the most ornate, spacious parts of these buildings *were* the most functional—the steps, the halls, the living-rooms, the fine staircases—it was these that contributed to society, that raised life above the exigencies of mere living to the plane of art, or at least style. There was a true bigness, a sort of impersonality, in the manner in which the houses were conceived. After an era of greed, roughness and panic, after an era of camping in charred or desolate ruins (as my Cromwellian ancestors did certainly) these new settlers who had been imposed on Ireland began to wish to add something to life. The security that they had, by the eighteenth century, however ignobly gained, they did not use quite ignobly. They began to feel, and exert, the European idea—to seek what was humanistic, classic and disciplined.

It is something to subscribe to an idea, even if one cannot live up to it. These country gentlemen liked sport, drink and card-playing very much better than they liked the arts—but they religiously stocked their libraries, set fine craftsmen to work on their ceilings and mantelpieces and interspersed their own family portraits with heroicized paintings of foreign scenes. Outdoors there was at first a good deal of negligence, but later one planned and planted demesnes. . . . All this cost money: many of these genial builders died badly in debt and left their families saddled with mansions that they could ill afford. Then, decline set in almost at once. A more modest plan of living would have made, in the end, for very much more peace: big houses that had begun in glory were soon only maintained by struggle and sacrifice. Sons were recalled from college, or never went there; daughters, undowered, stayed unwed; love-marriages had to be interdicted because money was needed to prop the roof. Husbands and wives struggled, shoulder to shoulder, to keep the estate anything like solvent, or, in the last issue, to hold creditors off; their children grew up *farouches,* haughty, quite ignorant of the outside world. And in this struggle for life, a struggle that goes on everywhere, that may be said, in fact, to *be* life itself, and should not therefore have anything terrible about it, the big house people were handicapped, shadowed and to an extent queered—by their pride, by their indignation at their decline and by their divorce from the countryside in whose heart their struggle was carried on. They would have been surprised to receive pity. I doubt, as a matter of fact, that they ever pitied themselves: they were obsessed, and to a degree exalted. They had begun as conquerors and were not disposed to let that tradition lapse. These big house people admit only one class-distinction: they instinctively 'place' a person who makes a poor mouth.

It is, I think, to the credit of big house people that they

concealed their struggles with such nonchalance and for so long continued to throw about what did not really amount to much weight. It is to their credit that, with grass almost up to their doors and hardly a sixpence to turn over, they continued to be resented by the rest of Ireland as being the heartless rich. Now this myth has broken down: I think everyone knows that life is not all jam in the big house. Nowadays, what I hear most commented on is the apparent futility of the sacrifice. New democratic Ireland no longer denounces the big house, but seems to marvel at it. Why fight to maintain life in a draughty barrack, in a demesne shorn of most of its other land, a demesne in which one can hardly keep down the thistles, far from neighbours, golf links, tennis clubs, cinemas, buses, railways, shops? 'What do you *do* all day? Isn't it very lonely? Do servants stay with you? Can you keep warm in winter? Isn't it very ghostly? How do you do your shopping?'

To most of these questions it would be hard to give a concrete and satisfactory answer. To some few of the big houses wealth and security have returned—or one should say had returned, for the war attacks these again. But in the majority life maintains itself by a series of fortuities. As I have heard many occupants say: 'I have no idea how we live, but we do.' Such people not only live but enjoy life. To the keeping afloat of the household not only the family but the servants contribute ingenuity and good-will. As on a ship out at sea, there is a sense of community. There is also—and this, I think, is the strength of such households—a very great feeling of independence: in the big house one does not feel overlooked; one lives by one's own standards, makes one's own laws and does not care, within fairly wide limits, what any-body outside the demesne wall thinks. This may tend to exaggerate, to the point of absurdity, the family's individual point of view: there are a thousand legends of eccentricity. But it does also make for a sort of hardiness and absence of social fear. And ennui, that threat to life in Ireland, is kept at bay by the constant exigencies, some of them unexpected, of the house and place. (This was not so in the more prosperous days—'Beautiful as it is, much as I love it,' wrote one of George Moore's ancestors about Moore Hall, 'I have not been able to exclude ennui from its pre-cincts.') No, life in the big house, in its circle of trees, is saturated with character: this is, I suppose, the element of the spell. The indefinite ghosts of the past, of the dead who lived here and pursued this same routine of life in these walls add something, a sort of order, a reason for living, to every minute and hour. This is the order, the form of life, the tradition to which big house people still sacrifice much.

From the point of view of the outside Irish world, does the big house justify its existence? I believe it could do so now as never before. As I said, the idea from which these houses sprang was, before everything, a social one. That idea, although lofty, was at first rigid and narrow—but it could extend itself, and it must if the big house is to play an alive part in the alive Ireland of to-day. What is fine about the social idea is that it means the subjugation of the personal to the impersonal. In the interest of good manners and good behaviour people learned to subdue their own feelings. The result was an easy and unsuspicious intercourse, to which everyone brought the best that they had—wit, knowledge, sympathy or personal beauty. Society—or, more simply, the getting-together of people—was meant to be at once a high pleasure and willing discipline, not just an occasion for self-display. The big, or big-seeming, rooms in the big houses are meant for just such pleasures of intercourse. They are meant for something more creative, and gayer, than grumbles, gossip or the tearing to pieces of acquaintances' characters. 'Can we not,' big, half-empty rooms seem to ask, 'be, as never before, sociable? Cannot we scrap the past, with its bitternesses and barriers, and all meet, throwing in what we have?'

There are difficulties—expensive 'entertainment,' for instance, cannot be given now. The distances *are* great—and an impalpable barrier stands between city and country Ireland. But there are buses and there are bicycles; we all eat and drink a good deal less, and would not find it any shame in a host not to offer what he has not got. The world around us is moving so rapidly that it is impossible to be dull-minded; we should all, more than ever, have a great deal to say; every newcomer, with his point of view, becomes an object of quite magnetic interest. Symbolically (though also matter-of-factly) the doors of the big houses stand open all day; it is only regretfully that they are barred up at night. The stranger is welcome, just as much as the friend—the stranger, in fact, *is* the friend if he does not show himself otherwise. But who ever walks in? Is it suspicion, hostility, irony that keep so much of Ireland away from the big house door? If this lasts, we

impoverish life all round. Or is it the fear that, if one goes into the
big house, one will have to be 'polite'? Well, why not *be* polite—
are not humane manners the crown of being human at all?
Politeness is not constriction; it is a grace: it is really no worse
than an exercise of the imagination on other people's behalf. And
are we to cut grace quite out of life?

The big house has much to learn—and it must learn if it is to
survive at all. But it also has much to give. The young people
who are taking on these big houses, who accept the burden and
continue the struggle are not content, now, to live for themselves
only; they will not be content, either, to live 'just for the house.'
The young cannot afford to be stupid—they expect the houses
they keep alive to inherit, in a changed world and under changed
conditions, the good life for which they were first built. The
good in the new can add to, not destroy, the good in the old.
From inside many big houses (and these will be the survivors)
barriers are being impatiently attacked. But it must be seen that
a barrier has two sides.

The Bell.

IV

PLAYS, PICTURES, PLACES

King Lear at Cambridge

Island Life

Royal Academy

Salzburg, 1937

London, 1940

Dover: 1 *June,* 1944

Folkestone, July, 1945

'KING LEAR' AT CAMBRIDGE

1938

King Lear might be called the plainest, the most comprehensibly sad of the Shakespearean tragedies. It starts at the level of the ordinary heart and eye. *Macbeth* or *Hamlet,* for instance, start at what is already a certain altitude of passion or intellect; they are based, like peaks, above the foothills of common experience; a special air is breathed from the moment the curtain rises; the characters have inherited tragic stature—we do not watch them attain it. Unless the mind is keyed up from the very start, unless ordinary terms and measures have been discarded, the tragedy may be perceived rather than felt. But *King Lear* opens upon a situation that (like an Old Testament story or a newspaper paragraph) engages interest directly, invites a naive moral judgment and involves the heart. The figures are, at the outset, hardly more than life-size; one does not have to stand back to take them in. Throughout the opening movement of the play, these figures are comprehensible in domestic terms. Though, as characters, they are simplified for their dramatic purpose, having each been pared down to a few elements, these elements are so rendered as to make the characters more immediately sympathetic or antipathetic than the characters in any other tragedy. Their behaviour, their action upon each other excites a strong personal feeling in the onlooker. Pathos is driven in.

This feeling of closeness to the characters in *King Lear* is essential, if the tragedy is to operate. The point of departure—the smiling kingdom, the court, the two families professedly ruled by love—must be felt in order to get, later, the sense of annihilation, of being outcast. All this Lear abandons—why, and for what? In his old age, because of his old age, he abandons power for feeling: the simple and proud act becomes an act of extravagance. By it he applies a test to what he does not suspect. This has to be watched, before it is fully felt—watched as by Kent, the foreseeing onlooker. Before the fatal transaction is completed, the terror has begun to kindle gradually: the parallel tragedy of Gloucester (*his* misinvestment, in his bastard Edmund) mounts at about the same rate. This love of love in the old, this need to celebrate the affections, to re-inherit life, this wilfully exposed heart, this recoil from what seems the insufficient fire—in Cordelia, in Edgar—must appear in the first scenes, still fairly quietly signalized in Lear's imperiousness, Gloucester's credulity. With an abandon more complete and fatal than the abandon in any sexual passion, Lear and Gloucester offer themselves to the ruthlessness of Lear's elder daughters, of Gloucester's bastard. These two victims believe ·that they are commending themselves to nature. Actually, nature has her proprieties; she stands back—as Cordelia stands back—from the extravagant demand. This demand, which seems to Lear to be inherent in nature, only extravagance, with interest behind it, meets. Falsely and momentarily satisfied, Lear rejects Cordelia as insufficient, Gloucester is turned against his more coldly begotten son.

Feeling cannot subsist on falseness: betrayal follows. The play turns on this axis of betrayal, and on one implicit question—what is the *nature* of nature? What (in man) are nature's properties? What is its moral colour? Is nature a sound ruling, or is it anarchy? Is nature in the heart, or in the heat of the blood? Is nature the force outside man, his anti-human ally, the force behind his begetting, the patron, the referee? What is natural, what is unnatural?

The moral position of nature in *King Lear* is different in regard to each of the characters. Edgar, the bastard, says: 'Thou, Nature, art my goddess.' Gloucester says: 'Nature finds herself scourged. . . . Love cools, friendships fall off, brothers divide. . . .' Lear says unkindness 'wrenched my frame of nature from its fixed place,' and hopes any child of the cruel Goneril's may be 'a thwart disnatured torment to her.' He asks: 'Is there any cause in nature that makes these hard hearts?' Regan reproves Lear: 'O, sir! you are old; Nature in you stands on the very verge of her confine: you should be ruled and led. . . .' Albany turns on Goneril for her treatment of Lear: 'I fear your disposition: that nature, which contemns its origin, cannot be border'd certain in itself. . . .'

The Fool is the line of reason ruled through the play. He succeeds Cordelia as the impartial voice, heard through the mounting quarrels, through the Heath scenes with their orchestration of storm and madness. Madness supplies the august and terrible distance in which Lear's figure at once recedes and towers. Feigned madness transports Edgar; he has been a plain character; his application to madness seems to open a door through which another self rushes: Poor Tom is a speaker behind his reason, a speaker who had been waiting while Edgar reasoned and vacillated. Tom's is the free speech of dissociation, Lear's the constricted speech of torture. Gloucester, blind, answers Lear, mad, with the voice of someone disorientated by the loss of a sense. Throughout the middle scenes—the Heath scenes, the mad scenes—these figures are driven, obliterated as though by the storm: their voices come from a distance.

Towards the end of Act IV, the figures begin to come into closer view again. It is a terrible morning after the storm, but morning. Goneril, Regan, Edmund intrigue, murder, but there are no more dæmons. Lear wakes to Cordelia's presence. The unnatural sinners are extinguished, leaving Kent and Albany. The stage is quiet when Lear approaches the audience, Cordelia dead in his arms, with his 'Howl, howl, howl, howl!' The extreme quiet, while the looking-glass does not mist, the feather does not stir, makes sadness conclusive—Cordelia's death vindicates nothing; it is a total loss, the answer to a question that never should have been asked.

All this appeared with its full force when, last week, at the Arts Theatre at Cambridge, the Marlowe Society and the A.D.C. presented *King Lear* in its entirety. The tragedy could not have been more fully realized, or played with greater lucidity. The anonymous and impersonal actors seemed to be saturated not only in their own parts but in the entire play. The acting was vital: a good deal of natural vigour had been schooled, though not schooled out of existence—the effect of this was that there were no obvious accents, no *tours de force*. Thus, these performances did *King Lear* a rare service: they offered an unobstructed channel for the rush of the play. Too often, the natural and imperative rhythm has been tampered with; the scenes have been rearranged—at Cambridge, they were played in their written order, and in this order their power is cumulative.

The movements and the grouping were excellent—remarkable in the Heath scenes, so easily incoherent, and in the final scene, with its pattern of static figures. Memorable also was blind Gloucester, with Edgar, where there was no cliff. The producer should be praised for his use of action—used to heighten and point a moment, never used distractingly. He also taught the actors to make their stillness significant, to make their silences tell, and to bring out movement by contrast. Not a scene opened or a figure entered without effect—and thus, in spite of the unromanticized playing, no passage was abstract or monotonous. *King Lear* must be an ordeal—to produce, to act or to see. Here we had both its height and its tenderness.

The New Statesman and Nation.

ISLAND LIFE

1938

Coincidence has produced, in this last week, two plays which, while they have no underlying resemblance, are alike in one thing: they both deal with emotion intensified by geographic conditions. In *Land's End* at the Westminster and *No More Music,* the London International Theatre Club production at the Duke of York's, the characters are, by isolation in the exact sense, driven in on each other and on themselves—Mr. F. L. Lucas's in a Cornish cliff-top house rocked by equinoctial gales, Miss Lehmann's in a West Indian island hotel. This makes what happens, in both cases, much more circumstantial, and destroys what is, in most plays, an initial unreality. In the general run of plays, a great hitch and annoyance is one's sense that outside life—that is to say, the general life of the characters, not related to what is happening immediately—has been unreally suspended, or cut off. The characters, placed for observation in a lit tank, without currents or shadows, cannot give either emotion or behaviour the value of their context in the whole of life—and at the same time, by their claim to be naturalistic, they lose poetic significance. In real life (or what is called real life) drama is almost impossible: one is not detached enough; there is no time; the interior tension that exists in most people seldom makes itself felt. The routine by which we live is soporific. 'Life-like' plays, that affect to deal with people in their habitual settings, practising their professions, occupying their homes, nearly always come down through not making routine felt, through ignoring its tremendous anti-dramatic power—that checks situations, that neutralizes character. Drawing-room drama, once, had its special privileges, and approached in its own way its peculiar reality. Now, the increasing plea for naturalism, for the common-sense view, for the ourselves-as-we-are play (often semi-sincere) has produced a predicament: if the non-poetic theatre is to have any importance it must, if not embrace, at least begin to account for the whole of life. The boards are no longer charmed.

No More Music, however, falsifies nothing. The characters have all left what passes for life with them at the other side of the world. They have already detached themselves from their settings by the deliberate act of taking ship, in January, for the West Indies. Mrs. Gobbett's committees are far away; family life no longer touches the introverted Hilda, and the vicissitudes of Mrs. Bloxham's London friends seem part of dream experience. Old Mr. Guthrie arranged some time ago to come here and die. For the duration of these people's visit, the lounge of Miss Leith's private hotel, the tropical light outside, the brilliant coast below have become the world, the sole world. A residential hotel lounge is a natural stage, always set for something to happen: its inhabitants live unconsciously keyed up. Therefore the entrance of Jan and Miriam has (as it would in life) a world-wide effect.

Jan Loder, the painter, and his mistress, Miriam, are born precipitants. Articulate, *désabusés,* tense with nervous emotion inside their self-made circle, they arrive one day off a steamer—and everything is changed. The temperature begins rising. The lounge enjoys music; old Mr. Guthrie grabs at life from the shadows; Hilda's exaltation and agony begin. Miriam, always hoping for a solution, has worked on Jan to come out here—but here, too, she is to suffer torments of clear sight. Jan continues to exercise, here as everywhere else, the indifferent power of the self-obsessed person: to know him is to suffer inside his orbit. His approach to the sealed-up Hilda is idle, but not quite meaningless even to him. He and Miriam are both static characters: they drill down into themselves but do not proceed. The last morning, after a night electric with storm and tragedy, leaves them much as they were. Hilda, washed out to sea, has been too dynamic for them. Dramatically, all this is excellent.

Miss Lehmann has kept, throughout the play, a balance between the banal and the heroic. The mood is, with a few breaks, astringent; the dialogue is pointed, vivid, light. Some monologues could be shortened; more could be left implicit—for the characters make their momentum and their direction felt from the first. Hilda, in particular, is once or twice more articulate than seems in character; her idiom is once or twice too like Miriam's. Actually, Miss Beatrix Lehmann's acting, with its command of violent silences, violent immobilities, could make Hilda palpable, almost, in dumb show. The casting of *No More Music* does not show one error: Mr. Jack Hawkins' Jan, Miss Jane Baxter's Miriam and Miss Margaret Rutherford's Miss Leith stay longest in the emotional memory, but in a cast in which no character is entirely minor, no actor has let Miss Lehmann down. The production and setting both heighten the atmosphere. The London International Theatre is to present this play at the Duke of York's for two more Sunday performances—after which, surely, it ought to have a regular run elsewhere?

In *Land's End,* at the Westminster, Mr. Lucas has attempted to rush the barrier that divides the discursive from the melodramatic play. His people, with the exception of Hector Galbraith, explorer, are of the type who say 'Such things do not happen.' Possibly Mrs. Galbraith is a more truly desperate character than her husband, who talks much too much in the second act before coming into play with pistols and whips. Mrs. Galbraith lives in a haze of talk; her two adolescent children love to define situations; her lover talks; her husband talks; her bat-like Cornish charwoman utters long maledictions. Mr. Lucas, in building up the drama from both sides, seems to distinguish too clearly between two sets of ideas: ideas which are not his own but which are dramatically plausible, and ideas which are his own but are not dramatic. Thus his own honest doubt hangs over his big scenes. Violence is imposed on his characters from the outside; it does not seem to spring from their own natures. There is a click of clockwork about Hector Galbraith; he is not quite mad enough not to be academic. His monologue, back to the fire, to the two trapped lovers should have one purpose only—to tighten the screw on them. Was this the time for pure ideas? Really it was not.

There are moments which are fine theatre—for instance, Mrs. Galbraith's languorous, intimate greeting, as she lies on the sofa with her back to the door, to someone she takes to be her lover back from the post, who is in fact her husband back, for blood, from Africa. There are some excellent pieces of Grand Guignol—the duel, with Mrs. Galbraith's gun nosing between the curtains. The quickness and tension of the third act, when everyone's future hangs on the girl Valentine, an Electra with a green conscience, lasts to the final curtain. It is the first act that drags, that needs cutting and tightening up. Miss Cathleen Nesbitt's Mrs. Galbraith is magnificent; Mr. Alan Napier does well as the civilized Hugh, and Mr. Cecil Trouncer as the savage Hector. Here, as in *No More Music,* the felt isolation makes for validity: there *is* no outside world.

The New Statesman and Nation.

P

ROYAL ACADEMY

1936

The Royal Academy has opened for the hundred and sixty-eighth time, to settle—at least for the early summer—a good deal of this nonsense about art. The grey court of Burlington House is packed with shiny cars; the scene looks alert, decided and very massive, like an annexe of Whitehall. There is no reason why art should be lowering or upsetting, should put into one's head ideas not already there or be a tactless mirror. The stairs inside Burlington House are broad as the stairs to heaven: at the top there is reassurance, or, at least, escape. May is no time to inquire what art is: if a group of important people did not know, there would be no Royal Academy. Art can be civic, jolly, reverent, tender, virile, coy. On the title page of the Academy's light blue catalogue a quotation from Bridges, like a fanciful heading to a menu, sets the tone of the show and settles the matter finally.

Once we know more or less what we are in for, no one is fonder of art than we English: is it not part of our heritage? Art teaches us to see life, so full of colour and quaintness that in our hurry we often overlook. When we totter out of the Royal Academy, everything that we look at for some time after composes into pictures in thick gold frames, which shows that we have developed the seeing eye. Art teaches us to observe the moods of nature and reminds us that nature is always going on. Art makes us sympathize with the lower orders by showing them in market places and pubs. Art helps us to find beauty by starring places or objects in which it may be found. There is no reason why art should not move with the times and explore our civilization, as well as nature, for spiritual influences: trams, esplanades and bungalows may be perfectly proper subjects if treated well. Every year our Academy becomes more broadminded. There is no harm in English painters glancing abroad and learning to paint a little like Monet, Utrillo or Van Gogh so long as they do not lose their normal point of view. Normality is a major part of our heritage: Americans by calling it normalcy show that they are not

normal in the true sense. It is the business of an artist to paint
objects recognizably, give moral pleasure and make art pay. If
it does not pay there must be something wrong with him; if it
does, he is taking his place in society. He should turn up at the
Private View looking as much like an artist as possible, in order
to contribute to the fun.

Every May, then, Burlington House opens its doors to give
art, like the Royal Family, its place in the heart of the nation, to
assert standards and discourage silly ideas. The Chinese, French,
Italian or Flemish pictures which hung there during the winter
have gone back where they belong. They are not quite forgotten;
they have affected fashion. At the Private View, younger ladies'
hats and collars remember them prettily; one or two of the glossy
pictures above the hat-line reflect their influence. The winter ex-
hibitions are education, proper to grim grey months. But at the
Royal Academy everything is much jollier; art not only uplifts,
she flatters and entertains. The most winning, perhaps the only
winning, feature of the crowd inside the Academy is that it is not
pretentious. It is here not because it ought to be, because the
B.B.C. or its high-class friends have been at it, but because this
is what it really enjoys. There is an honest exuberance which one
might call smug. Almost all the pictures beam with a mediocre
sincerity. They are by people empowered by command of a
medium to express, not a general truth (these are so hard to come
on, that to as much as discover one is the prerogative of genius:
even then, it takes decades to get a truth across) but a general
sentiment. These are pictures by people sincere above a certain
level, below which it is not wise to go. This month, Burlington
House is glossy and bland with pictures that represent the norm
of English honesty, susceptibility, power or wish to see. Many
people get upset—which is a credit to them and shows that they
have a soul—by bluebells, moonlight, a Scottish glen, a procession seen from a window, a tree in flower, nubbly sheep crossing
snow, a home in sunset, young children skipping along a beach:
they feel they wish they could paint. These happy exhibitors can.
That is to say, they can so treat with form and apply colour as to
give represented objects the ideality of a homesick Englishman's
memories, a clerk's regrets for a finished holiday.

The blandness of the whole is unnerving. The English must be
the most alarming race on earth; they ride down a minority so

unconsciously. An evenly wide zone of facetious tolerance protects
what few vital beliefs they have. You cannot be alien from them
in feeling or nationality without writhing under their fair play.
Their prudery of spirit is so infectious that to force them into the
open becomes embarrassing. They see themselves as St. George
got up as Old Bill. Their good-natured fun has disgruntled into
existence a minority that is too largely tedious, fractious or
second-rate. To dissent is not, unhappily, always to be excellent.
Minorities make themselves worlds which become provincial and
nearly watertight: there is a good deal of horrid, pert, minority
snobbishness. To run down the Royal Academy is too easy fun.
It is nothing but melancholy to see the greater part of the English
being fed the art they deserve. This annual national gesture, this
assent to art every May is grave enough to make one fidget, however detached one is. The English have dignity, they are not
nincompoops: why should this national show be such a farce?
There are three or four good pictures nearly every year; most of
the rest show a muddled vitality. The old hands know the tricks
of their trade too well, they can take their top notes without a
quiver, but the younger exhibitors have gone all out, however
misdirectedly. The public comes in perfectly good faith. August-
ness still hangs over the Private View.

The Private View is very august indeed. Everyone seems satisfied with themselves and art. On the lozenge-shaped centre
benches in each saloon sit very old grand people, having preserved in orris the elegance of decades ago. Doddering grand old
men nurse their silk hats. The farded bluish faces of grand old
women quiver with feather-shadows; feathers or yellow ermine
are round their necks; they look round like owls in daylight. The
thick unseated crowd moves round the lozenge benches like
stirred porridge. May 1, 1936, was Aprilish, sun rolled in infre-
quent waves through the high glass roofs. But the canvases
would have brightened a thunderstorm. Younger people,
though more mobile, were less dashing: a few orchids in button-
holes and small smart turning heads did not leaven the mass of
dowdiness. It was inconceivable that beings, all human, should
vary so very widely in shape and style, and so few be quite right.
In the congested human traffic, blocks determined the pictures of
the year. Where someone stopped they all stopped, as though
there had been an accident. Only the old sat on, like Trafalgar

lions. The noise, though stupefying, was not irreverent: the whole effect was cathedralish. Why disestablish art?

Fatigue and bemused respect for this rolled one flat. Pictures that I remember as being good looked far off, at the time, and related to nothing there—the late Miss Beatrice How's *L'Infirmière* (392), pictures by Miss Ethel Walker, Mr. Fitton, and a flower piece by Miss Beatrice Bland. I should rather see them elsewhere. I may have missed several others. Visibility, that day, seemed the chief merit. Mr. Simon Elwes has painted the Duke of York, heroic (150) and, very nicely, Sir Richard Sykes with a butler and perspective of cool rooms (415). Not far from the Duke of York, Mr. Ranken's *Portrait Group* (135) arrested the eye with the immense size of its canvas, the height of its blond young people, the alliance of voluptuousness and high prosperity. There is an impressive picture of Canadian fecundity. The punctuality with which Dame Laura Knight reproduces her circus pieces is amazing: I learn that her *Spring in Cornwall* would have been the picture of the year had it not been exhibited already. Otherwise she gave no reason to stop. Mr. Augustus John's two portraits (57, 168) stopped one inevitably. Mr. Munnings sent, this year, fewer horses and more landscapes. Considering all he got in, Mr. F. O. Salisbury's canvas for *The Heart of the Empire, 6 May, 1935* (163), is not really so very large. The outstanding Lavery picture was *Summer* (229). Sir D. Y. Cameron, Messrs. Lamorna Birch, Brockhurst, Russell Flint, and Connard showed their known conviction and verve. There was nothing out of place, like a Sickert. I saw not a portrait that could have displeased the sitter. There were the usual flower pieces and decent nudes, allegorical or otherwise. The Misses Zinkeisen's charming, dashing pictures were the best of the spreading *Vogue*-cover school. Child portraits show an increase in sensitivity. The Anning Bell manner is spreading too.

I hope no one will say the Academy is going off. This 1936 exhibition seemed to me very showy. Either blow the whole thing up or like it the way it is.

The New Statesman and Nation.

SALZBURG, 1937

By now the Festival will be over and everyone who was at it will be going away. Pressure will subside in the town crowded between two rocks and strung along the unnaturally quick river. A loud hum and a routine of excitement has been imposed by the visitors. I take the norm of Salzburg to be a perpetual Sunday afternoon. Lush fresh uncut grass grows in the gardens of the silent villas, and weeds lodge in the cracks in the steps of the municipal buildings. The stucco residential streets, and the shady faubourgs at the other side of the tunnel through the rock, kept right on through August their dusty hush, disturbed only by the occasional tinkling of a piano by some unmusical child. Already the metal of autumn was on the lime-trees, and down alleys and up the wooded height the powerful quiet of autumn seemed to be waiting to come out when everybody should go.

The Salzburgers, relaxing, may fritter away on each other what is left of their tired spontaneous charm. Pulling up square to their desks, they unlock the tills and tot up the final accounts. At the banks, no longer busy with changing foreigners' money, an involuntary understanding smile will communicate itself even to the cashiers. It has been a successful season.

A highly successful season. Everywhere was booked up. There was a great last-minute trade in tickets; the tout was in power; the late-comer paid through the nose. There was not even standing-room in the Café Bazar, where everybody felt bound to show up at least once, so that this place became a sort of social register. At the height of a day at the height of the season there was almost nowhere you could sit down, and certainly nowhere you could sit down without sitting by someone else, which made you feel what a gathering you were at. It was impossible not to share your café table, but less oppressive to do so with a complete foreigner. Those who secured standing-room in the Café Bazar could remain for hours craning their necks round, obliged to pay nothing, as drinks could not be served to them. The only place

214

where it was forbidden to stand was the main bridge with the
scarlet-and-white banners. If you stopped here to look at the
blue-glassy panorama of mountains, a policeman coaxed you to
move on. This was the only point at which Austrians interfered.
Otherwise they behaved like a nice school that has had a lecture
on good manners to a visiting team. Their shops were crowded
with special objects that could be of little interest to them.

Articles of native dress are chiefly sold to the visitors. A good
deal of excitement goes on before hotel mirrors during the first
phases of dressing up. Few visitors, thus got up, look con-
spicuously ridiculous, though men conscious of hairless pink
knees communicate their distress. The effect of the bunchy dress
with the searching diaphragm-line on women is pretty neutral.
It makes Englishwomen look like helpers at an English garden
fête. It shows off well the American exotic make-up, jewellery
and curled heads. It divides ex-débutantes sharply into two
classes, the self-consciously depraved and the merely self-conscious. The French only seem to buy such garments as seem to
them to have an intrinisic chic, such as off-white circular belted
frieze capes. These capes can only be worn by the unsloppy. The
dressing-up shows the visitors to be diligently merry; it shows that
they have money to throw about, which is good for their morale
and the morale of the town.

In Salzburg in August it is either very hot or very wet. In
September perhaps there is a nip in the air. The August weather
makes for a sort of gay lassitude: in the rain, which is dark brown
and torrential, you cannot go anywhere; in the heat you do not
want to. The river protests against this feeling of lassitude with
its neurotic speed. Livid, opaque as milk of magnesia, not
reflecting even the bluest sky, it tears between the weed-studded
embankments, split angrily by the piers of the main bridge. The
social dynamo is on its right bank. On its left bank, the grand and
silent part of the town is packed in under the towering bare rock.
Two funiculars play up and down this rock from sources almost
impossible to discover. One goes up to the fortress, the other up
to a restaurant. The heights between these two salients are
crowned by a forest-park, sylvan in character, full of glades and
dells, in which a sort of ghostly June persists. Peasants were busy
saving a second crop of hay there. Round the edge of the plateau
a chipped bench faces every extensive view. Hand in hand,

sentimental moral lovers in shorts and aprons make the place look like a nineteenth-century print.

After dark an inept searchlight wavers from this height, directs itself on the fortress, skids off it, picks out the façade of the cathedral, skids off that, fumbles with innocent slyness about the roofs of the city, catches now a dome, now a pavilion lodged up among the trees on the opposite height. From near the stance of the searchlight, when you are not at the Opera, you look down dizzily over a railing and see the Festspielhaus entrance throw out its mat of hard theatrical glare. There is the nerve of Salzburg.

Almost everyone admits to hunger during the Opera. To smoke in the intervals, you go out into the open-air theatre quarried by Reinhardt for the production of *Faust,* and stand looking up the rock in the dark. But out here you can purchase nothing to eat. Hunger is so exalting that during a last act you practically levitate. . . . I met nobody who had been lucky enough to see Toscanini or even Bruno Walter drive away from the Festspielhaus at the end. . . . The interior of the present Festspielhaus is arty-crafty (peasant style) and stuffy: none of the proposed changes can be for the worse. The dark wood beams ruled across the heavy ceiling give you an uneasy feeling in the scalp if you are claustrophobic in any way. But the Mozarteum is elegant inside, and the little Stadttheater is a gem.

The linked empty pale-coloured squares under the rock, round and behind the cathedral, have peculiar acoustics that make bells' echoes echo a long time and draw out the splash of the baroque fountain between weeping willows into a sigh. The façades and stretches of gravel are dazzling here. You are commanded by the grandness of the Prince Bishop. Tucked between the rock and another baroque church is a sunless cemetery of immense charnel elegance, with stone helmets on the tombs, and arcades of family vaults.

Favoured hours in Salzburg were at the Café Glockenspiel, whose flank adjoins the Cathedral square. It is from this café's veranda that you can most pleasantly watch dusk fall. The Glockenspiel tables are imperfectly screened from the square by exotic plants with long, ribbed leaves. At 6 P.M. the real Glockenspiel, or carillon, sweetly strikes out overhead the serenade from *Don Giovanni.* After dark they will floodlight the fountain with the cavorting stone horses. There is a smell of dust, awaiting to-

morrow's watercart. In the last light, humble figures slant across
the square from the humble streets. Chaste chilly mountain night
begins to possess Salzburg. This place and hour focuses my nostalgia, now I have gone away like everyone else. Salzburg, pale
with social tension, awaited silence and autumn, and I suppose
those are both flowing in now.

Night and Day.

LONDON, 1940

Early September morning in Oxford Street. The smell of charred
dust hangs on what should be crystal pure air. Sun, just up,
floods the once more innocent sky, strikes silver balloons and the
intact building-tops. The whole length of Oxford Street, west to
east, is empty, looks polished like a ballroom, glitters with
smashed glass. Down the distances, natural mists of morning are
brown with the last of smoke. Fumes still come from the shell of
a shop. At this corner where the burst gas main flaming floors
high made a scene like a hell in the night, you still feel heat. The
silence is now the enormous thing—it appears to amaze the street.
Sections and blocks have been roped off; there is no traffic; the
men in the helmets say not a person may pass (but some sneak
through). Besides the high explosives that did the work, this
quarter has been seeded with timebombs—so we are herded,
waiting for those to go off. This is the top of Oxford Street, near
where it joins the corner of Hyde Park at Marble Arch.

We people have come up out of the ground, or out from the
bottom floors of the damaged houses: we now see what we heard
happen throughout the night. Roped away from the rest of
London we seem to be on an island—when shall we be taken off?
Standing, as might the risen dead in the doors of tombs, in the
mouths of shelters, we have nothing to do but yawn at each other
or down the void of streets, meanwhile rubbing the smoke-smart
deeper into our eyes with our dirty fists. . . . It has been a dirty
night. The side has been ripped off one near block—the open
gash is nothing but dusty, colourless. (As bodies shed blood,

buildings shed mousey dust.) Up there the sun strikes a mirror over a mantelpiece; shreds of a carpet sag out over the void. An A.R.P. man, like a chamois, already runs up the debris; we stare. The charred taint thickens everyone's lips and tongues—what we want is bacon and eggs, coffee. We attempt little sorties—'Keep BACK, please! Keep OFF the street!' The hungry try to slake down with smoking. 'PLEASE—that cigarette *out*! Main gone— gas all over the place—d'*you* want to blow up London?' Cigarette trodden guiltily into the trodden glass. We loaf on and on in our cave-mouths; the sun goes on and on up. Some of us are dressed, some of us are not: pyjama-legs show below overcoats. There are some Poles, who having lost everything all over again sit down whenever and wherever they can. They are our seniors in this experience: we cannot but watch them. There are two or three unmistakable pairs of disturbed lovers—making one think 'Oh yes, how odd—love.' There are squads of ageless 'residents' from aquarium-like private hotels just round the corner. There are the nomads of two or three nights ago who, having been bombed out of where they were, pitched on this part, to be bombed out again. There is the very old gentleman wrapped up in the blanket, who had been heard to say, humbly, between the blasts in the night, 'The truth is, I have outlived my generation. . . .' We are none of us—except perhaps the Poles?—the very very poor: our predicament is not a great predicament. The lady in the fur coat has hair in two stiff little bedroomy grey plaits. She appeals for hair-pins: most of us have short hair—pins for her are extracted from one of the Poles' heads. Girls stepping further into the light look into pocket mirrors. 'Gosh,' they say remotely. Two or three people have, somehow, begun walking when one time-bomb goes off at Marble Arch. The street puffs itself empty; more glass splinters. Everyone laughs.

It is a fine morning and we are still alive.

This is the buoyant view of it—the theatrical sense of safety, the steady breath drawn. We shall be due, at to-night's siren, to feel our hearts once more tighten and sink. Soon after black-out we keep that date with fear. The howling ramping over the darkness, the lurch of the barrage opening, the obscure throb in the air. We *can* go underground—but for this to be any good you have to go very deep, and a number of us, fearful of being buried, prefer not to. Our own 'things'—tables, chairs, lamps—give one kind of confidence to us who stay in our own paper rooms. But when to-night the throb gathers over the roof we must not remember what we looked at this morning—these fuming utter glissades of ruin. No, these nights in September nowhere is pleasant. Where you stay is your own choice, how you feel is your fight.

However many people have crowded together, each has, while air whistles and solids rock, his or her accesses of solitude. We can do much for each other, but not all. Between bomb and bomb we are all together again: we all guess, more or less, what has been happening to all the others. Chatter bubbles up; or there is a cosy slumping sideways, to doze. Fear is not cumulative: each night it starts from scratch. On the other hand, resistance becomes a habit. And, better, it builds up a general fund.

Autumn seems a funny time to be bombed. By nature it is the hopeful start of the home year. The colours burning in the trees and weed-fires burning in the gardens ought to be enough. Autumn used to be a slow sentimental fête, with an edge of melancholy—the children going back to school, the evenings drawing in. Windows lit up earlier. Lanes in the country, squares in the city crisp with leaves. (This year, leaves are swept up with glass in them.) In autumn, where you live touches the heart—it is the worst time not to be living anywhere. This is the season in which to honour safety.

London feels all this this year most. To save something, she contracts round her wounds. Transport stoppages, roped-off districts, cut-off communications and 'dirty' nights now make her a city of villages—almost of village communes. Marylebone is my village. Friends who live outside it I think about but seldom see: *they* are sunk in the life of their own villages. We all have new friends: our neighbours. In Marylebone, shopping just before the black-out or making for home before the bombers begin to fill up the sky, we say, 'Well, good luck!' to each other. And every morning after the storm we go out to talk. News comes filtering through from the other villages. They say St. John's Wood had it worse than we did. Camden Town, on the other hand, got off light. Chelsea, it seems, was hot again. They say they brought 'one' down on Paddington Green. Has anybody been over to Piccadilly? A man from Hampstead was here a minute ago; he said . . . Mrs. X is a Pimlico woman; she's quite upset. Anybody know how it was in Kilburn? Somebody had a letter from Finsbury Park.

For one bad week, we were all turned out on account of time-bombs: exiled. We camped about London in other villages. (That was how I happened to be in Oxford Street, only to be once more dislodged from there.) When we were let home again we were full of stories, spent another morning picking up all the threads. The fishmonger said he had caught sight of me buying milk in Paddington. 'What, you were there too?' I asked. 'No,' he replied, 'I've got Finchley people; I was only over in Paddington looking after a friend.' We had all detested our week away: for instance, I had been worrying about my typewriter left uncovered in the dust blowing through our suddenly-emptied house; the fishmonger had been worrying about all that fish of his in the frig. with the power off. It had been necessary for several of us to slip through the barricades from time to time in order to feed cats.

Regent's Park where I live is still, at the time of writing, closed: officially, that is to say, we are not here. Just inside the gates an unexploded bomb makes a boil in the tarmac road. Around three sides of the Park, the Regency terraces look like scenery in an empty theatre: in the silence under the shut façades a week's drift of leaves flitters up and down. At nights, at my end of my terrace, I feel as though I were sleeping in one corner of a deserted palace. I had always placed this Park among the most civilized scenes on earth; the Nash pillars look as brittle as sugar—actually, which is wonderful, they have not cracked; though several of the terraces are gutted—blown-in shutters swing loose, ceilings lie on floors and a premature decay-smell comes from the rooms. A pediment has fallen on to a lawn. Illicitly, leading the existence of ghosts, we overlook the locked park.

Through the railings I watch dahlias blaze out their colour. Leaves fill the empty deck-chairs; in the sunshine water-fowl, used to so much attention, mope round the unpeopled rim of the lake. One morning a boy on a bicycle somehow got inside and bicycled round and round the silence, whistling 'It's a Happy, Happy Day.' The tune was taken up by six soldiers digging out a bomb. Now and then everything rips across; a detonation rattles remaining windows. The R.E. 'suicide squad' detonate, somewhere in the hinterland of this park, bombs dug up elsewhere. We have no feeling to spare.

DOVER: 1 JUNE, 1944

It is more than six hundred years since the Cinque Ports were given their Royal Charter. Hastings, Romney, Hythe, Dover, Sandwich—to call their names from west to east round the coast —their destiny was a proud one. Unique liberties made it; but there were unique calls to service too. The Cinque Ports gave England her first Navy—bold little cockleshells of ships, manned by the men of Sussex and men of Kent.

Of these proud five, only one, Dover, is still a port. Elsewhere, the natural harbours silted up, or the sea retreated. Romney, now locked in the grazing flats of the Marsh, is the most high-and-dry: over the wide main street and churchyard tombstones carved with sea-daring names, inland silence gathers. Or so I remember Romney, one heat-hazy June day before the war.

Silences can be as different as sounds. The silence I met in Dover, on the first day of this June, 1944, was charged, moment-ous, big with expectancy. Yes, the past was here: an unbroken past of fortifications and watchers dating back to the Romans. But the past seemed, with caught breath, to await the future. For four years, since France fell, Dover has watched, waited. Through the late summer of 1940, cut off from the rest of England by invisible barriers, she faced, across twenty-one miles of water, an enemy nothing had so far halted. She sent her children away, and her old people—or such of those as would go: Kent breeds a sturdy, contrary stock. That done, Dover battened down its hatches and waited. The Battle of Britain broke, and the world looked on. Then, as war became global, the salients shifted: eyes looked elsewhere. Dover, with her queer blend of grimness and equanimity, settled unnoticed into her wartime stride. Her ordeals, her problems remained her own.

Her own, and she has met them in her own way. Day and night since France fell, citizen watchers, Civilian Defence Wardens, have scanned, raked the French coast for first gunfire-flashes of a renewed bombardment. The two Observation Posts, connected by special lines with the town's Control Room, occupy heights at opposite sides of the city—the Castle, the Drop Redoubt. The glass-sided eyries command, over town and Channel, a spectacular view. Between them, squeezed narrow between the heights, grey war-tattered Dover extends the one way it can, up the river valley. Few, now, are the chimneys from which smoke rises. From the Redoubt's top, outside the O.P., I looked across at the Castle, flanked by the Roman lighthouse. Then I turned and looked straight down into the harbour. Below me floated invasion barges, like painted ships.

They had a strange light air, almost of unreality. Grouped by themselves on the dazzling water, they were near nothing by which one could rate their size. Their flat-bottomed shape made me think of punts—punts of other summers on a June river. Brought up close to my eye, as they were, by my field-glasses, their camouflage still made them difficult to see. Their look of lightness was not delusive—they are made, I learn, of canvas stretched over fine steel. My imagination found them as hard to focus as did my eyes. Much stranger than the first Cinque Port Navy were these ships for the future, ready to dip and right themselves under tons of weight. Painted canvas, waiting to carry history.

At my feet, gay indifferent yellow flowers waved in the cliff-top wind. A red ladybird, in its own little world of being, made its way slowly over a stone step. It was time to leave the Redoubt: we made our way down through tunnels, down twisting ramps, across bridges over the deep mined moats. The Redoubt was built to withstand Napoleon: to-day its guardrooms are ghostly, its battlements flower-grown.

I was down in the town again. Spring has come late to Dover: she has timed her glory for the eve of D-Day. Now, at the start of June, hawthorns and chestnuts are in full flower: in forsaken streets they mask the black windows of the blast-gutted houses. Red and white, the candles of the chestnuts seem alight with expectancy. . . . About noon a thin whitish film dissipated; the sun came out; brilliance of sunny green could be seen through ruins. Some residential areas of the town could not have been emptier—you cannot inhabit ruins. But the damaged machine of life has been kept going. Any outdoor movement I saw ran into the crease of the High Street, on which the old Maison Dieu—undamaged, Dover thanks God—looks down. To and fro past

Maison Dieu tower was a rapid thin flux of people about their business. Looking into those faces, those blue, alert and equable Kentish eyes, I saw what Dover understood—that she was on the eve of what she has waited for. Out of the mind of the world, out of the mind, even, of inland England, she has licked her wounds, enduring—for what?—for this? Her cycle completes itself; there was June 1940, now there is June 1944.

The High Street gives on the wiped-out market place, over-looked by one old café which has survived the bombing. Here, lunch. The gay, cracked, shaken building echoes the laughter of soldiers packed round its tables—I saw only one fellow-civilian, a very old man. The gimcrack elegance of the café's interior, with its pillars, its two or three still intact tarnished mirrors, somehow is Continental. And so, indefinably, are other parts of Dover. Many things here remind you that you are nearer to France than you are to London. France, bodily visible on clear days (I have met those in Dover who say they have read the time on the Calais clock) can never for long together, in war or in peace, be out of Dover's psychological view. For centuries, France's nearness has built up Dover's prosperity: prosperity now pays the tax on near-ness. Most of all, in these last mounting months, since the Allied battering of the Western Wall began, not only roaring skies but trembling earth has given Dover her part in the French ordeal.

'Bombs falling on France,' said a Dover woman, 'shake us up, somehow, more than bombs falling on this town. While our bombers go over, one cannot hear oneself think. Then, it seems only a minute later, one's bed rocks so violently that one has to clutch it. For some reason, it's dreadful—though it's got to be done. When one's been through it oneself, one can't help thinking of *them*.' She meant the French—whom Dover, these days, has so deep in its sympathies that it never names them.

I noticed another thing: Dover people speak of the coastline facing them as 'the German coast.' When they once more speak of 'the French coast,' that will mean something.

Dover is full of secrets. The existence of secrets has come to be part of the stuff of the townsfolks' lives. Towards the dock area, warning placards are up; guards are mounted half-way across the streets. But the guards have nobody to turn back, for, auto-matically, nobody goes that way. Unwatched, unquestioned, unhindered, mysterious activity goes on, behind in there. The position of the great guns trained on the Channel may be guessed at, but it is never spoken. There is a good deal Dover cannot help knowing—must not every citizen know what is in the harbour?—but taciturnity is the word. . . . The open roadway over the cliffs to Deal crosses a plateau bristling with rocket guns. Chalky white blisters in the plateau's turf show where enemy bombs fell (only just) wide—between the scars move placidly grazing sheep. British and American army lorries, travelling this clifftop road, carry loads too vast to be quite hidden, almost too long to take, with most skilful driving, the precipitous zigzag turns of the Castle hill. Yes, these are staring secrets—but not a man, woman or child would allow one to travel to the other side of the Downs. London is kept as ignorant of what goes on in Dover as might be Berlin.

This June opens upon a whole south of England vibrating with the final movements of soldiers. As I stood in Dover High Street, the built-up valley started to give out sound. All heads turned one way as the head of the convoy came round the bend. Shaking the narrow street, slowed by its many turns, the armoured file of vehicles roared past. Hollowed buildings echoed; remaining glass reflected the assault troops—balancing, riding, sprawling, swinging their legs over the backs of trucks. The green-and-brown raggy camouflage of their helmets blew like heroic plumage or savage hair. Their faces, in which the build of bone stood out not gaunt but tautly, were burned so dark that their eyes looked white—grinning, turning those light eyes this way and that, they returned the townspeople's glances as impersonally as Martians. There was something mythological about them, in the afternoon glare of the battered street. They rode and roared away out of view.

Their goodbyes have already been said; their own people no longer know where they are. They are to embark as secretly as though they were undertaking a crime. In these last, ghostly, unnumbered days before they go, only Dover, not knowing their names, blesses them. Old women look at them kindly; they are waved to by children born since the war.

Dover will wake to D-Day where she has woken many mornings before—in the caves honeycombing the seafront, in the tunnels bored into the hills. Caution, homelessness and by now, perhaps, habit make most of her population sleep underground.

Overground beds that rock as the Allied bombers hammer at France are few—for few are the roofs left. Along the humid chalk walls of tunnels, electric-lit, strange to the stranger's eye, run double-decker sleeping berths in their hundreds. The entrances to these dormitories inside hills look like mouseholes. I see those small black apertures at the foot of a white cliff pink-tufted with valerian. Better I liked the caves—once, smugglers' hide-outs; later, burgesses' cellars. Very dark, chilly after the outdoor heat, the cave I entered still smelled of wine—for a moment I fancied I heard vats dripping; then someone said: 'The alarm clocks. . . .' In the dark, on ledges above the rolled-up bedding—patchwork quilts, paisley eiderdowns, knitted blankets —clocks tick all day until their owners' return.

One morning—which morning?—will those alarms be needed? Will not some intimation run through the caves and tunnels, so that Dover, before opening its eyes, will know?

Written for the *Ministry of Information*.

FOLKESTONE: JULY, 1945

Folkestone—municipal borough, seaport and watering place— is seventy-one miles S.E. by E. of London, on the Southern Railway. Its population, just under 36,000 in 1931, remained more or less static up to the outbreak of this war. On the Kentish Cinque Port coast, Folkestone stands between Hythe and Dover; it is a 'corporate member' of the Cinque Port of Dover, under the 1330 charter. Dislike of satellite status is still under the Folkestone skin: few visitors who take it that Folkestone *is* a Cinque Port proper are corrected. Knit up with this is a post-1940 resentment: Folkestone considers Dover has been camera-hogging in the matter of front-line publicity. In another aspect, Folkestone remains subsidiary; she is within the parliamentary borough of Hythe, her other, very small, Cinque Port neighbour. In 1945, a Conservative was again returned with a 1,957 majority over the Labour candidate. Total electorate: 23,575. An Independent secured 3,152 votes.

The non-indigenous *rentier* 'residents' are, for the most part, not back. The indigenous Folkestoner is Jute-descended;

Q

generally fair, big-boned, broad-faced, armed with a clear stare, a hereditary front-liner with a strong burgess tradition.

Physically, the contours of Folkestone are marked to the point of theatricality: levels and gradients demarcate different quarters, symbolizing the social plan. The packet and fishing port are at the mouth of a valley, up whose west side clambers the 'old town,' crowned by the parish church. Along the trough of the valley run shopping streets that provision townspeople and the inland country. Watering place expansion, with a definite bid for the high class, entailed the development of the plateau to the west. This enjoys altitude: it is backed by chalk downs, has as its lip the Leas, and shelves reluctantly eastward into the lower town. The plateau, with its high, well-spaced buildings, and grid plan, is (or was) the expensive visitor and residential quarter. North of the Central Station lies Radnor Park, which once had prestige; beyond that stretch the unaspiring, inland, late-Victorian suburbs, Shorncliffe and Cheriton. These, with a yellow brick and gas-works agglomeration (industrial-looking, but without industries) in a hollow east of the Central Station, used to cater, during the summer pressure, for lodgers willing to take what they could get. Away on the East Cliff, across the valley from the plateau, there has been recent working-class house development. Along the flank of Shorncliffe and some way up the foot of the Downs extend sun-trap, flat-roofed villas and bungalows—these are a new coastal type, but have been extruded: Folkestone's sea front was built by 1900.

On the plateau the clock has stopped. You come out of the Central Station into a hush of avenues, empty perspectives under the slate-dark foliage of chestnuts; it is late summer, 1945. In 1940, with the fall of France, the residents moved out, the soldiers moved in. All hotels and most of the houses were requisitioned; houses not requisitioned were boarded up, to begin a slow internal decay. The area was closed to the outside world. From across the Channel, German guns opened up with an intermittent shelling that was to last until September, 1944. Before the Battle of Britain there had been tip-and-run raiding. Evacuation was urged, but was not compulsory. This produced another sharp demarcation: the plateau emptied; downtown Folkestone continued to carry on a skeleton life. (It should be said in fairness to the plateau that the town suffered requisitioning on a smaller scale.)

The plateau is self-contained, having its own numerous churches, theatre and shopping thoroughfare, Upper Sandgate Road. These now, after five years, compose a sort of Pompeii. The shops are blind behind rusty shutters; a church has been obliterated; the Pleasure Garden Theatre, taken over by N.A.A.F.I., stands in a lorry-flattened waste, and its satellite racquet courts and roller skating rink are now Army stores and canteens. In private and public gardens has perished, for five summers, uncut hay. A pillar box, functionless, has been boarded up. Ivy mats and clings to the steps of more than one private house, sending suckers over the sealed door.

Through this film of ghostliness shows the time-colour of, say, 1908. Actually, the architecture dates between 1870 and 1900; the older buildings being along the Leas, from which development moved inland. The Leas crescents and terraces are all high and of a gritty grey; some have a boxlike starkness, others are of the ornate mansard type. Behind are strata of late-Victorian gothic and baroque, dark red brick, lighter-patterned or with terra-cotta mouldings. All are set off by gardens. Closing the west end of the Leas, mammoth twin brick hotels record the high water mark of opulence. Down the avenues, other hotels ran to a pleasing, sugary, brittle white, and used to put out awnings and sling geraniums.

On the Leas, Folkestone staked her at one time successful bid to be the Beauty Spot of England, the Queen of the South Coast. From this high-hanging, once drawingroom-like promenade you can enjoy an enormous marine view and, on clear days, scan the French coast. Far down below, the tides suck at orange shingle. Lifts used to ply, and paths artfully zigzagged, up and down the cliff-face, notched with rustic nooks and hermetic winter-gardens. Leas and beach were disconnected in 1940 as a defence measure; the Leas, then closed, held concealed gun emplacements, observation posts, anti-invasion blocks (which went some way in depth inland) and, for the rest, wire.

The best days were late-Victorian and Edwardian. At that time, the Leas were held to deteriorate slightly, socially, at their east end. Here, it is true, is found a cosy nucleus of old burgess houses round the parish church; but equally you cannot ignore, below you, the harbour, the debouching lower town and proletarian harbour-neighbourhood beach. For years Folkestone, by arrangement with the railway company, succeeded in excluding the day tripper. Many of the Leas houses were then in part-time occupation by London families who brought their own staffs of servants down for the season. The west Leas, unstatedly, were private; from the houses there could emerge, on hot summer nights, ladies and gentlemen in evening dress, to stroll under swags of electric light. The conversion—well under way before 1914—of private houses into boarding houses, however exclusive, or maisonettes for the moderate *rentier*, represented the first phase of decline from the fashionable to the merely good-class. Before Edward VII died, many schools had obtained their hold on the plateau; crocodiles of girls in distinctive hat-bands and little boys in distinctive caps wound past one another, competing in politeness. In the 1914 war, many schools held their ground until a girl playing hockey was killed by a bomb. (In 1917, a bomb also dropped on the lower town, killing thirty-three shoppers.) This war, the schools were quicker off the mark.

1945 finds plateau Folkestone in the throes of another transition stage. All-out military occupation is at an end, but soldiers are still about—the place is a transit camp, for which hotels, many houses and the theatre remain requisitioned. De-requisitioned buildings stand stripped and bleached, as though after the passage of white ants. Residents, none the less, are beginning to come back; a Cheltenham van disgorges furniture opposite a front door; an unsettled-looking maid stares out of a window she has just finished cleaning. Jeeps and bath-chairs cross the otherwise trafficless avenues. The returning residents are almost all old. Torturing the silence, there is to be heard from under a line of chestnuts the action of a pneumatic drill; a man is at work loosening the 1940 spiked concrete roadblocks. A crane is to follow, extracting these like teeth. This marks the opening of another campaign —for visitors. From the Leas, the thickets of wire have been cleared, leaving cracked asphalt and parched bald soil. *Can* the illusion be coaxed back? Half-way down the perspective, two new little beds of scarlet geraniums, bringing tears to the eyes, blaze. A formation of deck-chairs, stridently rebottomed with fresh canvas, waits hopefully—empty. On the Leas I only see two ladies, sitting with their backs to the sea, staring at the military remains.

Anyhow, where would plateau visitors sleep? On the steps of one delusively bright hotel an apparent barman, white-coated, unofficially smokes a cigarette. But on his sleeve are a sergeant's stripes. This, he says, is an officers' transit club.

In her inch-by-inch fight back to normal, Folkestone has taken two knocks: a year ago her pier pavilion, which had survived war, burst into flames and was consumed; last June a tornado struck the town, tore the roof from a cinema and scored its own trail of damage over that left by bomb and shell. As a watering place, her past is short and her future problematical; as municipal borough and port, she rallies with striking speed. Life has run downhill into the town proper. Here, the shopping streets, stuffy, heavily-architected, teem with Folkestoners, soldiers, and visitors —on whose unaccustomed skins sun and salt have done violent work. The 'old town' took the greater part of the bombing; its toy-sized High Street twists steeply down to the port, between ruins of toy shops, pet shops, sweet shops, that at least one memory holds dear.

Port-side Folkestone looks Continental; it runs to blue-and-white-wash, arcades, caryatids and strident painted lettering. The summer's mine-warnings plaster ruins: be careful what you fall over, be careful what you pick up. The fish market is enjoying a boom: housewives crowd this part of the quays. Black lobsters heave on the stalls; plaice flop from hand to hand. A stall-holder who looks like a weight-lifter bids for the speed record for gutting fish. At the arches through to the market, a winkle table is doing trade—pins are no more: one serves the extracted winkle, Prunier-manner, in scollop shells. Veteran salts, sitting along the parapet, watch the scene which, war in, war out, has probably not changed much.

Behind the old men's backs, below them, anchored small craft ride bumping on the thick, pungent water. And a tanker is in. The harbour, with its long, deep-water pier, had berths for eight steamers: the 'Boulogne boat' used to leave twice daily. In 1945, there is a shuttle leave service between here and France—weather permitting: the pier has sustained damage. On the net of railway lines round the harbour, where boat trains used to shunt, one sees, here and there, static rolling stock. Port-level Folkestone holds one luxury hotel—never for season visitors, for the Channel traveller. This is now the headquarters of the transit camp; on its lawns guns still stand, tarpaulined. Café life—for visitors, fish-shoppers, Forces men and girls—concentrates on an awning-shaded projection into the harbour water; this place, serving tea and soft drinks, hums.

Folkestone's magnetic centre has, decidedly, shifted: it is now down here—one might say, back down here. Early-Victorian terraces, round the bend from the harbour, under and backing into the heights, lost caste when the plateau came into being. Facing them, we are back to the first focus, the original pleasure-town and watering-place idea. Opposite them lies the fun fair; its ruins hold the illusion the Leas have failed to regain. An empty circular floor, battle-ground of the Dodgems, has cracked and heaved up. Lorries stink and back between the pleasure booths; on the beach a crane rattles, scooping graves for the wire. Prams going down to the sea bump cross the rails for the shingle trucks. The dry cement bed of the swimming pool shows cracks; its metal and bottle-glass screen sags in. A hit steel and concrete pavilion looks like a crashed plane. Beatifically, however, the holiday people are circu-lating among the fun fair ruins. 'I always did like Folkestone,' one woman said. They sit, smoking, round the rim of the Dodgems, in groups imitating the sensation of a crowd. Bunches of sat-in deck-chairs tilt on the shelving shingle; flocks of cycling boys do stunts on the hard strip. Apart from the winkle table and too-small harbour café, I see no place for anyone to have tea. A shimmer of contentment, however, goes up from this end of the hot beach.

This is the last idyll of war, not the first of peace. It is essential for Folkestone to get going. War damage cannot account for everything; for years before this war she had been feeling the draught. From the point of view of to-day, she has disadvantages —difficulties of access to the sea, the extrusion of modern-type holiday building to miles inland. Pleasure-beach life is forced into unideal proximity with the harbour by the narrowing, as one goes west, of the strip between the Leas' base and the sea—over which the Leas' overhang is itself oppressive. Socially, the whole plateau set-up is out of date; there is frigid urbanity, a best-clothes compulsion. The sunbather and beachwear devotee has no outlet. The age level of visitors to the plateau had, pre-war, been shifting up; the steadies were Midland rich middle-aged middle class—*their* sons and daughters wanted something more *plage-y*: shorts, espadrilles, the drink after the swim. For the child of 1945 Folkestone bristles with barbed wire.

Contact—'The First Spring of Peace.'

V

A BROADCAST

Anthony Trollope—A New Judgment

ANTHONY TROLLOPE*

NARRATOR [*in level, descriptive voice*]: The walls are lined with books. On their backs, the firelight should be playing—but this is war-time: there is an electric radiator, with one bar lit, in the grate. As close as possible to the radiator, the study's owner reclines in an armchair. A fastidious, pleasant, elderly man. He is lost to the world, reading. He holds the book in long fingers. The door opens. A young man in battle-dress hesitates on the threshold before speaking.

WILLIAM: Uncle Jasper?

UNCLE JASPER [*startled*]: Who's that? Why, William! [*warmly*] William . . . Come in, come in, dear boy!

WILLIAM: Disturbing you?

UNCLE JASPER: I like it. Pull up that other chair. Cigarette?

WILLIAM [*in uncertain voice*]: Thanks, I . . .

UNCLE JASPER: Settle down, dear boy, settle down.

WILLIAM: Actually, I haven't got too much time. [*significantly*] Got a train to catch.

UNCLE JASPER [*vaguely*]: Train? [*change of tone—gravely*] Oh. You mean—you're off?

WILLIAM: Very soon—yes.

UNCLE JASPER: One does not ask where?

WILLIAM: We-ell . . .

UNCLE JASPER: But one makes a pretty good guess?

WILLIAM [*audibly grinning*]: One makes a pretty good guess.

UNCLE JASPER [*in tone of controlled feeling*]: Well, I'm glad you looked in, you know: it was nice of you.

WILLIAM [*inarticulate*]: Well, I mean to say . . . [*pause, with audible grin again*] Besides, I wanted to ask—

UNCLE JASPER [*quickly, pleased*]: What—anything *I* can do?

WILLIAM: Well, it's quite a thing to ask—[*with a rush*] Can I take a book?

UNCLE JASPER [*with instinctive reluctance*]: Take a book *away?*

---

* Written as a Broadcast in the B B.C.'s 'New Judgment' Series. First performed June, 1945. Subsequently published by the Oxford University Press.

WILLIAM: Well, it comes to that. . . . It *is* quite a thing to ask. And I don't want any old book; I want a Trollope. You know—Anthony Trollope.

UNCLE JASPER [*ironical*]: I know: Anthony Trollope.

WILLIAM: You don't think much of him?

UNCLE JASPER: He doesn't say much to me. That may be my fault: I'm not saying it's not. God forbid *I* should run down any honest man who gives honest pleasure. In fact, who has done so twice. He pleased his own generation—and so he should have done: he had got them taped. And, which seems a good deal odder, he pleases yours—I wish you could tell me why. *I* belong to the generation halfway between: in fact, by a funny coincidence, I was born the year Trollope died—1882. And frankly, William, by the time I was your age, which is to say in the early nineteen-hundreds, Trollope was so stone dead, so utterly off the map, that he might just as well not have been born at all. He'd out-stayed his welcome, with his most devoted readers; his reputation went with him down to the grave.

WILLIAM [*thoughtful*]: Funny . . .[*brightening*] It didn't stay there.

UNCLE JASPER [*absently*]: No . . . [*energetically*] Trollope died—in both senses—at the time when the English novel was coming into its own. Hardy, Meredith, Henry James were all in the field. Trollope—by his own admission—wrote for young ladies. Hardy, Meredith, James, wrote for adult minds; or at least, for minds that wanted to be adult. It may seem odd to you, William —in fact, I say this to you with some humility—but we young men, when *I* was a young man, surrounded as we were, to the outward eye, with all the good things of those piping times of peace, *did* look on life as a psychological battle. And into that battle we took our three novelists—Hardy, Meredith, James. Yes, those were the great names when I was your age. And frankly, where I am concerned, they're the great names still. And now? I see *you* go into actual battle carrying Trollope!

WILLIAM [*simple*]: I like him.

UNCLE JASPER: Wherefore, I take off my hat to him. *Not* as a novelist—that would be asking too much. Yes, I *have* tried one or two of his books these last few years, but I couldn't away with any of them. Plum duff, sheer plum duff! No, no, no, no—Henry James, as generous a critic as you wish, said about all for Trollope that could be said, in that essay on him in *Partial Portraits* . . .

'Strong, genial, abundant' . . . 'Something masterly in his large-fisted grip' . . . 'He represents to an admirable degree the natural decorum of the English spirit' . . . 'His complete appreciation of the ordinary' . . . Yes, that—all that. It took James's fine eye to see it. But he, even he, was forced to the last conclusion—and for him, as for me, it *was* the damning one—'Trollope's imagination had no light of its own.'

WILLIAM: And yet—you take off your hat to him?

UNCLE JASPER [*smile in voice*]: There must be *something* about any writer who lives twice. He's a double man. There's the Trollope his own generation knew, and the Trollope yours has found—or, perhaps, created?

WILLIAM: Created?

UNCLE JASPER: You don't think you give him something he hadn't got?

WILLIAM: I do think he's got something we've never had.

UNCLE JASPER [*reflective, struck*]: That's possible. Something you would have liked? Come to that, old Trollope immortalizes quite a few things I could do with myself. [*shivers*] On a day like *this,* I could do with one of those Plumstead Episcopi roaring fires. . . . The rooks in the elms, the port on the table. . . . [*abruptly*] Which do you want?

WILLIAM [*uncertain*]: Which?——

UNCLE JASPER: Which of the Trollope novels?

WILLIAM [*much relieved*]: Oh, you *have* got some of him, then? I began to wonder.

UNCLE JASPER [*dryly*]: If you move that sofa—which will involve moving the table first—I think you'll find three or four away in the corner, down on the bottom shelf. [*more dryly*] They were your great-aunt Emily's.

WILLIAM [*to sound of moving sofa*]: That old warhorse? Fancy me and Aunt Emily seeing with the same eye! [*pause: voice muffled, as from corner of bookshelves*] Yes, here we are . . .

UNCLE JASPER [*reflective*]: With far from the same eye. Aunt Emily wanted the testimonial——

WILLIAM: Testimonial——

UNCLE JASPER: To her own way of living. Whereas, you want——

WILLIAM [*amused*]: What do *I* want?

UNCLE JASPER: A picture book?

WILLIAM: A picture book . . . [*amused*] Well, I'll look at it in the train.

UNCLE JASPER: Very proper—he probably wrote it in the train.

Pause: Fade-in train noises—rather accentuated, as of train taking up-gradient. Gradually fade in, on top of these noises and in their rhythm, voice saying 'A picture book, a picture book, a picture book' . . . *The words should gain, slowly, more with each time of speaking, over train noises.*

Both Faded Out.

NARRATOR: William is very tired. He has had quite a day, saying so many good-byes in a short time. Kit stowed in the rack above him, he is dozing, arms folded, in a corner of the compartment—which is surprisingly empty. The book he was holding has slipped to the seat beside him. The mists of William's drowsiness clear and thin as, from time to time, he opens his eyes. Lit by bland winter afternoon sunshine, a landscape streams past the windows. A stone house with white window-frames, basking in the yellow light of a valley . . . A church spire . . . A man on horseback, trotting on the grass verge of a road . . . The lichened roofs of farm buildings . . . In the distance—the smoke of a little city, turned by the sun to gauze . . . And, rising above this—surely?—cathedral towers . . . Now, which cathedral can *that* be?

TROLLOPE [*a very deep voice, at once genial and diffident*]: Barchester, sir.

NARRATOR [*as though surprised*]: William must have slept through the stop at the last station. For, he finds, the seat opposite him, empty last time he looked, is now occupied. A big, clumsy man, with a bushy square beard, sits there, eyeing him over thick spectacles that have slipped some way down on his nose.

WILLIAM [*bewildered*]: This country we're going through—it's familiar. Yet I can't, somehow, place it.

TROLLOPE: Possibly not on the map; no, possibly not on the map. [*with detachment, after clearing throat*] A new shire I added to the English counties.

WILLIAM [*automatically*]: Really sir? [*apologetic laugh*] I'm afraid I'm not very bright to-day.

TROLLOPE: Much on your mind, no doubt? Well, well. Youth is never an easy time. Not for much would I live through my own again.

WILLIAM: If you'll excuse me, sir, you're the first person of—of anything like *your* age that I've ever heard say that!

TROLLOPE: Oh, heaven endows a number of us old fellows with remarkably kind, false memories. That wasn't so in my case. No, all through my good years—and they were many, for my turning-point came when I was twenty-seven; and I lived to be sixty-eight —I was liable, any night, to wake up sweating from the nightmare that I was young again. Idleness, inferiority, envy. The seamy side. Those are the things, you know, that you don't forget. They don't have to cripple you: they didn't cripple me. But it takes the rest of your remaining days to get up with what they have done to you. Let's say they give you, and leave you with, one particular manner of seeing life. You continue to see life that way, whatever comes. Yes, whatever comes. [*pause*] Industry, success, popularity, well-being. . . . The strong, well-lit desk and my pen flowing well ahead of the clock. . . . The peaches and roses in the garden; my boys' voices out there—my boys had a happy youth. . . . Cheques rolling in, bills paid, the bank balance mounting up. The dinner parties—oh, those dinner parties of the 'eighties!

Fade In

FIRST LADY [*against general background of tinkling glass, laughter and conversation—her voice flattering, arch*]: Now, Mr. Trollope, you wonderful, naughty man, I've got something ever so *serious* to say to you. You really *must* let Lily Dale marry Johnnie Eames! Agatha and I would be *heartbroken*. . . .

SECOND LADY [*more fluttering*]: Mr. Trollope, may I just ask you this? I have quite a favourite uncle who's an archdeacon, and he's astounded by your knowledge of clergymen. *I* said that perhaps your father was an archbishop?

FIRST LADY: In confidence—I so wonder—*has* your Lady Glencora any orginal in real life?

SECOND LADY: One can but blame her, of course—though [*wistfully*] Burgo Fitzgerald was *very* fascinating! [*increasingly daring*] Come, Mr. Trollope, I know you will never tell me, but how *do* you know so much about ladies' hearts?

FIRST LADY: And peers?

SECOND LADY: And politics?

FIRST LADY: And, even—*quite—low—life?*

Fade Out

TROLLOPE [*reflective*]: My glass refilled, camellias, charming bright eyes, warming rustle of silks. And, dearest prospect of all, my return home. . . . And those evenings at the Garrick—of which I became a member in '61. Having up to that time lived very little among men—having hitherto been banished from social gatherings—I enjoyed infinitely the gaiety of the Garrick: it was a festival to me to dine there. [*pause—very modestly*] I think that I became popular among those with whom I associated. I had long, for very long, been aware of a certain weakness in my own character, which I may call a craving for love. The Garrick Club was the first assemblage of men. . . .

Fade Out

Fade-in sounds of men's voices, laughter: A generally prosperous and port-winey background of sound, with a confident Bohemian animation.

FIRST MAN: Ha, ha—very good—excellent. Tell Thackeray.

SECOND MAN [*cutting in*]: You forget, the best of it was, that *The Times* next day. . . .

THIRD MAN [*very cordial*]: Aha—*here* comes the real good fellow. Evening, Trollope.

ALL [*to sounds of chairs being pushed back*]: Hello, Evening, Anything new? Was feeling *you* were about due in. Things going on well? Needless to ask *you* that! Dirty evening, out there. Come to the fire. Last come, first served. Whist—bring the table up. Look, Trollope, before you get down to whist—tell me this, Trollope . . . Trollope . . . Listen to this, Trollope . . . (*etc.*).

Fade-out Garrick

Fade-in subdued train sounds.

TROLLOPE [*picking up from point where voice left off*]: The first assemblage of men at which I felt myself to be popular.

WILLIAM [*resigned to the oddness of this, but thoughtful*]: You *are* Anthony Trollope?

TROLLOPE: Well, yes—I know myself by that name. [*pause*] I know myself, that's to say, at least not less well than I know my characters.

WILLIAM [*taken aback*]: Isn't that, sir, a funny way round to put it? Surely one more often hears an author say that he knows his characters almost as well as he knows himself?

TROLLOPE: Indeed? Then you must know some clever fellows. No—[*reflective pause*] It's been t'other way round with me. I've thought more about my characters than I have about myself. To be honest, I like 'em a good deal better. I much prefer their company to my own. For my own company, first, I had no taste—misery, loneliness, wretchedness thrust me into it. I'd escape from it at any moment I could—into daydreams, in which I was a quite different fellow. It was that, no doubt, that set up my first habit of spinning yarns.

WILLIAM [*thoughtful*]: But later, sir, once you'd got thoroughly launched, once you'd got a name, once you had started to do so well?

TROLLOPE: Oh, by then I had no time for my own company, I was a busy man—organized down to each moment of every day. I had a lot to get through, and I got through it. [*simply*] I was a happy man. And a happy, busy man isn't given to thinking about himself. That's an idler's trick—and a wretched, unhappy trick, if you ask me.

WILLIAM [*still perplexed*]: Still, *I* always did understand that all writers, from Shakespeare down, drew their characters out of what they knew of themselves. If that was not so in your case, where *did* your people come from? Archdeacon Grantly, Plantagenet Palliser, old Mr. Harding—to mention only a few. Heaven knows, they're foursquare and alive enough!

TROLLOPE: Oh, yes, they're alive all right. [*chuckles*] A sight more alive than I am! [*reflective pause, then vaguely*] Oh, they came along, you know; they just came along. . . .

WILLIAM: But, out of *where?*

TROLLOPE [*with genuine piety*]: Ask the Almighty, my boy. No sense in asking me. I put myself into the habit of steady and rapid writing, set myself to turn out a set number of pages daily—and, moreover, turned 'em out, every day. That being so, my people just—came along.

WILLIAM: You suggest, you know, that a novelist is a sort of medium. Sits down, takes up his pen, goes into a sort of trance——

TROLLOPE [*cuts in—shocked*]: What—spirits? That flimmery-flummery? God forbid!

WILLIAM [*eager, pursuing his own idea*]: Or, better still, a sort of receiving station—picking up and transmitting all sorts of things that are in the air?

TROLLOPE [*not shocked now, merely dubious*]: Oh well, there, you know, we're outside my province. I had—er . . . left England . . . before any of *that* came in. Still, from what I've been able to see—and I watch with interest—there might—'pon my word, there might—be something in what you say. [*reflective pause*] Scenes, places, people, yes, as I sat there writing, I saw them as sharply as though they *were* going on.

WILLIAM: And so, perhaps, they were, sir?

TROLLOPE [*still dubious; growling*]: Well, I don't know, I'm sure. [*sharply*] Mind, I'm not saying I didn't use my head. It may not have been a bright head, but it was a steady one. I worked out my plot at the start; I stuck to it—and, by Gad, I made the pack of 'em stick to it, what is more!

WILLIAM: Pack of whom?

TROLLOPE: The characters. Once or twice, one or two of 'em kicked their heels up, took ideas into their own heads. Sometimes, the ladies were the devil—as ladies can be the devil in real life. There were chapters, for instance, where I had a bit of trouble with that fine young widow, Eleanor Bold. Yes, writing a novel, my boy, is like driving pigs to market—you have one of them making a bolt down the wrong lane; another won't get over the right stile . . . However [*satisfied sigh*] we all got home in the end.

WILLIAM [*suddenly*]: Sir? May I be a bit impertinent?

TROLLOPE [*with unworried chuckle*]: Go on, my boy, go on.

WILLIAM: Well, you said just now—I don't know if you'll remember—that you knew yourself not less well than you knew your characters. You *then* proceeded to say that, first, you'd fled from yourself as from poison; and that, later on, you'd had no time for yourself. In that case—here's where I'm being impertinent—I don't see how you *can* know yourself at all.

TROLLOPE [*undisturbed*]: Yet I do, you know, yet I do. Yes, I know Anthony Trollope, for what he's worth. I kept learning about myself from my own characters. Some say that to be a father's an education—you may quite often recognize, in your children, bits of yourself you had never known were there. In the same way—and I should say even more so—I found it an education to be a novelist. My characters—the best of them, that's to say—were all more definite, more sure of themselves, more active, and —where they *were* admirable—more admirable than *I*, myself, had ever been in real life. [*chuckles*] My characters fairly marched in on me—took a look round, took stock, and made use of all that *I* had. Ah, they were cool hands. [*chuckles again*] They commandeered me—my pen, my reasoning powers. And, more than that, they drew on a lot in me—desires, scruples, aspirations, and daydreams—of whose existence *I* had not been aware.

WILLIAM: They stole a march on you?

TROLLOPE [*resignedly*]: Put it that way. [*pause*] The best of them were what, without knowing, I should have liked to be. The worst of them—in the moral sense, that's to say—were what, without knowing, I'd somehow avoided being. My Warden, for instance—old Mr. Harding, in the novel, was a personification of my own muddled wish to do right at any cost. Plantagenet Palliser—the political hero whose career reaches its climax in my *Prime Minister*—is not only my political ideal, but personifies my own lost political hopes. I did once, you know, stand for parliament: at the Beverley elections; I took a sickening knock, and from then on, I buried *my* hopes for ever. But from then on, also, Plantagenet Palliser grew. [*pause: sigh*] Well, well. . . . Who was the third you said?

WILLIAM [*eager*]: Archdeacon Grantly.

TROLLOPE [*between sigh and chuckle*]: The Archdeacon . . . A bad, bad man—over-ambitious, hard, self-important, in love with power? A decent fellow, loyal to those he loved, humane, even kindly, in some situations, just? . . . I can pass no judgment, you know, on the Archdeacon. He was the product of my moral consciousness. He raised, for me, questions *I* haven't answered yet.

WILLIAM: I suppose he cared for the world too much.

TROLLOPE [*after reflection, humbly*]: I cannot say *I* never cared for the world. . . . [*with return of confidence*] And I do say, I'd have been a fool if I hadn't.

WILLIAM: For me, it's not quite so simple. My world's in rather a mess.

TROLLOPE: So I understand. You are off to the wars, I see. Off to one of the fronts. War's everywhere—every place that you look.

WILLIAM [*impulsively*]: Do you know, Uncle Jasper says that's why so many people like me are reading your books again? He thinks —at least, I suspect he thinks so—that we're homesick for

R

anything right-and-tight. The whole way of life that this country outside the windows—this country we're running through now—suggests. The whole way of life that is quite, apparently, gone. When he let me take one of your books from his shelves just now, sir, he said—I hope you won't mind?—that I wanted a picture book.

TROLLOPE [*as though leaning forward*]: And you—*was* that what you wanted, eh?

WILLIAM: No, you know, he was wrong! Of course I *do* like, we all like, pictures of the old happy times————

TROLLOPE [*dubious*]: Altogether happy?

WILLIAM: Decent, at any rate. But I don't think, with us, that's the root of the thing. No. I think your novels are a support against the sort of *hopelessness* we're inclined to feel. As you say, the characters in your books are *active*. They keep on the move; and they make decisions. They know what they want, and they want what they want all out. If they don't get it they put such a good face on it, or keep such a flag flying, one is left to feel that they *have* won out, by the end. Your people are stronger than circumstances. Yes, I think I've got to the root of it—*that* must be what we're after in your books. It's essential for us, these days, to believe in people, and in their power to live. Not just in heroes or monsters, but in ordinary people with the knack of living ordinary lives. Now, all of your characters, Mr. Trollope—except one or two of the monsters like Mrs. Proudie—were ordinary, in a way that sticks out a mile. And you see, we long for what's ordinary.

TROLLOPE: So did I.

WILLIAM: You, sir? But————?

TROLLOPE: How else could I have painted the ordinary in such sublime colours? Can't you see, my brush was tipped, from the first, with a desire that I could not forget? War isolates *you*, my friend, for the time being, from your proper inheritance as a young Englishman. In my own youth, I knew the same isolation —and that its reasons were different, only made it more bitter. [*shamed half-laugh*] I was a gentleman's son who was, apparently, never to be a gentleman, and who knew of no way to be anything else. My father, consuming himself as he consumed our fortunes, remorselessly confronted me with an ideal which I could not approach. For my failure—which had been his failure—he hated

me and made me hate myself. He was at pains to place me where
I should suffer most—I enjoyed, I believe, the unique distinction
of being miserable—a butt, a failure—at *two* of the greatest
English Public Schools. At the two great schools, my father's
story was known—disclosed by his failure to pay my fees. All
those years I was surrounded by school-fellows who enjoyed
what I should have had—who were poised, successful, assured.
Could I fail to romanticize those other lives, those other futures,
so unlike mine? At eighteen, I was a shambling usher at a poor
school in Belgium. At nineteen, I was a clerk in the Post Office.
Yes, in time, I respectably worked my way up; but those first
years in the Post Office were—well, well . . . Idleness, debts and
squalor, interludes of too well-deserved disgrace. And all that—
can't you see it?—made ten times worse by my mirages, my
dream-pictures of other lives, built up out of those glimpses that
I had had?

WILLIAM [*slightly bewildered*]: I'm sorry, sir.

TROLLOPE [*sharply*]: Thanks, I don't ask for pity. I was merely—
explaining. [*pause*] How, once, I yearned for the ordinary like a
lover. How I came to depict cheerful, confident people, serene
homes, honoured positions, as a lover might depict his beloved's
face. However, however . . . [*lapse into sudden embarrassment—
then abruptly, with complete change of tone*] May I ask which of my
novels you've got there?

WILLIAM: *The Small House at Allington.*

TROLLOPE: Eh? My old eyes may deceive me, sir, but I *think*
you'll find you are wrong.

WILLIAM: Surely? . . . [*pause, then outcry*] Oh, gosh— *oh* gosh! This
would happen to *me*! Wrong book! That bottom shelf was dark;
and I was in a hurry. Here I am, now, stuck for the duration with
some mouldy old autobiography!

TROLLOPE [*dryly*]: Mine, I think.

WILLIAM [*flustered*]: Yours, sir? I'd no idea . . .

TROLLOPE [*with amused defiance*]: Well, I did. I wrote one. Cannot
regret it, either: did me the world of good. Of course, ruined me,
finished my good name. I'd left it with my son Henry, for posthumous publication, so he brought it out the year after I'd—
left the scene. Yes, my poor lad Henry, he had to face the music:
I felt bad about that—otherwise, I had a hearty laugh!

WILLIAM [*puzzled, diffident*]: Was it—er—scandalous, sir?

TROLLOPE [*chuckling*]: Scandalously honest! Or so it seemed to the lot who read it when it came out: 1883, you know—they were just beginning to have fine feelings. Felt that writers ought to be artists, and so on. Made 'em wince. My own lot, I think, would have understood—Thackeray, for instance; but he'd gone on ahead. And *your* lot, in its turn , I feel somehow, may understand. In fact, my boy, may I say there's no book of mine I would rather see you take with you to the battle? Read it, will you?—and *then* go back to the novels. Maybe I wrote it for you. It's the truth— or as near the truth as man ever came.

WILLIAM: Sir—[*no answer*] Mr. Trollope! [*slightly frantic*] Sir! [*pause—bemused voice*] He's—he's not—Have I been asleep then? It's getting dark . . .

> *Fade-in train noises for a few seconds, in same rhythm as before, accompanied by voice saying 'The Ordinary! The Ordinary—The Ordinary . . .'*

Fade Out

NARRATOR: Yes, it is getting dark. One can just see that the seat opposite William is no longer occupied—if it ever was. Outside the carriage windows the winter country is fading, flowing into the dusk. Perhaps, indeed, we have crossed the Barset border and are back in the numbered English counties again. The sunshine, timeless, mellow, and bland, that fell on Trollope's spires and roofs and roads and manorial gates is gone.

UNCLE JASPER'S VOICE [*as though quoting*]: 'Trollope's imagination had no light of its own.'

NARRATOR: No: only genius sheds light. Faithful talent receives the plain light of nature, holds it, reflects it back. Trollope holds up a mirror in which English faces, seasons, and scenes remain. It is a mirror, not distorting, not flattering; with only one magic quality—retention. Can one wonder it should reassure William to look across the years, and find, in the Trollope mirror, faces so like his own? [*pause*] It was not the clumsy and grubby boy, or the seedy clerk, that the world remembered. The big, burly, genial, likeable chap; the unflagging, successful author; the esteemed Civil Servant; the hard rider to hounds; the prosaically happy husband and father—this was the image left. This was the image that was, in time, to bore Uncle Jasper and his more finely strung generation. *Were* there two Trollopes? Uncle Jasper, off-hand, has thrown us out the idea. The anxious outcast, the successful man of the world—was the first, perhaps, never quite absorbed and lost in the second? Is it the wistful outsider, somewhere in Trollope's writing, who gives that mirage-illusion to the ordinary scene?

Is it the mirage that William seeks? . . .

Yes, it is dark in the railway carriage. The train bears on to his destination William, now sleeping deeply, without a dream—head dropped forward over his folded arms. The *Autobiography* has slipped from his hold again—this time, to the floor. The pages blow over rapidly, in a draught. So the last paragraph is exposed for a moment—it is too dark to read it . . .

TROLLOPE'S VOICE [*from the distance and with a solemn impersonality*]: 'Now I stretch out my hand and from the further shore I bid adieu to all who have cared to read the many words I have written.' . . . Now I stretch out my hand . . .

VI

TWO PIECES FROM ORION

Notes on Writing a Novel

Out of a Book

NOTES ON WRITING A NOVEL

PLOT.—*Essential. The Pre-Essential.*

PLOT might seem to be a matter of choice. It is not. The particular plot is something the novelist is driven to. It is what is left after the whittling-away of alternatives. The novelist is confronted, at a moment (or at what appears to be the moment: actually its extension may be indefinite) by the impossibility of saying what is to be said in any other way.

He is forced towards his plot. By what? By the 'what is to be said.' What is 'what is to be said?' A mass of subjective matter that has accumulated—impressions received, feelings about experience, distorted results of ordinary observation, and something else—*x*. This matter is *extra* matter. It is superfluous to the non-writing life of the writer. It is luggage left in the hall between two journeys, as opposed to the perpetual furniture of rooms. It is destined to be elsewhere. It cannot move till its destination is known. Plot is the knowing of destination.

Plot is diction. Action of language, language of action.

Plot is story. It is also 'a story' in the nursery sense = lie. The novel lies, in saying that something happened that did not. It must, therefore, contain uncontradictable truth, to warrant the original lie.

Story involves action. Action towards an end not to be foreseen (by the reader) but also towards an end which, having *been* reached, must be seen to have been from the start inevitable.

Action by whom? The Characters (see CHARACTERS). Action in view of what, and because of what? The 'what is to be said.'

What about the idea that the function of action is to *express* the characters? This is wrong. The characters are there to provide the action. Each character is created, and must only be so created, as to give his or her action (or rather, contributory part in the novel's action) verisimilitude.

What about the idea that plot should be ingenious, complicated —a display of ingenuity remarkable enough to command attention? If more than such a display, what? Tension, or mystification towards tension, are good for emphasis. For their own sakes, bad.

Plot must further the novel towards its object. What object? The non-poetic statement of a poetic truth.

Have not all poetic truths been already stated? The essence of a poetic truth is that no statement of it can be final.

Plot, story, is in itself un-poetic. At best it can only be not anti-poetic. It cannot claim a single poetic licence. It must be reasoned—onward from the moment when its none-otherness, its only-possibleness has become apparent. Novelist must always have one foot, sheer circumstantiality, to stand on, whatever the other foot may be doing. (*N.B.*—Much to be learnt from story-telling to children. Much to be learnt from the detective story—especially non-irrelevance. (See RELEVANCE.))

Flaubert's '*Il faut intéresser.*' Stress on manner of telling: keep in mind, 'I will a tale *unfold.*' Interest of watching silk handker-chief drawn from conjuror's watch.

Plot must not cease to move forward. (See ADVANCE.) The *actual* speed of the movement must be even. *Apparent* variations in speed are good, necessary, but there must be no actual varia-tions in speed. To obtain those apparent variations is part of the illusion-task of the novel. Variations in texture can be made to give the effect of variations in speed. Why are *apparent* variations in speed necessary? (a) For emphasis. (b) For non-resistance, or 'give,' to the nervous time-variations of the reader. Why is *actual* evenness, non-variation, of speed necessary? For the sake of internal evenness for its own sake. Perfection of evenness = per-fection of control. The evenness of the speed should be the even-ness inseparable from tautness. The tautness of the taut string is equal (or even) all along and at any part of the string's length.

CHARACTERS

Are the characters, then, to be constructed to formula—the formula pre-decided by the plot? Are they to be drawn, cut out, jointed, wired, in order to be manipulated for the plot?

No. There is no question as to whether this would be right or wrong. It would be impossible. One cannot 'make' characters, only marionettes. The manipulated movement of the marionette is not the 'action' necessary for plot. Characterless action is not action at all, in the plot sense. It is the indivisibility of the act from the actor, and the inevitability of *that* act on the part of *that* actor, that gives action verisimilitude. Without that, action is without force or reason. Forceless, reasonless action disrupts plot. The term 'creation of character' (or characters) is misleading. Characters pre-exist. They are *found*. They reveal themselves slowly to the novelist's perception—as might fellow-travellers seated opposite one in a very dimly-lit railway carriage.

The novelist's perceptions of his characters take place *in the course of the actual writing of the novel*. To an extent, the novelist is in the same position as his reader. But his perceptions should be always just in advance.

The ideal way of presenting character is to invite perception.

In what do the characters pre-exist? I should say, in the mass of matter (see PLOT) that had accumulated before the inception of the novel.

(*N.B.*—The unanswerability of the question, from an outsider: 'Are the characters in your novel invented, or are they from real life?' Obviously, neither is true. The outsider's notion of 'real life' and the novelist's are hopelessly apart.)

How, then, is the pre-existing character—with its own inner spring of action, its contrarieties—to be made to play a preassigned rôle? In relation to character, or characters, once these have been contemplated, *plot* must at once seem over-rigid, arbitrary.

What about the statement (in relation to PLOT) that 'each character is created in order, and only in order, that he or she may supply the required action?' To begin with, strike out 'created.' Better, the character is *recognized* (by the novelist) by the signs he or she gives of unique capacity to act in a certain way, which 'certain way' fulfils a need of the plot.

The character is there (in the novel) for the sake of the action he or she is to contribute to the plot. Yes. But also, he or she exists *outside* the action being contributed to the plot.

Without that existence of the character outside the (necessarily limited) action, the action itself would be invalid.

Action is the simplification (for story purposes) of complexity. For each one act, there are an x number of rejected alternatives. It is the palpable presence of the alternatives that gives action interest. Therefore, in each of the characters, while he or she is acting, the play and pull of alternatives must be felt. It is in being seen to be capable of alternatives that the character becomes, for the reader, valid.

Roughly, the action of a character should be unpredictable before it has been shown, inevitable when it has been shown. In the first half of a novel, the unpredictability should be the more striking. In the second half, the inevitability should be the more striking.

(Most exceptions to this are, however, masterpiece-novels. In *War and Peace, L'Éducation Sentimentale* and *La Recherche du Temps Perdu,* unpredictability dominates up to the end.)

The character's prominence in the novel (pre-decided by the plot) decides the character's range—of alternatives. The novelist must allot (to the point of rationing) psychological space. The 'hero,' 'heroine' and 'villain' (if any) are, by agreement, allowed most range. They are entitled, for the portrayal of their alternatives, to time and space. Placing the characters in receding order to their importance to the plot, the number of their alternatives may be seen to diminish. What E. M. Forster has called the 'flat' character has no alternatives at all.

The ideal novel is without 'flat' characters.

Characters must *materialize*—*i.e.*, must have a palpable physical reality. They must be not only see-able (visualizable); they must be to be felt. Power to give physical reality is probably a matter of the extent and nature of the novelist's physical sensibility, or susceptibility. In the main, English novelists are weak in this, as compared to French and Russians. Why?

Hopelessness of categoric 'description.' Why? Because this is static. Physical personality belongs to action: cannot be separated from it. Pictures must be in movement. Eyes, hands, stature, etc., must appear, and only appear, *in play.* Reaction to physical personality is part of action—love, or sexual passages, only more marked application of this general rule.

(Conrad an example of strong, non-sexual use of physical personality.)

The materialization (in the above sense) of the character for the novelist must be instantaneous. It happens. No effort of will—and obviously no effort of intellect—can induce it. The novelist can *use* a character that has not yet materialized. But the unmaterialized character represents an enemy pocket in an area that has been otherwise cleared. This cannot go on for long. It produces a halt in plot.

When the materialization *has* happened, the chapters written before it happened will almost certainly have to be recast. From the plot point of view, they will be found invalid.

Also, it is essential that for the reader the materialization of the character should begin early. I say begin, because for the *reader* it may, without harm, be gradual.

Is it from this failure, or tendency to fail, in materialization that the English novelist depends so much on engaging emotional sympathy for his characters?

Ruling sympathy out, a novel must contain at least one *magnetic* character. At least one character capable of keying the reader up, as though he (the reader) were in the presence of someone he is in love with. This is not a rule of salemanship but a pre-essential of *interest*. The character must do to the reader what he has done to the novelist—magnetize towards himself perceptions, sense-impressions, desires.

The unfortunate case is, where the character has, obviously, acted magnetically upon the author, but fails to do so upon the reader.

There must be combustion. Plot depends for its movement on internal combustion.

Physically, characters are almost always copies, or composite copies. Traits, gestures, etc., are searched for in, and assembled from, the novelist's memory. Or, a picture, a photograph or the cinema screen may be drawn on. Nothing physical can be *invented*. (Invented physique stigmatizes the inferior novel.) Proust (in last volume) speaks of this assemblage of traits. Though much may be lifted from a specific person in 'real life,' no person in 'real life' could supply everything (physical) necessary for the character in the novel. No such person could have just that exact degree of physical intensity required for the character.

Greatness of characters is the measure of the unconscious greatness of the novelist's vision. They are 'true' in so far as he is occupied with poetic truth. Their degrees in realness show the degrees of his concentration.

SCENE—*Is a derivative of Plot. Gives actuality to Plot.*

Nothing can happen nowhere. The locale of the happening always colours the happening, and often, to a degree, shapes it.

Plot having pre-decided what is to happen, scene, scenes,

must be so found, so chosen, as to give the happening the desired force.

Scene, being physical, is, like the physical traits of the characters, generally a copy, or a composite copy. It, too, is assembled—out of memories which, in the first place, may have had no rational connection with one another. Again, pictures, photographs, the screen are sources of supply. Also dreams.

Almost anything drawn from 'real life'—house, town, room, park, landscape—will almost certainly be found to require *some* distortion for the purposes of the plot. Remote memories, already distorted by the imagination, are most useful for the purposes of scene. Unfamiliar or once-seen places yield more than do familiar, often-seen places.

Wholly invented scene is as unsatisfactory (thin) as wholly invented physique for a character.

Scene, much more than character, is inside the novelist's conscious power. More than any other constituent of the novel, it makes him conscious *of* his power.

This can be dangerous. The weak novelist is always, compensatorily, scene-minded. (Jane Austen's economy of scene-painting, and her abstentions from it in what might be expected contexts, could in itself be proof of her mastery of the novel.)

Scene is only justified in the novel where it can be shown, or at least felt, to act upon action or character. In fact, where it has dramatic use.

Where not intended for dramatic use, scene is a sheer slower-down. Its staticness is a dead weight. It cannot make part of the plot's movement by being shown *in play*. (Thunderstorms, the sea, landscape flying past car or railway-carriage windows are not scene but happenings.)

The deadeningness of straight and prolonged 'description' is as apparent with regard to scene as it is with regard to character. Scene must be evoked. For its details relevance (see RELEVANCE) is essential. Scene must, like the characters, not fail to materialize. In this it follows the same law—instantaneous for the novelist, gradual for the reader.

In 'setting a scene' the novelist directs, or attempts to direct, the reader's visual imagination. He must allow for the fact that the reader's memories will not correspond with his own. Or, at least, not at all far along the way.

DIALOGUE.—*Must* (1) Further Plot. (2) Express Character.

Should not on any account be a vehicle for ideas for their own sake. Ideas only permissible where they provide a key to the character who expresses them.

Dialogue requires more art than does any other constituent of the novel. Art in the *celare artem* sense. Art in the trickery, self-justifying distortion sense. Why? Because dialogue must appear realistic without being so. Actual realism—the lifting, as it were, of passages from a stenographer's take-down of a 'real life' conversation—would be disruptive. Of what? Of the illusion of the novel. In 'real life' everything is diluted; in the novel everything is condensed.

What are the realistic qualities to be imitated (or faked) in novel dialogue?—Spontaneity. Artless or hit-or-miss arrival at words used. Ambiguity (speaker not sure, himself, what he means). Effect of choking (as in engine): more to be said than can come through. Irrelevance. Allusiveness. Erraticness: unpredictable course. Repercussion.

What must novel dialogue, behind mask of these faked realistic qualities, really be and do? It must be pointed, intentional, relevant. It must crystallize situation. It must express character. It must advance plot.

During dialogue, the characters confront one another. The confrontation is in itself an occasion. Each one of these occasions, throughout the novel, is unique. Since the last confrontation, something has changed, advanced. What is being said is the effect of something that has happened; at the same time, what is being said *is in itself something happening,* which will in turn, leave its effect.

Dialogue is the ideal means of showing what is between the characters. It crystallizes relationships. It *should,* ideally, so be effective as to make analysis or explanation of the relationships between the characters unnecessary.

Short of a small range of physical acts—a fight, murder, love-making—dialogue is the most vigorous and visible inter-action of which characters in a novel are capable. Speech is what the characters *do to each other.*

Dialogue provides means for the psychological materialization of the characters. It should short-circuit description of mental traits. Every sentence in dialogue should be descriptive of the character who is speaking. Idiom, tempo, and shape of each spoken sentence should be calculated by novelist, towards this descriptive end.

Dialogue is the first case of the novelist's need for notation from real life. Remarks or turns of phrase indicatory of class, age, degree of intellectual pretension, *idées reçues,* nature and strength of governing fantasy, sexual temperament, persecution-sense or acumen (fortuitous arrival at general or poetic truth) should be collected. (*N.B.*—Proust, example of this semi-conscious notation and putting to use of it.)

All the above, from *class* to *acumen,* may already have been established, with regard to each character, by a direct statement by the novelist to the reader. It is still, however, the business of dialogue to show these factors, or qualities, in play.

There must be present in dialogue—*i.e.,* in each sentence spoken by each character—*either* (a) calculation, or (b) involuntary self-revelation.

Each piece of dialogue *must* be 'something happening.' Dialogue *may* justify its presence by being 'illustrative'—but this secondary use of it must be watched closely, challenged. Illustrativeness can be stretched too far. Like straight description, it then becomes static, a dead weight—halting the movement of the plot. The 'amusing' for its *own* sake, should above all be censored. So should infatuation with any idiom.

The functional use of dialogue for the plot must be the first thing in the novelist's mind. Where functional usefulness cannot be established, dialogue must be left out.

What is this functional use? That of a bridge.

Dialogue is the thin bridge which must, from time to time, carry the entire weight of the novel. Two things to be kept in mind—(a) the bridge is there to permit *advance,* (b) the bridge must be strong enough for the weight.

Failure in any one piece of dialogue is a loss, at once to the continuity and the comprehensibility of the novel.

Characters should, on the whole, be under rather than over articulate. What they *intend* to say should be more evident, more striking (because of its greater inner importance to the plot) than what they arrive at *saying.*

ANGLE

The question of *angle* comes up twice over in the novel.
Angle has two senses—(a) visual, (b) moral.

(a) *Visual Angle.*—This has been much discussed—particularly
I think by Henry James. Where is the camera-eye to be located?
(1) In the breast or brow of *one* of the characters? This is, of
course, simplifying and integrating. But it imposes on the novel
the limitations of the 'I'—whether the first person is explicitly
used or not. Also, with regard to any matter that the specific
character does not (cannot) know, it involves the novelist in long
cumbrous passages of cogitation, speculation and guesses. *E.g.*—
of any character other than the specific (or virtual) 'I' it must
always be 'he appeared to feel,' 'he could be seen to see,' rather
than 'he felt,' 'he saw.' (2) In the breast or brow of a succession
of characters? This is better. It *must*, if used, involve very careful,
considered division of the characters, by the novelist, in the
seeing and the *seen*. Certain characters gain in importance and
magnetism by being only *seen*: this makes them more romantic,
fatal-seeming, sinister. In fact, no character in which these
qualities are, for the plot, essential should be allowed to enter the
seeing class. (3) In the breast or brow of omniscient story-teller
(the novelist)? This, though appearing naïve, would appear best.
The novelist should retain right of entry, at will, into any of the
characters: their memories, sensations and thought-processes
should remain his, to requisition for appropriate use. What
conditions 'appropriateness'? The demands of the plot. Even
so, the novelist must not lose sight of point made above—the
gain in necessary effect, for some characters, of their remaining
seen—their remaining closed, apparently, even to the omniscience
of the novelist.

The cinema, with its actual camera-work, is interesting study
for the novelist. In a good film, the camera's movement, angle
and distance have all worked towards one thing—the fullest
possible realization of the director's idea, the completest possible
surrounding of the subject. Any trick is justified if it adds a statement. With both film and novel, plot is the pre-imperative. The
novelist's relation to the novel is that of the director's relation to
the film. The cinema, cinema-going has no doubt built up in
novelists a great authoritarianism. This seems to me good.

(b) *Moral Angle.*—This too often means, pre-assumptions—social, political, sexual, national, æsthetic, and so on. These may all exist, sunk at different depths, in the same novelist. Their existence cannot fail to be palpable; and their nature determines, more than anything else, the sympatheticness or antipatheticness of a given novel to a given circle of readers.

Pre-assumptions are bad. They limit the novel to a given circle of readers. They cause the novel to act immorally *on* that given circle. (The lady asking the librarian for a 'nice' novel to take home is, virtually, asking for a novel whose pre-assumptions will be identical with her own.) Outside the given circle, a novel's pre-assumptions must invalidate it for all other readers. The increasingly bad smell of most pre-assumptions probably accounts for the growing prestige of the detective story: the detective story works on the single, and universally acceptable, pre-assumption that an act of violence is anti-social, and that the doer, in the name of injured society, must be traced.

Great novelists write without pre-assumption. They write from outside their own nationality, class or sex.

To write thus should be the ambition of any novelist who wishes to state poetic truth.

Does this mean he must have no angle, no moral view-point? No, surely. Without these, he would be (a) incapable of maintaining the *conviction* necessary for the novel; (b) incapable of *lighting* the characters, who to be seen at all must necessarily be seen in a moral light.

From what source, then, must the conviction come? and from *what* morality is to come the light to be cast on the characters?

The conviction must come from certainty of the validity of the truth the novel is to present. The 'moral light' has not, actually, a moral source; it is moral (morally powerful) according to the strength of its power of revelation. Revelation of what? The virtuousness or non-virtuousness of the action of the character. What is virtue in action? Truth in action. Truth by what ruling, in relation to what? Truth by the ruling of, and in relation to, the inherent poetic truth that the novel states.

The presence, and action, of the poetic truth is the motive (or motor) morality of the novel.

The direction of the action of the poetic truth provides—in

fact, *is*—the moral angle of the novel. If he remains with that truth in view, the novelist has no option as to his angle.

The action, or continuous line of action, of a character is 'bad' in so far as it runs counter to, resists, or attempts to deny, the action of the poetic truth. It is predisposition towards such action that constitutes 'badness' in a character.

'Good' action, or 'goodness' in the character, from pre-disposition towards such action, is movement along with, expressive of and contributory to, the action of the poetic truth.

If the novelist's moral angle is (a) decided by recognition of the poetic truth, and (b) maintained by the necessity of stating the truth by showing the truth's action, it will be, as it should be, impersonal. It will be, and (from the 'interest' point of view) will be able to stand being, pure of pre-assumptions—national, social, sexual, etc.

(*N.B.*—'Humour' is the weak point in the front against pre-assumptions. Almost all English humour shows social (sometimes, now, backed by political) pre-assumptions. (Extreme cases—that the lower, or employed, classes are quaint or funny— that aristocrats, served by butlers, are absurd. National pre-assumptions show in treatment of foreigners.)

ADVANCE

It has been said that plot must advance; that the underlying (or inner) speed of the advance must be even. How is this arrived at?

(1) Obviously, first, by the succession, the succeedingness, of events or happenings. It is to be remembered that *everything* put on record at all—an image, a word spoken, an interior movement of thought or feeling on the part of a character—is an event or happening. These proceed out of one another, give birth to one another, in a continuity that must be (a) obvious, (b) unbroken.

(2) Every happening cannot be described, stated. The reader must be made to feel that what has not been described or stated has, none the less, happened. How? By the showing of subsequent events or happenings whose source *could* only have been in what has not actually been stated. Tuesday is Tuesday by virtue of being the day following Monday. The stated Tuesday must be shown as a derivative of the unstated Monday.

(3) For the sake of emphasis, time must be falsified. But

the novelist's consciousness of the subjective, arbitrary and emotional nature of the falsification should be evident to the reader. Against this falsification—in fact, increasing the force of its effect by contrast—a clock should be heard always impassively ticking away at the same speed. The passage of time, and its demarcation, should be a factor in plot. The either concentration or even or uneven spacing-out of events along time is important. The statement 'Ten years had passed,' or the statement 'It was now the next day'—each of these is an event.

(4) Characters most of all promote, by showing, the advance of the plot. How? By the advances, from act to act, in their action. By their showing (by emotional or physical changes) the effects both of action and of the passage of time. The diminution of the character's alternatives shows (because it is the work of) advance —by the end of a novel the character's alternatives, many at the beginning, have been reduced to almost none. In the novel, everything that happens happens either *to* or *because* of one of the characters. By the end of the novel, the character has, like the silk worm at work on the cocoon, spun itself out. Completed action is marked by the exhaustion (from one point of view) of the character. Throughout the novel, each character is expending potentiality. This expense of potentiality must be felt.

(5) Scene promotes, or contributes to, advance by its freshness. Generically, it is fresh, striking, from being unlike the scene before. It is the new 'here and now.' Once a scene ceases to offer freshness, it is a point-blank enemy to advance. Frequent change of scene *not* being an imperative of the novel—in fact, many novels by choice, and by wise choice, limiting themselves severely in this matter—how is there to continue to be freshness? By means of ever-differing presentation. Differing because of what? Season of year, time of day, effects of a happening (*e.g.*, with house, rise or fall in family fortunes, an arrival, a departure, a death), beholding character's mood. At the first presentation, the *scene* has freshness; afterwards, the freshness must be in the *presentation.* The same scene can, by means of a series of presentations, each having freshness, be made to ripen, mature, to actually advance. The *static* properties in scene can be good for advance when so stressed as to show advance by contrast—advance on the part of the characters. Striking 'unchangingness' gives useful emphasis to change. Change should not be a factor, at once, in

both scene and character; either unchanged character should see, or be seen against, changed scene, or changed character should see, or be seen, against unchanged scene. *Two* changes obviously cancel each other out, and would cancel each other's contribution to the advance of plot.

RELEVANCE

Relevance—the question of it—is the headache of novel-writing.

As has been said, the model for relevance is the well-constructed detective story: nothing is 'in' that does not tell. But the detective story is, or would appear to be, simplified by having *fact* as its kernel. The detective story makes towards concrete truth; the novel makes towards abstract truth.

With the detective story, the question 'relevant to *what*?' can be answered by the intelligence. With the novel, the same question must constantly, and in every context, be referred to the intuition. The intelligence, in a subsequent check over, may detect, but cannot itself put right, blunders, lapses or false starts on the part of the intuition.

In the notes on Plot, Character, Scene and Dialogue, everything has come to turn, by the end, on relevance. It is seen that all other relevances are subsidiary to the relevance of the plot—*i.e.*, the relevance to itself that the plot demands. It is as contributory, in fact relevant, to plot that character, scene and dialogue are examined. To be perfectly contributory, these three must be perfectly relevant. If character, scene or dialogue has been weakened by anything irrelevant *to itself*, it can only be imperfectly relevant—which must mean, to a degree disruptive—to the plot.

The main hope for character (for each character) is that it should be magnetic—*i.e.*, that it should *attract* its parts. This living propensity of the character to assemble itself, to integrate itself, to make itself in order to *be* itself will not, obviously, be resisted by the novelist. The magnetic, or magnetizing, character can be trusted as to what is relevant *to itself*. The trouble comes when what is relevant to the character is found to be not relevant to the plot. At this point, the novelist must adjudicate. It is possible that the character may be right; it is possible that there may be some flaw in the novelist's sense of what is relevant to the plot.

Again, the character may, in fact must, decide one half of the question of relevance in dialogue. The character attracts to itself the right, in fact the only possible, idiom, tempo and phraseology for *that* particular character in speech. In so far as dialogue is *illustrative,* the character's, or characters', pull on it must not be resisted.

But in so far as dialogue must be 'something happening'—part of action, a means of advancing plot—the other half of the question of dialogue-relevance comes up. Here, the pull from the characters may conflict with the pull from the plot. Here again the novelist must adjudicate. The recasting and recasting of dialogue that is so often necessary is, probably, the search for ideal compromise.

Relevance in scene is more straightforward. Chiefly, the novelist must control his infatuation with his own visual power. *No* non-contributory image, must be the rule. Contributory to what? To the mood of the 'now,' the mood that either projects or reflects action. It is a good main rule that objects—chairs, trees, glasses, mountains, cushions—introduced into the novel should be stage-properties, necessary for 'business.' It will be also re-called that the well-set stage shows many objects *not* actually necessary for 'business,' but that these have a right to place by being descriptive—explanatory. In a play, the absence of the narrating voice makes it necessary to establish the class, period and general psychology of the characters by means of objects that can be seen. In the novel, such putting of objects to a descriptive (explanatory) use is excellent—alternative to the narrator's voice.

In scene then, relevance demands either usefulness for action or else explanatory power in what is shown. There is no doubt that with some writers (Balzac, sometimes Arnold Bennett) categoricalness, in the presentation of scene, is effective. The aim is, usually, to suggest, by multiplication and exactitude of detail, either a scene's material oppressiveness or its intrinsic authority. But in general, for the purposes of most novelists, the number of objects genuinely necessary for explanation will be found to be very small.

Irrelevance, in any part, is a cloud and a drag on, a weakener of, the novel. It dilutes meaning. Relevance crystallizes meaning.

The novelist's—any writer's—object is, to whittle down his meaning to the exactest and finest possible point. What, of course, is fatal is when he does not know what he does mean: he has no point to sharpen.

Much irrelevance is introduced into novels by the writer's vague hope that at least some of this *may* turn out to be relevant, after all. A good deal of what might be called provisional writing goes to the first drafts of first chapters of most novels. At a point in the novel's progress, relevance becomes clearer. The provisional chapters are then recast.

The most striking fault in work by young or beginning novelists, submitted for criticism, is irrelevance—due either to infatuation or indecision. To direct such an author's attention to the imperative of relevance is certainly the most useful—and possibly the only—help that can be given.

Orion II, 1945.

OUT OF A BOOK

I know that I have in my make-up layers of synthetic experience, and that the most powerful of my memories are only half true.

Reduced to the minimum, to the what did happen, my life would be unrecognizable by me. Those layers of fictitious memory densify as they go deeper down. And this surely must be the case with everyone else who reads deeply, ravenously, unthinkingly, sensuously, as a child. The overlapping and haunting of life by fiction began, of course, before there was anything to be got from the printed page; it began from the day one was old enough to be told a story or shown a picture book. It went on up to the age when a bookish attitude towards books began to be inculcated by education. The young person is then thrown out of Eden; for evermore his brain is to stand posted between his self and the story. Appreciation of literature is the end of magic: in place of the virgin susceptibility to what is written he is given taste, something to be refined and trained.

Happily, the Eden, like a natal climate, can be unconsciously remembered, and the magic stored up in those years goes on secreting under to-day's chosen sensations and calculated thoughts. What entered the system during childhood remains; and remains indistinguishable from the life of those years because it *was* the greater part of the life. Probably children, if they said what they thought, would be much franker about the insufficiency of so-called real life to the requirements of those who demand to be really alive. Nothing but the story can meet the untried nature's need and capacity for the whole. Of course one cannot narrow down children to the reading child; but I could not as a child, and I cannot now, conceive what the non-reading child must be like inside. Outdoor children were incomprehensible to me when I was their age, and I still find them dull; I could not, and cannot, find out what makes them do what they do, or why they like what they like; and of such children now they are grown up I can only say that I cannot conceive what they remember, if they do remember—for how can even the senses carry imprints when there was no story? The non-reading active children were not stupid; they had their senses. Nor was it the clever children who read most, or who were at any rate the ones who inhaled fiction— quite apart there were always the horrible little students, future grown-ups, who pursued knowledge. The light-headed reading child and the outdoor child had more in common (in fact, the life of sensation) than either had with the student. Readers of my kind were the heady ones, the sensationalists—recognizing one another at sight we were banded together inside a climate of our own. Landscapes or insides of houses or streets or gardens, outings or even fatigue duties all took the cast of the book we were circulating at the time; and the reading made of us an electric ring. Books were story or story-poetry books: we were unaware that there could be any others.

Some of the heady group remained wonderfully proof against education: having never graduated these are the disreputable grown-ups who snap up shiny magazines and garner and carry home from libraries fiction that the critics ignore. They read as we all once read—because they must: without fiction, either life would be insufficient or the winds from the north would blow too cold. They read as we all read when we were twelve; but unfortunately the magic has been adulterated; the dependence has become ignominious—it becomes an enormity, inside the full-sized body, to read without the brain. Now the stories they seek go on being children's stories, only with sex added to the formula; and somehow the addition queers everything. These readers, all the same, are the great malleable bulk, the majority, the greater public— hence best-sellers, with their partly artful, partly unconscious play on a magic that has gone stale. The only above-board grown-up children's stories are detective stories.

No, it is not only our fate but our business to lose innocence, and once we have lost that it is futile to attempt a picnic in Eden. One kind of power to read, or power that reading had over us, is gone. And not only that: it is a mistake to as much as re-open the books of childhood—they are bare ruined choirs. Everything has evaporated from those words, leaving them meaningless on the page. This is the case, for me, even with Dickens—I cannot read him now because I read him exhaustively as a child. Though I did not in those years read all his books, I cannot now read any that I did not read then—there is no more oxygen left, for me, anywhere in the atmosphere of his writing. The boredom I seem to feel as I pursue the plots is, really, a flagging of my intellect in this (by me) forever used up and devitalized air. I came to an end with Dickens when I had absorbed him into myself.

Yes, one stripped bare the books of one's childhood to make oneself—it is inevitable that there should be nothing left when one goes back to them. The fickleness of children and very young persons shocks their elders—children abandon people, for instance, without a flicker, with a simplicity that really ought not to be hurting: the abandoned one has been either a 'best' friend or an object of hero-worship, and the more emotionally fruitful and fanciful the relationship, the more complete the break. 'Where is So-and-so these days? I don't seem to have heard anything about him (or her) for a long time. Haven't you two got any more plans?'—'Oh, I can't be bothered.' What applies to people applies to books, and for the same reason: everything that was wanted has been taken; only the husk or, still worse, mortifying repetition remains. The child is on the make—rapacious, mobile and single-minded. If the exhausted book survives physical abandonment—being given away or left out in the garden in the rain— it languishes on in its owner's indifferent keeping; however, once memory and sentiment have had time to set in and gather about it, it is safe. I still keep a row of books I loved as a child— but I neither wish nor dare to touch them.

What do I mean by those books making myself? In the first place, they were power-testing athletics for my imagination— cross-country runs into strange country, sprints, long and high jumps. It was exhilarating to discover what one could feel: the discovery itself was an advance. Then, by successively 'being' a character in every book I read, I doubled the meaning of everything that happened in my otherwise constricted life. Books introduced me to, and magnified, desire and danger. They represented life, with a conclusiveness I had no reason to challenge, as an affair of mysteries and attractions, in which each object or place or face was in itself a volume of promises and deceptions, and in which nothing was impossible. Books made me see everything that I saw either as a symbol or as having its place in a mythology—in fact, reading gave bias to my observations of everything in the between-times when I was not reading. And obviously, the characters in the books gave prototypes under which, for evermore, to assemble all living people. This did not

by any means simplify people for me; it had the reverse effect, and
I was glad that it should—the characters who came out of my
childish reading to obsess me were the incalculable ones, who
always moved in a blur of potentialities. It appeared that nobody
who mattered was capable of being explained. Thus was inculcated a feeling for the dark horse. I can trace in all people whom
I have loved a succession from book characters—not from one
only, from a fusion of many. 'Millions of strange shadows on
you tend.'

Also the expectation, the search, was geographic. I was and I
am still on the look out for places where something happened:
the quivering needle swings in turn to a prospect of country, a
town unwrapping itself from folds of landscape or seen across
water, or a significant house. Such places are haunted—scenes
of acute sensation for someone, vicariously me. My identity, so
far as I can pin it down at all, resides among these implacable
likes or dislikes, these subjections to magnetism spaced out
between ever-widening lacunæ of indifference. I feel certain that
if I *could* read my way back, analytically, through the books of my
childhood, the clues to everything could be found.

The child lives in the book; but just as much the book lives in
the child. I mean that, admittedly, the process of reading is
reciprocal; the book is no more than a formula, to be furnished
out with images out of the reader's mind. At any age, the reader
must come across: the child reader is the most eager and quick
to do so; he not only lends to the story, he flings into the story
the whole of his sensuous experience which from being limited is
the more intense. Book dishes draw saliva to the mouth; book
fears raise gooseflesh and make the palms clammy; book suspense
make the cheeks burn and the heart thump. Still more, at the
very touch of a phrase there is a surge of brilliant visual images:
the child rushes up the scenery for the story. When the story, as
so often happens, demands what has not yet come into stock,
indefatigable makeshifts are arrived at—as when a play that calls
for elaborate staging is performed by an enterprising little company with scanty equipment and few drop-scenes. Extension (to
draw an iceberg out of a fishmonger's ice-block) or multiplication
(to make a thin, known wood into a trackless forest) goes on. For
castles, gorges, or anything else spectacular out of art or nature,
recollections of picture postcards, posters or travel albums are

drawn on; and, of course, the child to-day has amassed a whole
further scenic stock from the cinema. This provision of a con-
vincing *where* for the story is a reflex.

For the child, any real-life scene that has once been sucked into
the ambience of the story is affected, or infected, forever. The
road, cross-roads, corner of a wood, cliff, flight of steps, town
square, quayside or door in a wall keeps a transmuted existence:
it has not only given body to fiction, it has partaken of fiction's
body. Such a thing, place or scene cannot again be walked past
indifferently; it exerts a pull and sets up a tremor; and it is to indent
the memory for life. It is at these points, indeed, that what I have
called synthetic experience has its sources. Into that experience
come relationships, involving valid emotion, between the child
reader and book characters; a residuum of the book will be in all
other emotions that are to follow.

In reverse, there are the real-life places—towns, seaports,
suburbs of London—unknown to the child, though heard of,
which become 'real' through being also in books. For instance,
after *David Copperfield* I could not hear either Dover or Yar-
mouth mentioned, in the most ordinary context, without excitement: I had a line on them. Towns that were in books, and the
routes between them travelled by characters, stood out in relief
on the neutral map of England. Not a Londoner, I was continuously filling in and starring my map of the environs—at
Richmond lived Sir Percy, the Scarlet Pimpernel, and his wife
Marguerite, who fainted into a bed of heliotrope in her riverside
garden; at Highgate, the Steerforths and Rosa Dartle; at Black-
heath and Lewisham, the E. Nesbit children. When I came to
read 'Kipps,' I was made dizzy by the discovery that I had, for
years, been living in two places, Hythe and Folkestone, that were
in a book. Historic places one was taken to see meant no more
and no less to me than this; history was fiction—it took me a long
time to be able to see that it gained anything further from being
'true.'

Though not all reading children grow up to be writers, I take
it that most creative writers must in their day have been reading
children. All through creative writing there must run a sense of
dishonesty and of debt. In fact, is there such a thing, any more,
as creative writing? The imagination, which may appear to bear
such individual fruit, is rooted in a compost of forgotten books.

The apparent choices of art are nothing but addictions, pre-dis-positions: where did these come from, how were they formed? The æsthetic is nothing but a return to images that will allow nothing to take their place; the æsthetic is nothing but an attempt to disguise and glorify the enforced return. All susceptibility belongs to the age of magic, the Eden where fact and fiction were the same; the imaginative writer was the imaginative child, who relied for life upon being lied to—and how, now, is he to separate the lies from his consciousness of life? If he be a novelist, all his psychology is merely a new parade of the old mythology. We have relied on our childhoods, on the sensations of childhood, because we mistake vividness for purity; actually, the story was there first—one is forced to see that it was the story that apparelled everything in celestial light. It could lead to madness to look back and back for the true primary impression or sensation; those we did ever experience we have forgotten—we only remember that to which something was added. Almost no experience, how-ever much simplified by the distance of time, is to be vouched for as being wholly my own—*did* I live through that, or was I told that it happened, or did I read it? When I write, I am re-creating what was created for me. The gladness of vision, in writing, is my own gladness, but not at my own vision. I may see, for in-stance, a road running uphill, a skyline, a figure coming slowly over the hill—the approach of the figure is momentous, accom-panied by fear or rapture or fear of rapture or a rapture of fear. But who and how is this? Am I sure this is not a figure out of a book?

Orion III, 1946.

Kind Lady

COLLECTED IMPRESSIONS (269 pp.) —
Elizabeth Bowen—Knopf ($3.50).

Elizabeth Bowen is a fine novelist, as she proved in her *To the North* and *The Death of the Heart*; but she has written some very poor book reviews. Kindness of heart that does her credit as a woman sometimes blinkers her as a critic. Many of these *Collected Impressions* are reprinted reviews recording her pleasure with some very ordinary books, and they will explain why her British fellow authors wait eagerly for her notices of their work. It is rarely that she lets anything pass without a kind word, quotable on a book jacket.

Yet for all her egalitarian treatment of geese and swans, she writes with such grace and elegance that she is always worth reading. Her own virtues bring her home even when she is farthest off the beam. It is a joy to read her preface to 19th Century Sheridan Le Fanu's *Uncle Silas;* seen through the delicate, complex lenses of the Bowen prose, it seems a masterpiece. But anyone who takes the preface away from his eye, and looks squarely at the book, will see only a first-rate thriller about a mid-Victorian miss pursued by a bogeyman.

The best sections of *Collected Impressions* are those which deal with damp-rotted Irish country houses, with Author Bowen's school days, and with her own maxims on novel writing. Samples:

What is the object of a novel? "The non-poetic statement of a poetic truth." At what point does the novelist get his perceptions about his characters? "In the course of the actual writing of the novel . . . The novelist is in the same position as his reader. But his perceptions should be always just in advance." What is the novelist's—or any writer's—object? "To whittle down his meaning to the exactest and finest possible point. What, of course, is fatal is when he does not know what he does mean: he has no point to sharpen."

V. S. Pritchett, the best critic in Britain today, has called these and the rest of her pungencies the only really instructive statement on novel writing that he knows. Carpers may feel that she merely tells how to write like Elizabeth Bowen if you have the luck to be Elizabeth Bowen. But even that is something which few writers writing of their craft have managed to do.